Y0-BVN-820

# RELIGIOUS BUSINESS
## Essays on Australian Aboriginal Spirituality

This remarkable collection is drawn from the Charles Strong Memorial Lectures in comparative religion. Bringing the insights of anthropology, history and theology to a range of topics, the book reveals the complexity, diversity and dynamism within Aboriginal religion. The topics covered include ethical concepts, women's religious experience, religious expression in art, the dialogue between Aborigines and Christianity, the incorporation of Ned Kelly into Aboriginal myths, and the religious background to the Mabo case. The distinguished team of contributors includes Diane Bell, Ronald M. Berndt, Deborah Bird Rose, Frank Brennan, Max Charlesworth, Rosemary Crumlin, Nonie Sharp, W.E.H. Stanner, Tony Swain and Peter Willis. Spanning twenty years, the book traces the development of scholarship in the area, and also provides crucial background to the current land rights and reconciliation debates.

Max Charlesworth is Emeritus Professor of Philosophy at Deakin University, where he was formerly Dean of Humanities. He has been a visiting professor at universities in the USA, Canada and Belgium. He has written extensively on the philosophy of religion, and his publications include *Religion in Aboriginal Australia* (co-editor), *Ancestor Spirits* and *Religious Inventions*, published by Cambridge in 1997. In 1991 he was appointed Officer of the Order of Australia.

# RELIGIOUS BUSINESS

## Essays on Australian Aboriginal Spirituality

*Edited by Max Charlesworth*

PUBLISHED BY THE PRESS SYNDICATE OF THE UNIVERSITY OF CAMBRIDGE
The Pitt Building, Trumpington Street, Cambridge, United Kingdom

CAMBRIDGE UNIVERSITY PRESS
The Edinburgh Building, Cambridge CB2 2RU, UK http://www.cup.cam.ac.uk
40 West 20th Street, New York, NY 10011–4211, USA http://www.cup.org
10 Stamford Road, Oakleigh, Melbourne 3166, Australia



First published 1998

Printed in Australia by Brown Prior Anderson

Typeset in Goudy Old Style 11/13 pt

*A catalogue record for this book is available from the British Library*

*Library of Congress Cataloguing in Publication data*

Religious business: essays on Australian Aboriginal spirituality/
edited by Max Charlesworth
p. cm.
"The essays which make up this collection were given as lectures
in a continuing series on comparative religion sponsored by the
Charles Strong Memorial Trust over the last twenty years" – Introd.
Includes bibliographical references and index.
ISBN 0-521-63347-8 (hb: alk. paper). – ISBN 0-521-63352-4 (pbk.
: alk. paper)
1. Australian aborigines – Religion. 2. Australia – Religion.
I. Charlesworth, M.J. (Maxwell John). 1925 – . II. Charles Strong
Memorial Trust.
BL2610.R48 1998
299'.9215–dc21 98–4099

ISBN 0 521 63347 8 hardback
ISBN 0 521 63352 4 paperback

Publication of this work was assisted by a
grant from the Charles Strong Memorial Trust.

# CONTENTS

# ILLUSTRATIONS



# COLOUR PLATES

# CONTRIBUTORS

**Diane Bell** is the Henry R. Luce Professor of Religion, Economic Development and Social Justice at the College of the Holy Cross, Worcester, Mass., USA. Formerly Professor of Australian Studies at Deakin University, Victoria, she has undertaken extensive fieldwork in various Aboriginal communities. Her books include *Radically Speaking: Feminism Reclaimed* (co-editor 1996), *Gendered Fields: Women, Men and Enthnography* (co-editor 1993), *Daughters of the Dreaming* (1983/1993), *Religion in Aboriginal Australia* (co-editor 1983).

**Ronald Berndt** was, until his retirement in 1982, Foundation Professor of Anthropology in the University of Western Australia. He is the author and editor of a large number of works on Aboriginal Australia including *Kunapipi* (1951), *Djanggawul* (1952) and *Australian Aboriginal Religion* (1974). R.M. Berndt died in 1990.

**Frank Brennan**, AO, is a Catholic priest in the Society of Jesus. A lawyer by training, he has worked extensively in the area of Aboriginal land rights and he has acted as adviser on Aboriginal Affairs to the Queensland Catholic Bishops. His works include *Sharing the Country: The Case for an Agreement between Black and White Australians*, Penguin Books, Australia, 1991.

**Max Charlesworth**, AO, is a former Professor of Philosophy at Deakin University. He has written a number of works on the philosophy of religion. He is co-editor of *Religion in Aboriginal Australia* (1983) and co-author of *Ancestor Spirits: Aspects of Australian Aboriginal Life and Spirituality* (1990). His most recent book is *Religious Inventions* (1997).

**Rosemary Crumlin** is a member of the Sisters of Mercy (Parramatta), a Roman Catholic religious order. She has a background in art history and is the co-editor of *Images of Religion in Australian Art*. She was the curator of the exhibition under the same name and she has worked with artists from Aboriginal Communities at Balgo, Turkey Creek and other locations in Western Australia and the Northern Territory.

**Deborah Bird Rose** is an anthropologist who has been working in Australia since 1980. Formerly a Visiting Fellow at the Humanities Research Centre at the Australian National University, she is now at the Northern Australia Research Unit in Darwin. She is the author of many articles on Aboriginal religion, co-editor of *Aboriginal Australians and Christian Missions*, and author of *Dingo Makes us Human: Life and Land in the Aboriginal Australian Culture* (1992).

**Nonie Sharp** is a senior lecturer in the School of Sociology and Anthropology, La Trobe University, Victoria. She has done extensive research on Torres Strait Islander peoples (see *Stars of Tagai: The Torres Strait Islanders* 1993), and on the implications of the Mabo decision (see *No Ordinary Judgment: Mabo the Murray Islanders' Land Case* 1995).

**W.E.H. Stanner**, 1905–1982, was Professor of Anthropology and Sociology at the Institute of Advanced Studies, Australian National University, until 1970. He wrote extensively on all aspects of Aboriginal life and his works include *On Aboriginal Religion* (1962) and the collection of essays *White Man Got No Dreaming* (1979).

**Tony Swain** is a lecturer in Religious Studies at the University of Sydney. In 1983–4 he did fieldwork with the Warlpiri people at Yuendumu. He is the author of *Interpreting Aboriginal Religion*, *'On Understanding' Australian Aboriginal Religion* and *A Place for Strangers: Towards a History of Australian Aboriginal Being* (1993).

**Peter Willis** is a lecturer in Aboriginal Studies and Adult Education at the University of South Australia. After a decade as a missionary and community development worker in the Kimberley region, he was subsequently a co-ordinator at the Institute of Aboriginal Development in Alice Springs.

# IN MEMORY OF COLIN BADGER

This volume of lectures is dedicated to the memory of Colin Badger who was the key figure in the formation and development of the Charles Strong Memorial Trust.

In 1938 Colin Badger was appointed as Director of University Extension at the University of Melbourne. In that capacity he came into contact with representatives of the Australian Church, an independent progressive congregation run by the Rev. Charles Strong. Colin was asked to speak several times to the congregation. On the first occasion he met Charles Strong in person. Soon afterwards Strong became ill, and died in February, 1942.

With the death of Strong the Australian Church gradually declined and the church property had to be sold. Badger suggested that the State Government purchase the property and make it into a cultural centre. Eventually the Premier of Victoria, John Cain, was persuaded to buy the building, which became the Russell Street Theatre in 1960.

The proceeds of the sale of property were then set aside to provide a suitable memorial for Charles Strong, and Colin Badger was invited to join the Trustees of the Australian Church to plan this memorial. The task was not simple, since Strong had been a fervent advocate of many causes, including penal reform, women's rights, world peace, Aboriginal welfare and a range of other social justice issues. Strong was also an intellectual whose challenging sermons appealed to many of the academics of his day.

The proposal of a Mrs Alabaster, which finally won the approval of the planning committee, was that a trust be established to study comparative religion in Australia, another of the topics which interested Charles Strong.

The Australian Church was officially dissolved in February 1957. In 1958 the sum of 27,500 pounds Australian was placed with the Perpetual Executors and Trustees Association of Australia as managing agent for the Charles Strong Memorial Trust, an arrangement which continues today.

The question of how the revenue from the Trust fund ought to be spent was a matter of considerable debate.The possibility of funding a chair in comparative religion at one of the Australian universities was explored, but was found to be too costly. At this stage, moreover, Australian universities remained suspicious of the academic study of religion.

At Badger's suggestion, the Trust functioned with a core of three trustees who were legally responsible for the Trust funds and a council with representatives of various educational bodies. This arrangement proved too unwieldy and the council was soon replaced by an advisory committee of interested academics, which now meets once a year.

Among the original group of academics was Professor John Bowman of the University of Melbourne, who greatly influenced and encouraged Colin Badger in the early years of the Trust.

Since religion studies had not yet been established as a recognised academic field in Australian universities or colleges of advanced education, Badger and the members of the Trust brought well-known scholars from abroad to give lectures in comparative religion, and to thereby promote an interest in the field. The first of these was Professor Houston Smith, a world famous scholar whose tour of Australia was a great success. His visit, as well as the later visits of international figures like Professor Cantwell Smith, played a part in the eventual introduction of Religion Studies into Australian tertiary institutions. I count myself as one of the first beneficiaries of this development, being privileged to introduce religion studies at the Adelaide College of Advanced Education in 1974. We who teach religion studies in Australia can thank Colin Badger and the Trust, at least in part, for the progress that has been made in this field.

We must also thank Colin Badger for researching, writing and publishing a popular volume on the life and work of Charles Strong. The papers of Strong and the Australian Church are in the archives in Canberra for anyone who wishes to continue the work begun by Colin.

Badger was the chairperson and the driving force of the Trust from its inception until he resigned in 1979 as chairperson and I was asked to take his place. Until 1990, when he resigned as Trustee, he continued to provide the wisdom and guidance we all came to appreciate.

I first met Colin Badger in connection with a Strong Trust lecture in Sydney in 1975 and I thereafter counted Colin not only as a partner in the promotion of comparative religion, but also as a friend whose wit and tales about the great men and women at the University of Melbourne made him a delightful companion.

In the 1980s religion studies flourished in many academic institutions in Australia and Colin could see some of the fruits of his labours. With this development, Badger supported the policy that we promote Australian scholars in the field rather than introduce foreign scholars on a regular basis. This change enabled the Trust to fund two Strong Trust lecturers each year and to have their lectures published. A significant aspect of this policy was to promote the study of Aboriginal religions as a legitimate field in its own right. This volume, which is dedicated to Colin Badger, is the result of that policy and represents a valuable collection of papers on Aboriginal religion delivered over the past twenty years.

Colin Badger died in 1995, having contributed significantly to the formation of the Charles Strong Trust, the promotion of the empathetic study of Aboriginal religion and the creation of a body of scholarly literature that will benefit that field of study for years to come. This present volume is representative of that literature and we are honoured to dedicate it to Colin's memory.

*Dr Norman Habel*
*Chair, Charles Strong Memorial Trust*

# INTRODUCTION

*Max Charlesworth*

The essays which make up this collection were given as lectures in a continuing series on comparative religion sponsored by the Charles Strong Memorial Trust over the last twenty years. The Trust was established in memory of the remarkable Scots clergyman and scholar, Charles Strong (1844–1942), who came to Australia in 1875 as minister of the Scots Church, Melbourne. Strong had boldly unconventional views about Christianity and, after much debate and conflict, he was formally ostracised in 1883 by the Presbyterian Church. He then founded the Australian Church in 1885, which continued until Strong's death in 1942.

Charles Strong had a lifelong interest in comparative religion and the Trust was set up in 1956 to promote scholarship in this area by inviting overseas authorities to Australia and by sponsoring lectures by local scholars. (In this the Trust has maintained a close association over a number of years with the Australian Association for the Study of Religion.) Given its modest resources, the work of the Trust has had a notable effect. At the same time one must lament the fact that the various Australian churches, and Australian academic scholars in general have, comparatively speaking, taken so little interest in non-Christian religions, despite the fact that Australia is located in a region – South East Asia – of extraordinary religious vitality and diversity.

A number of the lectures sponsored by the Trust have been concerned with Australian Aboriginal religious ideas and it is these lectures which have been collected here.[1] Unfortunately, it has not been possible to include the Charles Strong Lectures recently given by two Australian Aboriginal women, Vicki Walker and Elizabeth Pike. The authors, after consideration, decided that their lectures would be better suited to publication in another form.

## THE STUDY OF ABORIGINAL RELIGIONS

The history of the study of Australian Aboriginal religions has been a rather chequered one. In the late nineteenth century and the first half of the twentieth century it was largely assumed that Aboriginal cultures and their religions were quintessentially 'primitive' and of antiquarian interest only. The idea that Aboriginal religious systems could be seriously compared to Christianity, or Judaism, or Islam, or Buddhism would have seemed laughable until the 1950s.

Late nineteenth-century thought was dominated by the idea of evolutionary development from simple forms to complex forms in nature, biology and human history and institutions. In this perspective the history of religions was seen as a progressive development from non-rational or 'pre-logical' or 'magical' modes of thought to the more complex and sophisticated rational modes of the great world religions – Hinduism, Buddhism, Taoism, Judaism, Christianity, Islam. So called 'primitive' religions were seen by Frazer (author of *The Golden Bough*), Robertson Smith, Durkheim and Mauss as belonging to the simple or 'elementary' stage of development in human consciousness, and Australian Aboriginal religions were accordingly seen in the same perspective. As Sir James Frazer wrote in the later nineteenth century: 'Among the Aborigines of Australia, the rudest savages as to whom we possess accurate information, magic is universally practised, whereas religion, in the sense of a propitiation of the higher powers, seems to be unknown'.[2] Unfortunately, the findings of late nineteenth- and early twentieth-century ethnographic observers such as Howitt, Baldwin Spencer, Gillen, Pastor Strehlow and others came on stream, so to speak, just at the time when the evolutionary idea was at its most dominant. Marcel Mauss, Durkheim's collaborator, described Spencer and Gillen's work, *The Native Tribes of Central Australia*, as 'one of the most important books of ethnography and descriptive sociology of which we know . . . the picture they give us of social and religious organisation is one of the most complete with which anthropology has provided us'.[3] After Durkheim's great (if misguided) work, *The Elementary Forms of Religious Life: The Totemic System in Australia* (1912), Australian Aborigines were seen as exemplars of the most elementary form of social organisation with the most elementary religious beliefs and practices. (Some 50 years later W.E.H. Stanner, in his magisterial essay 'Reflections on Durkheim and Aboriginal Religion',[4] was to provide a devastating critique of Durhkeim's thesis that religion was a function of society. Durkheim's 'society', Stanner argued, was a 'figment' to which, in Ginsberg's words, he attributed 'powers and qualities as mysterious and baffling as any assigned to the gods by the religions of the world'.[5])

To early twentieth-century scholars of that era it would have seemed absurd to think that Aboriginal religious systems could be approached in the same way that scholars approached the great world religions – Judaism, Christianity, Islam, Hinduism, Buddhism, Taoism – or that Aboriginal religious ideas could have contemporary relevance. Almost all the early studies of Aboriginal religious ideas were done by anthropologists (both amateur and professional) who mostly belonged to the school of what came to be called British social anthropology and who (with some shining exceptions) had, as noted, a generally evolutionist and positivistic view of religion. For them religion in general was, as compared with science, an inferior form of human consciousness and, as we have seen, Aboriginal religions in particular were viewed as the most 'elementary' or 'primitive' form of religious experience.[6] It took almost 80 years for Australian Aboriginal religions to escape from that characterisation and for scholars to recognise that Aboriginal religions were belief-systems of considerable sophistication and seriousness.[7]

## CHRISTIAN MISSIONARIES

Apart from the anthropologists, the Christian missionaries (of various persuasions) were the main group interested in Aboriginal religious beliefs and practices. Although the relationship between missionaries and Aborigines was by no means as dismal as has sometimes been painted, an historic chance was missed by the Christian churches to encounter and dialogue with and learn from the indigenous religions in Australia. In 1659 the Catholic Church's Sacred Congregation for the Propagation of the Faith instructed missionaries in the following enlightened terms:

> Do not regard it as your task, and do not bring any pressure to bear upon people, to change their manners, customs and uses, unless they are

> evidently contrary to religion and sound morals. What could be more absurd than to transport France, Spain, Italy, or some other European country to China? Do not introduce all that to them, but only the faith, which does not despise or destroy the manners and customs of any people, always supposing that they are not evil, but rather wishes to see them preserved unharmed.[8]

Unfortunately, this instruction was honoured more in the breach than the observance, especially in those countries such as Australia where the missionaries had followed the flag of the nineteenth-century colonising powers.

It was an unquestioned assumption among the early nineteenth-century Christian missionaries that civilisation and Christianity were inextricably linked. European civilisation would lead to the reception of the religious and moral doctrine of Christianity, and conversion to Christianity would result in the civilising of native peoples. Unfortunately, in Australia neither the civilising nor the Christianising projects were successful (as compared, say, with missionary activities in Melanesia and Polynesia) and Jean Woolmington's melancholy summing up is a just one:

> While the dedication and faith of the missionaries is not in doubt, their understanding of Aboriginal culture and spirituality was almost non-existent. Indeed, they were quick to condemn any signs of Aboriginal customs as wickedness and superstition. Mainly of humble origins themselves, the missionaries lacked the educational background which might have enabled them to appreciate and understand a culture so different from their own. Not understanding, they condemned; and were unable to comprehend the Aborigines' rejection of them and their religion.[9]

Happily there are now signs of a more ecumenical attitude by missionaries towards indigenous religious beliefs with the recognition that white Christians have just as much to learn from Aboriginal religion and spirituality as Aborigines from Christians. As the traditional formula has it, faith requires understanding (*fides quaerens intellectum*) and an ecumenical faith must be based upon an ecumenical understanding. However, much remains to be done if a 'two ways' (Aboriginal and Christian) spirituality is to become a reality.

It is worthwhile noting that most of the early missionaries had, inevitably, a monotheistic bias and they identified the local spirit beings ('Baiame', 'Bundjil', 'Daramulan' and others) with a Supreme Being or

God. Ernest Worms, the distinguished German Catholic missionary, had been deeply influenced by the ideas of the German scholar Wilhelm Schmidt, who argued that monotheism was the highest form of religion.[10] The Lutheran missionary, Pastor Carl Strehlow (father of the great anthropologist T.G.H. Strehlow) also argued that the Arrernte had a strictly monotheistic idea of God.[11] It has indeed been argued that Spencer and Gillen invented the idea of the 'Dreaming' in order to prevent this monotheistic interpretation of Arrernte belief. So Morphy says, Pastor Strehlow's interpretations 'were a prescription for the conversion of the Arrernte away from their indigenous practices towards Christianity, and a denial of the validity of Aboriginal religion.'[12]

In a remarkable study the Canadian anthropologist David H. Turner has suggested that from the beginning Aboriginal peoples made a quasi-deliberate option against any form of monism and monotheism so as to escape, if one can so put it, the malign social and cultural consequences that monism and monotheism would bring in their train – monarchy and hierarchy, tribalism/nationalism, exclusivism, the centralisation of power and authority, and violence.[13] Whatever may be said about this, it is true that Aboriginal thought seems to have been profoundly antipathetic to any form of monistic worldview and that the failure of Christianity (or at least the Christianity of the early missionaries) with regard to the Australian Aborigines is closely connected with this.

## ASSUMPTIONS ABOUT ABORIGINAL RELIGIONS

To return to the anthropological views of late nineteenth- and early twentieth-century scholars: allied with the evolutionary view there were a number of other factors which distorted white European views of Australian religions and prevented the latter from being taken seriously. First, there was the unquestioned assumption that Australian Aboriginal culture and religion was a unitary phenomenon. We now realise that there were and are profound differences between the various Aboriginal 'peoples' and that we have to speak of Aboriginal cultures and religions in the plural. When Captain Cook arrived in Australia the total Aboriginal population was approximately 750,000 divided into some 500 distinct groups using more than 200 distinct languages (though they belonged to a common linguistic family).

It is difficult to estimate the distinct religious groupings that obtained but it was clearly a considerable number. No doubt, as with

Australian languages, there was a family resemblance between them and certain ideas – the role of the Ancestor Spirits, the concept of the 'Dreaming', the sacredness of 'the land', certain myths like that of the Rainbow Snake – were common to most Aboriginal religious systems. But as has been said, there were also profound differences between Aboriginal cultures – Pintubi, Warlpiri, Yolngu, Pitjantjatjara, Arrernte etc. – and their religions.

A second assumption which distorted earlier views of Aboriginal religions was that they were essentially conservative and unchanging and 'timeless'. But there is now a great deal of evidence that there has always been much significant innovation and reinterpretation and creative adaptation in Australian religions. One has to distinguish between the public rhetoric of traditional Aborigines, which gives the impression that Aboriginal religions are devoted to the faithful replication of the primordial design laid down by the Ancestor Spirits, and on the other hand the actual reality of Aboriginal life and practice, where there is a continual process of experimentation and invention and development.[14] The most notable expression of that development has been the creative extrapolation of the Aboriginal concept of 'the land'. Originally, the land primarily represented the local territories given by the Ancestor Spirits to the various clans and peoples. But from the 1960s onwards, mainly due to the land rights movement, the concept of 'the land' became more generalised. After the Federal Government's enactment of the Northern Territory Aboriginal Land Rights Act (1974), land councils were set up and the central religious idea of the land became the basis of a movement of what can only be called Aboriginal liberation. This culminated in the revolutionary decisions of the Australian High Court in the Mabo case and the Wik case, where the 'spiritual attachment' of Aborigines to their land was formally recognised as the basis for 'native title to land'.

A third distorting assumption has been that Aboriginal cultures have been seen as predominantly 'male', in that power resided in the hands of the initiated and older men, and the central religious ceremonies and rituals were similarly controlled by men. But as Diane Bell and others have made clear, the role of women in Aboriginal cultural and religious life is far from being a subordinate one. In most Aboriginal groups, women have their own autonomous religious domain which men may not enter.

## CONTEMPORARY VIEWS

In general then anthropological approaches to Aboriginal cultures powerfully shaped the picture that white Europeans in Australia in the early part of the twentieth century had of those cultures and their religious systems. However, while those earlier views still exert considerable influence, they have to some extent been counterbalanced by certain contemporary views envisaging the possibility, as has just been mentioned, of an ecumenical exchange or even synthesis between Australian Aboriginal spirituality and Christianity.[15] A symbiotic exchange between the two, it has been argued, will provide a religious vision for the new Australia of the next millennium. Central to this is the idea of *dadirri*, an attitude of contemplative listening and waiting, as the Aboriginal thinker Miriam Rose Ungunmer-Baumann has called it.[16] (It is worth noting here Deborah Bird Rose's meditative reflections on 'the land' in her recent book *Nourishing Terrains: Australian Aboriginal Views of Landscape and Wilderness*.[17])

However, one must at the same time recognise the formidable difficulties standing in the way of such a synthesis. It is easy enough to discern general analogies between Aboriginal and Christian religious ideas and experiences (the 'sacramental' view of life and 'green' environmental values, for example), and it is also easy to select attractive bits from each and to stitch together some kind of eclectic and sentimental religious amalgam. Finding a deeper basis for Aboriginal–Christian dialogue is, however, not easy at all, given the radical cultural and social differences between indigenous cultures and white Australian culture, and also given the *sui generis* character of Australian Aboriginal religious systems. Thus, at the cultural level, we have on the traditional Aboriginal side a hunter-gatherer or forager economy with basic social units or 'bands' of 100–200 people, and with an extremely simple technology allied to an astonishingly complex system of social relationships. Each band has a strongly religious or spiritual affiliation to its own territory but, apart from general links with other regional groups, has no sense of belonging to an Australia-wide pan-Aboriginal community.

On the other hand, anthropological and other research over the last 30 years or so has made us aware of how unique and sophisticated Aboriginal religious systems are. In these religious systems there are no gods: the ancestor spirits who shaped the territories or 'countries' and gave a moral and religious and ceremonial 'Law' to each group 'at the beginning of things', and who impregnated particular sites with spiritual power, are certainly not gods and do not even function as moral and spiritual exemplars. It is these local sites, which have been entrusted by the ancestor spirits to particular groups, and not the land in general, which are the mediators of what Christians would call 'divine grace'. To use an analogy, just as in the Christian scheme Jesus is the mediator of God's supernatural power or grace, so in Australian Aboriginal religions the particular land sites are the mediators of vitalistic power (a kind of *élan vital*) if they are cared for and approached in the appropriate way. As a recent writer, Tony Swain, has nicely put it, Aboriginal religions are 'geosophical' in that spiritual power and wisdom is linked to places. As Swain says, 'Warlpiri religious identity is more a question of geography than theology'.[18]

In the light of these differences it is hard to see how the basic themes of Christianity might be meaningfully translated into Australian Aboriginal religious contexts and vice versa, without doing violence to the one or the other, although of course there are general analogies and resemblances. Perhaps we just have to recognise, and accept, that there are two irreducibly different Australian religious visions or spiritualities, very much as we now accept that there are two irreducibly different Australian legal systems and land tenure systems and art systems.

However, at the practical ('lived experience') level there are all kinds of interchanges and mutual adaptations between Aboriginal and non-Aboriginal religions and there is as noted before, a burgeoning literature in this field, some of it 'pop' in style but much of it serious. (It is interesting to note that the main interest is in 'spirituality' and not in 'religion' since the latter term has been compromised by its past.) It is worthwhile remarking here the recent publication of a text prepared by a group of Aboriginal leaders ('Rainbow Spirit Elders') entitled *Rainbow Spirit Theology: Towards an Australian Aboriginal Theology*.[19] This text has the aim of 'integrating the traditions of Aboriginal culture with the traditions of Christianity'.

What gives one hope that there can be some real ecumenical religious interchange is that there has been just such an exchange in contemporary Australian Aboriginal painting, as witness the astonishing translation of traditional Aboriginal motifs, designs, styles and religious/spiritual and mythological content into works of art that powerfully resonate with mysterious meanings for white Europeans. Of course, a New York art buyer sees Aboriginal paintings very differently from the traditional Aboriginal artists who made them, but clearly something real is also transmitted across the cultural and religious gap. (One thinks for instance of Rosemary Crumlin's superb *Aboriginal Art and Spirituality*,[20] and John Cawte's work on Arnhem Land religion and art, *The Universe of the Warramirri*.[21])

## THE LECTURES

To return to the lectures collected here: W.E.H. Stanner was one of the first to take Aboriginal religious phenomena seriously and his essay in this volume, 'Some Aspects of Aboriginal Religion', written in 1976, is an excellent example of the new approach. That approach is evident in all the other essays in this collection. Thus the late Ronald M. Berndt's study, 'A Profile of Good and Bad in Australian Aboriginal Religion' (1979), shows how central a role ethical ideas play in Aboriginal religious thought, although they are presented and conceptualised in a very different way from European and Christian ethical ideas. Again, Diane Bell's essay 'Aboriginal Women and the Religious Experience' (1982) argues that the religious experience and spirituality of Aboriginal women is radically different from that of men. 'Women's business' serves a distinct social and cultural function and is generally hidden from men's scrutiny, including white male anthropologists and other observers.

In Tony Swain's essay 'On "Understanding" Australian Aboriginal Religion' (1985), it is suggested that we need to devise a method of inquiry which will allow us to understand what Aboriginal beliefs and practices mean for Aborigines themselves. The theoretical understandings of earlier anthropologists and sociologists were largely external and reductive in their approaches to Aboriginal religions and we require a more imaginative and empathetic approach.

In her evocative discussion, 'Aboriginal Spirituality: Land as Holder of Story and Myth in Recent Aboriginal Art' (1994), Rosemary Crumlin is concerned to show how certain contemporary Aboriginal artists have attempted to incarnate religious ideas and symbols (both Aboriginal and Christian) in forms that derive from Aboriginal sources. Crumlin rejects those styles of Aboriginal Christian art which are 'little better than other Christian art in churches' and which, she says, are 'emotionally weak and heavily derivative from a corrupted Renaissance figurative tradition' and which bear heavily 'the persuasion of the missionary'. An analogous theme emerges in Deborah Bird Rose's essay, 'Ned Kelly Died for our Sins', which analyses how the historical European myths of Captain Cook and Ned Kelly have been appropriated by contemporary Aboriginal myth makers. Once again, it is the inventive vitality and capacity to change and innovate which is the mark of authentic Aboriginal religious thought, and we must reject the old idea that Aboriginal cultures and religions are deeply conservative and 'fundamentalist', and resistant to change and development.

Peter Willis, in 'Riders in the Chariot: Aboriginal Conversion to Christianity in Remote Australia' (1988), reflects upon the symbiotic exchange between Christian missionaries and Aboriginal groups around Kununurra in north-western Australia. According to Willis the Aboriginal groups are not the passive subjects of Christian missionary activity; rather, the Aborigines use the latter for their own religious purposes. The Aborigines, Willis says, 'did not replace their religion with Christianity. They rather located it within categories of their own religious world'.

Finally, two essays emphasise how crucial Aboriginal religious ideas are to the debate about Aboriginal land rights and 'native title' to land. To most white Europeans the issues about Aboriginal land are matters of property law; but to Aborigines those same issues are bound up with deep religious and spiritual concerns. Frank Brennan's essay, 'Land Rights: The Religious Factor' (1993), expertly sketches the background to the revolutionary decision of the Australian High Court in the Mabo case (1992). And Nonie Sharp's essay, 'Malo's Law in Court: The Religious Background to the Mabo Case' (1994), analyses the Meriam people's oral religious–legal tradition known as Malo's Law.

## STANNER'S APPROACH

It is remarkable to note how pervasive Stanner's ideas and general approach are in almost all the essays collected here. In a sense Stanner's central themes form a powerful link between those essays. As Howard Morphy has observed, Stanner 'moved the agenda towards the way in which Aboriginal people experience the world', and his understanding of Aboriginal society and religion was 'a means of changing public opinion and advocating Aboriginal rights'.[22] In an historical memoir of the Australian anthropologists at the London School of Economics in the 1930s Stanner recounts that there was a great deal of concern with demonstrating that 'practical anthropology' could benefit indigenous communities. 'We were', he says, 'it seems to me, as impassioned and as interested in political activism as the young anthropologists who demand "relevance" and "commitment" today.'[23]

Non-Aboriginal Australians are slowly and painfully recognising the fact that, right from the beginning of Australian society, it has been 'multi-cultural'. Despite many attempts to exclude the Aborigines by violence, or 'benign neglect', or by breaking up the structures of Aboriginal social life, or by quasi-legal devices (*terra nullius*), the co-existence of Aboriginal cultures (some of which are more than 50,000 years old) and the main white European culture sharing the same country for last 200 years, is a fact of life which both sides have to come to terms with and mutually profit from. That conviction runs through all the essays in this collection and it is hoped that they will contribute to further creative progress in reconciliation and the meeting of Aboriginal and non-Aboriginal minds and spirits. The recent debate provoked by the historic decisions of the Australian High Court in the Mabo and Wik cases *a propos* of native title to land, has made it crystal clear that Aboriginal religious beliefs about and attitudes towards 'the land' are absolutely crucial to any discussion of the implications of the High Court's decisions and indeed to the whole process of 'reconciliation'. In this sense the study of Aboriginal religions is not just a remote academic activity but something of the utmost practical and political relevance at the present time.

At the end of 1997, after the Senate debate on 'native title', the situation on Aboriginal land rights remains confused. Unfortunately, the Prime Minister's 'Ten Point Plan' to amend the post-Mabo Native Title Act has served only to polarise positions on all sides with the consequence that the situation will remain unresolved until late 1998. The actual Senate debate was disappointing in that very little reference was made to the religious or spiritual basis of Aboriginal land rights or to the radical differences in land use by Aboriginal peoples on the one hand and, on the other hand, by white pastoralists and miners.

Equally, apart from the 'stolen children' issue, the Senate debate paid little attention to the sad and brutal history of Aboriginal dispossession of their lands and of white attempts to justify those acts of dispossession. One is left with the dispiriting impression that most white Australians – both political leaders and the general populace – seem to be ignorant of the true reality of the white occupation of Australia and what C.D. Rowley has called 'the destruction of

Aboriginal society'. That occupation and destruction were very similar to what took place during the nineteenth century and the early twentieth century under the regimes of the European colonialist powers in Africa, China, Indo-China, Oceania and the Americas.

No doubt, in Australia, there were some oases of benevolence, where Aborigines were treated humanely by the white settlers, but the prevailing situation was one where Aborigines were evicted from their lands without any real compensation (save for the famous 'flour, sugar and tea' and the annual gift of a blanket). Generally, Aborigines were treated by pastoralists as chattels and kept in a position of virtual slavery where their wives and daughters were often sexually exploited; again, they were subjected to spasmodic massacres and arbitrary detention, while their children were often removed 'for their own good'. 'Genocide' is not a word which should be used lightly but this pattern of cruel repression resulted in the near extinction of many Aboriginal groups and the disappearance of their languages, kinship systems, and above all their rich and complex religions. (Ironically, it has been religious factors that have, as noted before, been central to the recent movement of Aboriginal liberation in all its aspects.) At all events, if wc balk at the use of the term 'genocide', the effect was undeniably genocidal.[24]

## NOTES

1 An earlier collection of essays on other religions was published in 1987, Robert B. Crotty (ed.), *The Charles Strong Lectures 1972–1984*, E.J. Brill, Leiden.

2 James Frazer, *The Golden Bough*, abridged edition, Macmillan, London, 1960, p. 72.

3 Cited in S. Lukes, *Emile Durkheim – His Life and Work, A Historical and Critical Study*, Penguin, London, 1975, p. 452. In a recent essay, Howard Morphy has mounted an enthusiastic defence of Spencer's and Gillen's views of the Australian Aborigines. See 'Gillen – A Man of Science' in John Mulvaney, Howard Morphy and Alison Petch (eds) *My Dear Spencer: The Letters of F.J. Gillen to Baldwin Spencer*, Hyland House, Melbourne, 1997, p. 28: 'Those who see Spencer and Gillen's research simply as being guided by Frazer's and Tylor's theoretical prescriptions fail to account for the fact that their enthnography, as much as anything else, moved the agenda of anthropology beyond nineteenth-century theories, and fail to explain why their work has lasted not as an example of evolutionary theory but as the

foundation of modern fieldwork-based anthropology'. Morphy admits, however, that 'despite this relatively sophisticated perspective on evolutionary theory, Spencer and Gillen in the end left Aboriginal religion in the Frazerian pigeon hole of magic' (p. 36).

4 In M. Freedman (ed.), *Social Organisation: Essays Presented to Raymond Firth*, Cass, London, 1967, p. 240.

5 W.E.H. Stanner, 'Reflections on Durkheim and Aboriginal Religion', in Freedman (ed.), *Social Organisation.*

6 For a more detailed account see the introduction in Max Charlesworth, Howard Morphy, Diane Bell, Kenneth Maddock (eds) *Religion in Aboriginal Australia*, University of Queensland Press, St Lucia, 1984.

7 For an excellent survey of white European and Australian Aboriginal misunderstandings and interactions see Tim Bonyhady and Tom Griffiths (eds) *Prehistory to Politics: John Mulvaney, The Humanities and the Public Intellectual*, Melbourne University Press, Melbourne, 1996. The essays 'In search of Australian antiquity' by Tom Griffiths, and 'Making history: imagining Aborigines and Australia' by Bain Attwood, are especially valuable.

8 Cited by Kenelm Burrridge in his perceptive essay 'Aborigines and Christianity: An Overview' in Tony Swain and Deborah Bird Rose (eds) *Aboriginal Australians and Christian Missions: Ethnographic and Historical Studies*, The Australian Association for the Study of Religions, Adelaide, 1988. This is by far the best source on Christian–Aboriginal relationships in Australia.

9 Jean Woolmington, 'Writing on the Sand; The First Mission to Aborigines in Eastern Australia', in Tony Swain and Deborah Bird Rose (eds) *Aboriginal Australians and Christian Missions*, p. 89. See also in the same volume, Erich Kolig, 'Mission Not Accomplished: Christianity in the Kimberleys', p. 388: 'Aborigines did not so much reject Christianity because of a logical incompatibility of Christian belief elements with their traditional worldview but because of . . . a perceived lack of relevance of the offered belief to the needs and conditions of real life'.

10 E.A.Worms, *Australian Aboriginal Religion*, Spectrum Press, Melbourne, 1986, translated by M.J. Wilson, D. Donovan and Max Charlesworth. Though Worms admits (p. 106) that none of these spirit beings possess 'absolute and undivided power over all spiritual and material beings'.

11 Howard Morphy, 'Empiricism to Metaphysics: In Defence of the Concept of the Dreamtime' in Bonyhady and Griffiths (eds) *Prehistory to Politics*, p. 171.

12 Morphy, 'Empiricism to Metaphysics', p. 171.

13 David H. Turner, *Life Before Genesis, A Conclusion: An Understanding of the Significance of Australian Aboriginal Culture*, Peter Lang, New York, 1985. On the social and cultural consequences of Judaic monotheism see the striking study, *The Curse of Cain: The Violent Legacy of Monotheism*, by Regina M. Schwartz, University of Chicago Press, Chicago, 1997.

14 See Max Charlesworth, 'The Invention of Australian Aboriginal Religion', in *Religious Inventions: Four Essays*, Cambridge University Press, Cambridge, 1997.

15 For an excellent example see Eugene Stockton, *The Aboriginal Gift: Spirituality for a Nation*, E.J. Dwyer, Alexandria, 1995.
16 *Compass Theology Review* 1–2 (1988), pp. 9–11. See also Stockton, *The Aboriginal Gift*, ch. 9.
17 Australian Heritage Commission, Canberra, 1996.
18 Tony Swain, 'The Ghost of Space: Reflections on Warlpiri Christian Iconography and Ritual', in Tony Swain and Deborah Bird Rose (eds) *Aboriginal Australians and Christian Missions*, pp. 459–60.
19 Rainbow Spirit Elders, *Rainbow Spirit Theology: Towards an Australian Aboriginal Theology*, HarperCollins Religious, Blackburn, 1997.
20 Collins Dove, Melbourne, 1991.
21 New South Wales University Press, Kensington, 1993.
22 Howard Morphy, 'Empiricism to Metaphysics', in Bonyhady and Griffiths (eds) *Prehistory to Politics*, p. 182.
23 'Not by Eastern Windows Only: Anthropological Advice to Australian Governments in 1938', *Aboriginal History* 3 (1979), p. 46.
24 The U.N. Convention on the Prevention and Punishment of Genocide (1948) set out five defining marks of 'genocide': (1) killing members of the group; (2) causing serious bodily or mental harm; (3) deliberately inflicting on the group conditions of life calculated to bring about its physical destruction; (4) imposing measures intended to prevent birth within the group; (5) forcibly transferring children to another group.
Research on white settlers and Aboriginal relationships is very extensive. C.D. Rowley's three volumes, *The Destruction of Aboriginal Society*, Australian National University (ANU) Press, Canberra, 1970; *Outcasts in White Australia*, ANU Press, Canberra, 1972; *The Remote Aborigines*, ANU Press, Canberra 1972, are foundational. See also W.E.H. Stanner, *White Man Got No Dreaming: Essays 1938–1973*, ANU Press, Canberra, 1979, and the excellent studies by Henry Reynolds, *The Other Side of the Frontier*, Penguin, Ringwood, Vic., 1990, *The Law of the Land*, Penguin, Ringwood,Vic., 1992, and *Fate of a Free People: A Radical Re-examination of the Tasmanian Wars*, Penguin, Ringwood, Vic., 1995. One might also mention the perceptive account by Noel Loos, *Invasion and Resistance: Aboriginal–European Relations on the North Queensland Frontier 1865–1897*, ANU Press, Canberra, 1982. Finally, one must also note the monumental work, *Bringing Them Home: Report of the National Enquiry into the Separation of Aboriginal and Torres Strait Islander Children from their Families*, Commonwealth of Australia, 1997.

CHAPTER ONE

# Some Aspects of Aboriginal Religion

*W.E.H. Stanner*

## I

There may still be some who question the rightness of including Aboriginal beliefs, acts and objects within the scholarly scope of comparative religion. In this lecture I will contend that all the intellectual requirements can be, and long have been, amply satisfied.

If, for the purpose, I adopt William James's dictum[1] – that the word 'religion' cannot stand for any single principle or essence, but is rather a collective name – it will not be in deference to the sceptics, but rather in acknowledgment of two things: the Aboriginal materials are too various and subtle for our present stage of professional insight, and we cannot yet make powerful general statements on a continental scale. I will therefore aim only at a broadly informative sketch.

If Aboriginal culture had an architectonic idea I would say that it was a belief that all living people, clan by clan, or lineage by lineage, were linked patrilineally with ancestral beings by inherent and imperishable bonds through territories and totems which were either the handiwork or parts of the continuing being of the ancestors themselves. This belief was held in faith, not as an 'official truth' or dogma, but as part of a body of patent truth about the universe that no one in his right mind would have thought of trying to bring to the bar of proof. The faith was self-authenticating. The very existence of the clans or clan-like groups, the physical features of the countryside, the world of animate and inanimate things, were held to make the truth, as received, visible. Even the somewhat abstract categories into which some people were grouped – the sections, subsections and moieties (which took us a good hundred years to begin to understand) – were thought corroborative. Customs, usages, even the fact of language and dialect were taken to be evidential: after all, who but the ancestral beings had taught men the ways of living and speaking? Songs, stories, dances, mimes and rites of high solemnity, deep secrecy, and sometimes of holy status, gave powerful buttress. As far as we know, there was no impulse, and no one tried, to break out from the vast circularity of these reasonings. Yet there was a dynamism at work, to which I will draw attention from time to time.

My main purpose is to discuss the tetrad already mentioned – living people, their countries, their totems and their ancestors – together with the inherent and imperishable bonds between them, and the philosophical ground on which the related entities alone have full meaning. I will hope that by so doing I may throw some further light on a religious outlook which, in the words of my good friend the late Fr E.A. Worms, 'penetrates all facets of Aboriginal life and has little to fear from distinctions which are both abstract and disunitive and which we, with our philosophic education, often make'.[2]

Some years ago I tried to sum up in about half a dozen propositions the understanding I then had of Aboriginal religion. There is nothing in them that I now want to unsay. But there is much that I could wish to have said better, so as to bring out the strength and beauty of the outlook I was trying to express. Since I have been led to believe that the subject is rather unfamiliar to many who are present, it may be useful for me to go through the propositions once again, amending them slightly as I do.

1 The Aborigines universally believed that ancestral beings had left a world full of signs of their beneficent intent towards the men they had also brought into being. The wisdom about living given to men, cherished by traditional experience, could interpret these outward and visible signs as saying that men's lives had to follow a perennial pattern and, if they did so, men could live always under an assurance of providence.

2 The human person, compound of body and several spiritual principles or elements, had value in himself and for others, and there were spirits who cared.

3 The main religious cults were concerned to renew and conserve life, including the life-force that kept animating the world in

which men subsisted and with which they were bonded in body, soul and spirit.

4 The material part of life, and of man himself, was under spiritual authority, and the souls of the dead shared in maintaining the authority and the providence over them.

5 The core of religious practice was to bring the life of a man under a discipline that required him to understand the sacred tradition of his group and to conform his life to the pattern ordained by that tradition.

6 The underlying philosophy of the religion was one of assent to the received terms of life; that is to say, it inculcated a strong disposition to accept life as a mixture of good with bad, of joy with suffering, but to celebrate it notwithstanding.

7 The major cults inculcated a sense of mystery by symbolisms pointing to ultimate or metaphysical realities which were thought to show themselves by signs.

I added that these propositions, if true, were evidence that the Aborigines 'had taken, indeed, had gone far beyond, the longest and most difficult step towards the formation of a truly religious outlook' in that 'they had found in the world about them what they took to be signs of intent toward men, and they had transformed those signs into assurances of life under mystical nurture. Their symbolic observances towards the signs, in rites of several kinds, were in essence acts of faith towards the ground of that assurance'.[3]

By and large, these statements still seem to me true, in a general sense, of the Australian scene taken widely, although I am the first to admit that they have been dated and by-passed by much recent thought and writing on the more esoteric aspects of myths, particularly their hidden logic and semantic structures. But each of my statements, and every idea in them, needs a sort of concordance, before that kind of analysis is possible. Let me illustrate the point by reference to the first sentence of the first proposition: 'the Aborigines universally believed that ancestral beings had left a world full of signs of their beneficent intent towards the men they had also brought into being'. I will draw the material of a sketch from the published works of an Adelaide scholar whose primacy is acknowledged, and who has put in his debt every person who is interested in the Aborigines and in their unique religion – T.G.H. Strehlow.[4]

It would seem from Professor Strehlow's writings that some of the Aranda-speaking peoples of central Australia could be said to have believed there were three domains of the primordial world: the sky, the surface of the earth, and the within of the earth.

> In the sky were a nameless Father and his wives and children. He and his sons were emu-footed, his womenfolk dog-footed. All were young and sempiternal, there being no death. They were self-existent, undescended from anyone. Father ('Great Father', Strehlow calls him) had reddish skin and shining blond hair; his sons were strong and comely, his daughters full-bosomed and beautiful, his wives with the grace of young girls. They lived to themselves, self-sufficiently, in a land perennially green, free from drought, and full of trees, fruits, flowers and birds, but no other animals. The Milky Way was a river flowing through the sky, its course bordered by stars, which were the sky-beings' camp fires. Their glow threw a dim light on the surface of the earth. But the sky-beings had no interest in the earth or its beings, and had no power over them.
>
> The terrestrial domain was dark, being sunless, and moonless, lacking even an Evening Star. It was also cold, featureless and desolate, without plants or animals. But there was a sort of life upon it in the form of innumerable diminutive beings, somewhat human-like but barely foetal, and clumped together at many places. They were immobile and helpless; their fingers and toes were webbed together; and each had nose, eyes and mouth closed. They were alive but unable to develop, age, decay or die.
>
> In the third, the subterrestrial, domain there was veritable human-kind, in the form of a great many mature persons of both sexes. While being truly human they were also superhuman, or at least more than human in that, intermixed with their essential humanity, were animal, plant and other vital life-principles and capacities. These beings, in the words of Professor Strehlow, had been 'born out of their own eternity'. They lay under the surface of the earth, as they always had, deeply asleep.
>
> Spontaneously, they awoke and, of their own will, broke through to the surface. As they did so, the sun rose and brought light and warmth. The sometime sleepers now revealed, or assumed, a four-fold distribution. One group had the forms of animals but thought and acted like human beings. A second looked like perfectly formed human beings but had inward affinities with species of animals and could change at will into them. A third was human in form but had plant affinities: they fed exclusively upon the affine species but did not – could not – take on the form. A fourth group, the smallest, were human in form with neither the animal nor plant affinities.
>
> All the sometime sleepers were like men and women of today in that they had similar thoughts, strivings and feelings, could be hurt and suffer

> pain, could age and in a certain physical sense die although a part of them, a second soul, could not die. Otherwise they were free of the limitations, restrictions and inhibitions that affect today's men and women. Some of them acted violently, cruelly and unfairly but not always with impunity. Some came to downfall from having tried to do so: the good and the bad in living were beginning to define themselves.
>
> Perhaps the greatest difference of the awakened sleepers was a truly superhuman creative capacity and/or energy which enabled them to work marvels that men now cannot emulate. They wandered widely working such marvels. Some went to help the protean earth-beings. They cut the huddled clusters into distinct individuals, freeing them from their physical disabilities, separating the sexes, and teaching them the arts of living as true men and women in the changed world now being brought about by other wakened sleepers, who were in their several ways bringing about all the distinctive features of the earth, indeed, of the cosmos.
>
> At length the superhumans wearied. Some went into the earth; others turned into sacred objects, or into hills, rocks, trees, water-holes and other things, and resumed their deep sleep. Some went into the sky where, unlike the celestial beings, they remained interested in the affairs and able to affect men's lives on earth. The sun, moon and planets now became set upon their courses. Every place at which the sleepers had emerged, or made camp, or had performed a prodigy, or returned to sleep, even the tracks they had made as they wandered, became charged forever with their being, and with the powers or principles they possessed, and were marked eternally by *tjurunga* or other symbols and signs. Before the final disappearance from the visible plane, they composed songs, stories and ceremonies now used to commemorate what had happened. The rights to such property, corporeal and incorporeal, were bequeathed to persons or groups according to an immutable plan of descent or attribution. The heavy secrets of replenishing the world from each such place, by annual, seasonal or occasional rites, with the life-giving powers ordained for it, went each to its proper custodian, or a plan as immutable and as sacrosanct.
>
> When all this had been done, in the words of our authority, 'the world of labour, pain and death that men and women have known ever since, came into being'.[5]

Now, this is not a word-by-word translation of any particular myth. It is an arrangement and a paraphrase of elements occurring in a number of myths which could be widely paralleled and in one form or another were possibly universal in Australia. Together they make a ground of understanding against which one must seek an insight into the Aboriginal *Weltanschauung* (worldview), while avoiding the errors of the conventional wisdom of cap, gown and cloth of the past. One can but marvel that scholars of the highest distinction should have been able to see in such myths, but a short time ago, only 'dark stories' (Tylor), a sort of disease of language, 'the dark shadow that language throws upon thought' (Max Muller), or 'strange stories, not to say absurd and incomprehensible' (Lévy-Bruhl). One might marvel rather more at the judgment expressed in a worthy text published for the Society for Promoting Christian Knowledge at about the same time: that Aboriginal 'mental capacity does not admit of their grasping the higher truths of pure religion'.[6]

Let us look briefly at the idea, the structure and the composition of a totality of three domains against the background of these examples of rationalist and Christian superbia. A schema of overworld, underworld and a tween-domain is not a novelty in mythology. One might say almost the same of an equation of overworld with the ideal, the underworld with the causative, and the tween-domain with actuality. Perhaps, again, the Aboriginal idiom is not all that remarkable in having made the 'underworld', or the 'underneath', or the 'inside' the locus of spontaneity and energy, and of creative, disturbing and other like forces in human affairs. But it does seem to me a work of imagination and of intellectual force to have made the 'inside' or 'underneath' the symbol of sleep. It is also frequently an Aboriginal metaphor of 'secrecy' or 'privacy' and perhaps even of 'sacredness' too. To have gone on to make dreaming, as the activity of sleep, into the master-symbol to which the whole corpus of Aboriginal religious life vibrated, was in my opinion still more impressive. The Dreaming, as activity, is represented as a continuing highway between ancestral superman and living man, between the life-givers and the life, the countries, the totems and totem-places they gave to living men, between subliminal reality and immediate reality, and between the There-and-Then of the beginnings of all things and relevances and the Here-and-Now of their continuations. On this material alone it seems to me that a sufficient answer could be given to the Christian critic I have quoted, and to the other writer whom he quoted approvingly as referring to a race 'intellectually, as physically . . . poor and weak . . . ignorant beyond comparison . . . abjectly subject to terror, yet have not acquired a mythology, nor any one general superstition'.[7]

Now, I have no wish, in correcting old misunderstandings, to go to the other extreme, but I am not alone in finding beauty, gravity and insight in much of the material I am discussing. May I perhaps go a little farther, and suggest that in the doctrine I have been summarising there is an implicit theory of something very like the unconscious? That is, a theory that elemental forces, antecedent to the formation of the mature human being in society, operate below the level of the waking or conscious mind by continuing perennially through sleep and dream, as major determinants of conscious human conduct.

We are, remember, a society of book-worms. The absence of an Aboriginal tradition of literacy has enabled us to patronise a people whose languages are now revealing to professional linguists a semantic subtlety, a conceptual richness, and a categorial quiddity that in the next five or ten years will bring about a Copernican change in our understanding of Aboriginal culture and, incidentally, in our self-perception of what we did from 1788 onward. Pending that time, let us consider what the doctrine of three domains seems to 'say' through its imagery, including its spatial imagery.

It depicts the sky-beings as other than men (because they walk on animal feet, do not die, and so on) but not as wholly other (because of so many human attributes). It depicts them as high above the earth, far removed from it, and thus transcending it, exemplifying social life, idealised and unconditioned, as it might be in freedom from limits. It depicts them as self-existent beings, beginningless, underived from anyone, and self-responsible; beings who are and were 'from everlasting'; beings who are as and where they were 'before the hills in order stood or earth received her frame'. So the conception deepens to one of transcendent and eternal beings, other than men but not wholly other, living an unconditioned life, but characterised by disinterest in true men and an absence of power over them.

The imagery, again often spatial and perhaps somewhat less ambiguous in a temporal sense, depicts the earth-beings who were to become true men as having been less than men but as having had a beginning as men at a point in time. They were made into men by a power beyond themselves; this theme becomes wholly explicit in the initiation rites: no boy 'becomes' a man; other men 'make' him a man. The assertions in the myths seem to say that the inert earth-beings did not become, like their transformers, greater than men, but were transposed from one modality to another, though still ultimately dependent on the transforming power. The change was from an inactive and potential modality to an active and kinetic modality. The imagery together with the assertions seem to say that life was actualised for such beings in some sense in division and strife, and under restraint and limit, not in the conditions of constancy and ideality of the sky-beings. Nor, because of their mortal element, were they to be ever-existing and never-changing in anything like the same sense.

The imagery depicting the earth-sleepers is more complex than I can condense suitably. It seems to me profoundly suggestive. Their spatial locus suggests immanence rather than transcendence. A philosopher or theologian of Aboriginal religion would have much to contemplate in that difference. The earth-sleepers were like the sky-beings in having been 'self-existent', other than men but not wholly other, though in a different sense. They were unlike the sky-beings in having true human feelings, interest in and (by attribution) compassion for earth-beings, and in having a moral or quasi-moral property mystifyingly linked with their ever-existing and never-ending properties, which are theirs – though in a strange modality – since, when they came on earth, they developed and distributed multiple self-differences which persisted inexhaustibly everywhere, yet their identities and powers remained as before.

I would suggest that, with a minimum of attribution, sufficient resonances come from such data to encourage us to believe that we are beginning to know what the Aborigines are talking about. Let me then go forward to talk about six ideas which, whoever else may have had them, in my opinion are also authentically Aboriginal, and had a major place in their religious outlook.

1 All Aboriginal myths postulated that some sort of entity *pre*-existed independently before the cosmos was transformed into the system and the state in which it now exists (at least until we Europeans came like meteorites). Nowhere in the myths was there any suggestion of that extraordinary idea of a creation *ex nihilo*. To Aborigines something always was; the something had an arrangement or at least a structure; in some sense, it involved both space and time; but no one, as far as our good knowledge goes, seems to have seen as problematical or intellectually interesting how the pre-existent entity or its division into three had come to be as they were. It sufficed, that something was, with an implicit order amongst its given things; and that it was *re*ordered and *transformed* by posited means and agents so as to take on an explicit structure in which men had a determinate place.

2 The second idea was that power or energy was part of the primordial scene. The Aboriginal conception, at least inferentially,

appears to have encompassed both the ideas of potential and of kinetic power, inasmuch as it was a basic postulate that the capacity of potential or applied power in things and places (including drawings, paintings, spells, songs) was there for release by the 'right' people. Hence, of course, the enormous and unshakeable attachment of the 'right men' to their ancestral 'countries'.

3 A third idea, much more difficult to express, was that the power itself, and the right to use it, were both speciated and individuated. Any and every kangaroo-man, if that is the totemic group we are speaking about, having the right ritual, which might take many years to acquire, could release from the sacred site the life-essence stored and potential there, so as to become kinetic in the form of actual kangaroos, not just this or that particular kangaroo but all and any kangaroos of that particular kind that were, are or may be. This seems to me to mean that the Aboriginal world was one of plural identities and a world of universals also.

4 But – and this was the fourth great idea – the world was, or was made, one of determinate relationships in which the relevance of anything to anything else was established. The sometime sleepers had linked the earth-beings as men everlastingly with themselves and with some at least of the sky-beings. They had put the three domains on a common framework and network of historical, substantial, spiritual and mystical ties. By 'historical' I refer to the supposedly unbroken lines of descent from the first true men through named persons known to have lived as men 'in history'. By 'substantial' I refer to the supposition that the country of each descent group, and its waters and food, had from the beginning given soul and body to clansmen, and had from the beginning been the last repository of their bones or ashes, and the everlasting home of their souls. By 'spiritual' I refer to the belief that at least one of the several elements of which, in Aboriginal thought, the 'person' is compound, connected him to clansmen through some incorporal entity with everything in the country which was 'his'. By 'mystical' I again draw on William James: I refer to 'a state of consciousness which seems to deepen and enlarge the ontological sense of life', not as a 'mere reproach, to throw at any opinion which we regard as vague and vast and sentimental, and without a base in fact or logic.[8]

5 A fifth idea was that the human will has always played a decisive part in men's affairs. The earth-sleepers irrupted on to earth of their

own will and returned to sleep of their own will. Spirit-children impregnate women (or find pregnant women) and malignant spirits intervene in men's lives of their own will. All the myths make much of the fact of private will and of the conduct that may be said to express it – from stubbornness and indifference to egotism, pride, jealousy, cruelty, deceit and treachery.

6 A sixth idea had to do with the founding drama of the cosmology. A great event occurred with calamitous consequences of the 'forever after' kind. The particular event may be represented as an error, foolish or culpable, inexplicable or left unexplained. It usually concerns death, how it became a necessity needlessly, or at least with some kind of option foregone. The clear suggestion is that men were not meant to die.

Now, I do not think it could reasonably be said that I have imposed these viewpoints on the material. I have tried to avoid attribution, though whether I have wholly succeeded may be in question. I put them forward as being at the least implicit postulates of the religious outlook, contributing towards what Feibleman, the philosopher, might have called the 'implicit dominant ontology', or ethos.[9] It seems to me no inconsiderable feat of mind to have conceived of an independently pre-existing entity transformed into a world of relevances, and therefore into a moral system, by a cosmic force immanent in men but somehow still transcendent over them. Given the physical conditions of life, the tenets concerning death, and the somewhat anarchic polity, it seems to me a psychological achievement of a high order to have developed an art of life so strongly characterised by humour and jollity. These things, together with the confidence in their power to survive, the practice of a life-long discipline of body and mind as a mark of their valuation of man both as flesh and as spirit, and the repetitive celebration – no less joyous a word will do – of the continuance of their way of life, seem to me to argue powerfully for a re-assessment of some of our past depreciation.

## II

I have felt that I could safely assume in such a gathering a good deal of general knowledge of Aboriginal society, in particular of the wider structure resting on and connecting the small, localised descent-groups (the 'clans' or 'patrilineages' I have referred to). It is plainly impossible for me even to summarise the scene made by thousands of such small groups, each possessing its own territory, its own idiosyncratic heritage of stories, songs, sacred places and ceremonies, and each a focus of order within a wider structure of variable social intercourse. There is much about this 'wider structure in which society and external nature are brought together and a system of organised relations established, in myth and ritual, between human beings and natural species or phenomena' that, for full appreciation, needs more general information than I have any right to assume. All I can hope to do is to make some side-long gestures as I turn now to a second important field. I shall consider the subject of ritual to try to discover whether it could help to clarify what was 'religious' in the content of the Aboriginal *Weltanschauung*.

There are immediate difficulties. At present there is no agreed nomenclature for the different kinds of ritual and no agreed classification. What precisely do we intend to denote by 'initiation' or 'totemism' or 'increase' rites? Many efforts are being made to think things out again. Some of Eliade's (and mine) have been described as 'an enterprise which seems to consist partly at least of translating the native idiom of thought into the technical language of metaphysics and theology'.[10] The critic seemed to feel that he was not tinkering with the 'native idiom of thought' in proceeding to discuss the subject of 'totemic myth' as 'the relation of the individual to the object-world, and libidinal cathexis as the defence used by human beings to bear the deprivation of object-loss or separation'.[11] The languages of positivist philosophy and psychoanalytics are not less 'technical' and may do as much violence in 'translating the native idiom' as any specialist language. What, essentially, I and some others are trying to do is to weaken the ethnicity of our approach, including the Christian approach, so as to be able to accommodate Aboriginal perceptions of life and world, and their intimate concerns with both.

For a long time scholars have tended to see the major rituals as in four groups: (1) 'commemorative' or 'historical' rites, (2) 'increase' rites, (3) 'initiation' rites, and (4) death and mortuary rites. The list pleases no one, for several reasons. In some sense, all the rites have a historical and a commemorative implication. As Meggitt has pointed out the so-called 'increase' rites are ill-named: their purpose is to maintain the supplies of natural species at their usual level, to support the normal order of nature, not to increase it. Both Elkin and Berndt would, I think, give the concept of 'initiation' a somewhat more restricted application than I do, in order – as I read them – to enhance the fact that some senior rites are much more 'revelatory' than 'initiatory' in purpose. They, and others, also are persuaded that we should recognise a special class of initiatory rites as 'fertility cults', such as the Kunapipi cult, which has attained an extraordinarily wide distribution. And are not death and mortuary rites in some sense 'initiations' also? There are also some residual forms of behaviour that are hard to know where to put, for example, some forms of magic, and meetings of very senior men to anoint, repair and contemplate sacred objects. The material is surprisingly rich and complex, with scores if not hundreds of locality-patterns. The 'dynamism' to which I referred earlier was very much at work here. Just as the rock-paintings may by 'over-painting' show a long temporal sequence of art-styles, so we are certain now that there have been historical changes of ritual-styles, over an unknown but possibly very long span of time. Professor Berndt recently made a courageous attempt to put the facts of the whole continent into perspective. He set up tentatively four main regional patterns, with intermediate and transitional forms. But after what might have been 40,000 years of development it is now difficult to isolate patterns which are mutually exclusive for significant defining properties. We should go on with the task and profit from his painstaking and exhaustive approach since there is certainly no Australianist who knows the material better than Berndt.

It is common ground to all anthropologists, I would imagine, that all rites of the kinds mentioned were concerned in one way or another with the most precious good of all, life itself, and more particularly with the continuance of life; and that the rites had a natural distribution along the course of the life-cycle of males. There was also an explicit comprehension that the continuance of life depended upon a power or powers external to men and beyond them. One is tempted to say that the rites were 'religious' in the measure in which, implicitly or explicitly, they acknowledged that dependence.

The historical or commemorative rites were consciously concerned to honour the particular ancestral life-givers of this or that clan or clan-like group, such as the father-son couple of subsections of tribes like the Waramunga. They did so often though not necessarily at the very places, now held to be deeply sacred, where the ancestors were credited with having emerged from the earth, or returned to it, leaving sacred tokens of their presence or passage. The ceremonies might be most spectacular and devout, including the drawing of blood, and using unstintingly the full treasury of song, story, mime, dance and icon, including the making of superb ground-paintings.

The 'increase' or maintenance rites were consciously concerned to ensure the normal flow of the kinds of life specific to each of the sacred places reputed to have been endowed with the life-potential of that totemic species. The ceremonies might be again spectacularly beautiful and devout, or merely notional, but always were a way of venerating the totemic ancestors and the site.

The classical initiation rites were consciously concerned to induct males by stages into the fellowship of the most senior men who understood the religious mysteries in part or in whole. The ultimate purpose was to ensure the passage to and retention by the rightful persons of the knowledge required for the continuance of life. These rites have sometimes been referred to as age-grading ceremonies, but in my opinion this is something of a misnomer because although the novices who went through a rite on a particular occasion were roughly of the same age, were sometimes known by a common term, and were closely bonded by the experience, they were graded by age only in a secondary way: what really graded them was their degree of religious knowledge.

I should interpolate here that the oldest and most knowledgeable ritualists might spend long periods, without any novices or postulants being present, reverently handling and contemplating the sacra. They were consciously concerned to nurture, revere, protect and preserve the physical embodiments or tokens of the persons and/or powers of ancestral beings, and with the exegesis of their import for living men.

The last group of rites – at death and later at burial – were consciously concerned with two tasks: to enable the ghost of a dying or dead clansman to be quit of earthly ties, and to shepherd his immortal soul towards and into the place within his clan-country where his bones could lie at peace, and whence (the doctrine varied a great deal) his or an equivalent spirit might again animate a human host.

It is clear from this cursory survey that all the major rites can be related functionally to the life-cycle of a person, a clan-member, except to the fact of birth; that is a puzzle in itself. Aboriginal attention centred on the fact of conception, or at least the proof of pregnancy. It is also clear that study is reaching a point at which it may be as important to push inquiry intensively as extensively. The task of continental inquiry, including the broad comparison of regional cults like the Kunapipi, the Djunggawon, and the Jabaduruwa, to name three only, is obviously a fascinating one and I can well understand yielding to it. But I prefer to ask questions of a sharper kind. In what way, if at all, does the ground so far covered bring us nearer a grasp of what was specifically 'religious' about the rites mentioned?

## III

The material seems to establish beyond question that the Aborigines acknowledged that men's lives were under a power or force beyond themselves; that they venerated the places where such power or force was believed to concentrate; that they imposed a self-discipline to maintain a received tradition relating to the provenance and care of such power; and that part of the discipline was to maintain what might be called a 'religious economy'. The elements of belief and action were in a sense an 'address' to the givers of life. There was no element of direct petition, so that to speak of 'prayer' would be to go too far, just as it would be to speak of 'worship'. But I agree that we are dealing with lives of religious devotion.

I have probably said enough of the first two matters – the recognition of dependence on powers beyond themselves, and the veneration of the places where the powers are present or represented. Let me say something further of the two others – the initiatory ordeals and the religious economy.

Everyone has heard about the tossings of boys in the air, the smoking and toasting over fires, the head-biting, the physical beatings, the tooth evulsion, the cicatrization, the circumcision, the subincision, and so on. They have often been made to appear as bizarre savageries; indeed, I have been most surprised to learn that there are still suggestions of mere cruelty and bloodlust as the bases of such practices. These acts always had a social context and observed certain public conditions. A boy or youth about to be initiated was set apart from all that was mundane and ordinary: in a sense, he was made 'sacred' for the occasion. He was brought to the forefront of community attention, and for weeks or months became the cynosure of all eyes and thoughts. During that time, and on successive initiatory occasions, he was put in the care of guardians or instructors, whose task it was to prepare him and bring him in safety, well-being and good heart to his ordeal. At every stage he had close at hand comfort, encouragement, sustenance and protection while undergoing the isolation, privation, discipline, anxiety, fear and pain – quite often extreme fear and excruciating pain

– that were his lot. A theory of 'callousness' and 'deliberate cruelty' is quite inconsistent with these and other concomitant facts. A boy, to my knowledge, was never circumcised by his own father, brother, or grandfather. The surgery was done by a member of another clan, who could operate with more detachment. I was told that no father could bear to inflict such pain on his own son. I saw fathers and brothers, distracted by grief, abuse and throw spears towards the operators. The rite of subincision differs. I did not myself see it but I was told that men of a man's own clan might join with others in performing the first operation, but that men were commonly seized by a sort of ecstasy to enlarge their own subincisions to draw blood for a ritual purpose. These facts are also recorded.

I suggest that in all this there was a spectrum. At one extreme, physical ordeals were *imposed* on boys and youths as preparative tests and as sanctifying acts. At the other end, men of some religious standing were *invited* to submit to ordeals as meritorious acts of asceticism and self-mortification. We are not entitled to overlook the differences. To the best of my knowledge, many men shrank from the agony of subincision and from the further ordeal – a worse agony, if possible – of having one or two finger nails torn out to make religious merit great enough to fit a man to make new sacra. But others accepted and passed the test – their religious status and repute were higher. So it is pretty clear that the spectrum had about it something of a *gradient* too: it measured degree of devotion to the self-disciplinary demands of the religious life. It would be more consistent with the evidence of the actual content and context of the rites to say that pain was inflicted, not from mere cruelty or blood-lust, but in a sorrowful public duty towards religious novices or postulants, and from ecstatic motives amongst the older and more devout. Men who cut *their own* arm-veins to pour blood on novices or on sacred objects and places, or lacerated *their own* sex-organs for similar purposes, were surely not affected by 'blood-lust': they were making an offer and gift of one of the symbols of life – at their own cost – to the novice or to whatever symbol was the recipient.

Now, to the fourth point – what I called 'the religious economy'. I have led my remarks to a point which in my opinion offers to students a true subject of comparative religion, one susceptible of detached scientific study: the analysis of Aboriginal ritual for a comparison of the liturgical formularies used throughout Australia. I have argued that there is no justification in the evidence we possess for dealing in concepts of 'prayer', 'worship', 'sin', 'guilt', 'grace', salvation' and so on, but there is a half-explicit concept of men co-operating ritually with unseen powers at holy places and on high occasions, to further a life-pattern believed to have been ordained by its founders, and of doing so under an assurance of a continuing flow of benefits. Some of the rites we have been considering plainly had a liturgical character, in that they were organised works of public – as distinct from private – duty, deference and even reverence towards, and of faith in, an otherworldly provenance of human well-being.

It has been said that 'the living heart of the Christian Church' can be found in its liturgy, and that 'an exchange of prayers and graces is the very substance of the liturgical life'.[12] In this minimal and aphoristic form one can perhaps see what might be called 'the Christian economy of salvation', the salvation of souls being the supreme benefit of the exchange. The Aboriginal 'economy' was one under which souls were kept in circulation from clan-country to clan-country through clansman after clansman, the continuance of The Dreaming being the supreme benefit obtained through liturgical acts of dutiful observance.

The conception I have formed can be put simply. There were two data to which Aboriginal life conformed: a cosmic datum and a social datum. Under the cosmology a soul, which could never die, entered a human being. Under the same cosmology soul and human host were linked indissolubly until the host died. During life, body and soul were kept together by developmental and integrative rites necessitated by the social datum. To do so was the chief religious art of life. As a man grew up, was initiated, and assumed all the duties and privileges of a full man, his spiritual development was attained by religious disciplines at great personal cost. The cost expressed the value of what was gained. When death came, a man's undying soul and his bones or ashes completed the cycle by returning to his 'bone and soul country'. Under this religious system human society and cosmos were made and kept correlative.

I have remarked elsewhere that only a blindness of the mind's eye prevented Europeans in the past from seeing that 'the ritual uses of water, blood, earth and other substances, in combination with words, gestures, chants, songs and dances, all having for the Aborigines a compelling quality' were not 'mere barbarisms' but had a sacramental quality.[13] I went on to add that 'one doubts if anywhere could be found more vivid illustrations of a belief in spiritual power laying hold of material things and ennobling them under a timeless purpose in which men feel they have a place'. Obviously, one has to look beyond the symbols to what is symbolised; behind the spoken images of myth, the acted images and gestures of rite, and the graven or painted images of art, to what they stand for; beyond the chrism of blood and ochre to what they point to, within the Aboriginal *Weltanschauung*.

During the lead-up to the Yirrkala land case I was present when the old man Mathaman, who had dared to sue Her Majesty and the Nabalco Company, was preparing to die. The 'right men' painted on his chest, with ochre and blood, the design that pointed beyond itself to things sacred and mystical to his clan. The industrial and commercial world made by the Commonwealth and Nabalco was roaring all around but if ever a man died at peace with The Dreaming, in spite of the ruin overtaking his people, it was Mathaman.

## IV

I turn now to my last topic: the new-found interest in the 'philosophy' of Aboriginal religious thought and life. The misgivings expressed by the late Fr Worms about looking at the Aboriginal data through Western philosophical spectacles are of course not new. Durkheim made a general criticism many years ago. He said that all philosophers since Socrates had become used to relating reality to a combination of concepts in the belief that they were explaining life by reducing it to a system of abstract, logically related ideas. What they saw, he said, was only the general framework in which things are related, not the vitality that makes things move. To live, he said, is not to think, but to act. The train of our ideas is a reflection of the events which we experience.

The criticism was renewed recently by a young American sociologist, who referred also to 'an implicit component of Western anthropocentrism in most philosophical systems' constructed by Western philosophers.[14] This had led to a 'culture-bound' philosophy that 'talks about man, his nature and artefacts without adequate empirical foundations'. The result is 'a product of the philosophical experience of Western civilization' made up of 'constructs abstracted from notions of men taken *in vacuo*'. He closed his argument with the statement: 'to consider man apart from his social setting is to leave a gap in all philosophical generalizations concerning man and human knowledge'.

I have no great confidence in my ability to clarify the discussion of this difficult topic but it is obviously of much import for the subject of this lecture. Let me say then that the great difficulty which I see involves the distinction, radical separation, even in certain circumstances opposition, between 'subject' and 'object'. The postulate that 'out there', external to and independent of the knowing or experiencing 'subject', is a 'reality' concerning which the subject forms 'objective knowledge' excluding all 'subjectivity', is simply incongruent with Aboriginal mentality in certain situations of life. When an Aboriginal identifies, say, his clan-totem and its sacred site, he is not 'pointing' to 'something' which is 'out there' and 'external' to him, but 'not him': he is identifying a part of his inwardness as a human being, a part of the plan of his life in society, a condition of his placement and activity in a manifold of existence in a cosmic scheme. We have to do what we can to try to 'see' the Aboriginal's intersubjective reality, made up of facts known to everyone in his community, and upheld by them as public, objective, true and valid, not just for him, or just for him for the moment, but for everyone, everywhere, at all times. According to the Aboriginal theory of 'reality', living and dead, human beings and animal beings, persons and things, persons and environment, can and do compenetrate each other. I meant as much by my earlier remark that between the elements of the tetrad there were, in Aboriginal understanding, historical, substantial, essential and mystical links that were inherent and imperishable. Our categories are too Procrustean, our abstractions too dry and spare, our intellectual habits too desiccated for the material we have to handle. Yet with care and patience something may be achieved.

It is appropriate that the first serious essay should have come from A.P. Elkin, for long the ranking Australianist, whose insight into Aboriginal mentality and culture has ripened over half a century.[15] I offer my comments with the most full respect.

He begins by pointing out how much Aboriginal thought takes for granted the ultimate origins of the world, the earth, the sky, the sea, and life itself. The heroic personages now regarded as 'totemic ancestors' are believed to have made the world, not by a creation *ex nihilo*, but by what he describes as 'a transformation and a revealing of what already exists'. That 'transformation' and 'revealing', he says, still happen in every religious ritual, for example in initiation rites. He says that what is made available to the novice in such rites is 'the essence of the non-appearing', which he likens to the Kantian *noumena*, which are intellectual or intuited things. He likens it also to the Ionians' *physis*, the principle or *Arche* of all things, 'the sustaining ground of man and his universe'. Thus, for Elkin, The Dreaming is in cosmogonical terms 'the ever-present, unseen ground of being – of existence'.

From cosmogony he passes to cosmology. The cosmos is The Dreaming as it appears in phenomena. It is the universal ground of every particular, unlimited by space or time.

Elkin appears to wish to show Aboriginal thinkers as having wrestled with most of the perennial philosophical problems: the one and the many, the particular and the universal, time and duration, the conditioned and the conditioning, and so on. In order to do so he draws on parallels with some of the pre-Socratic philosophers (e.g. Thales and Heraclitus), some of the moderns (Leibniz, Kant and Bergson) and even finds some analogies in Hindu thought. Some of the propositions that emerge are that 'man and natural species and phenomena are considered parts of one and the same social, moral and psychological order or structural system', which is very reminiscent of Radcliffe-Brown's view; that 'man and all that exists not only have a common source in The Dreaming but also constitute a personalized system'; and that that is why 'contingencies can be interpreted and met, and even forestalled, through behaviour of a ritualized or formal pattern'.

He then goes on to consider some questions of epistemology: the Aboriginal categories of causation, time, space, number and – perhaps a little strangely – property. I have no time to go into details but will indicate only his main observations.

As to causation, Elkin appears to embed the discussion in the context of the 'personalized system' already mentioned. I believe he means by this that some events put into operation by personal, spiritistic and magical activities by ritual, were countered by the same means. He seems to say that what we call 'cause' was the facilitation by ritual means of invisible *noumena* to become visible. An illustration was the use of totemic ritual to release the life-principle from totemic sites. Probably I have not understood this part of the exposition, but it seems to be Elkin's opinion that Aboriginal thinkers had not conceived of cause as 'a linkage of preceding events together with the total context of situations' but thought instead of 'personal and spiritistic and magical causes, seen or unseen, nearby or at a distance'.

As to time, Elkin accepts that the Aboriginal does 'recognise a past as distinct from the immediacy of today' but it is not a past that stretches very far back – at the most two or three generations – and 'it is not a past that is gone forever'. Elkin explains that under this conception 'man and natural phenomena do not exist now, and events do not happen now, as a result of a chain of events extending back to a long-past period – a 'Dreamtime' – a beginning. They exist and they happen because that Dreamtime is also here and now. It is The Dreaming, the condition or ground of existence'. He draws a formidably difficult picture in explanation. It is a picture of time, not as 'a horizontal line extending back horizontally through a series of pasts but rather of a vertical line in which the past underlies and is within the present'. It is an argument, as I understand it, that time was not a feature of the Aboriginal cosmos; that 'chronological distance' did not exist for them; and that all existence cycled, being replenished from The Dreaming, which was inexhaustible.

It seems to me that Elkin is saying that time for the Aborigines was not 'real' or 'objective'; not quantitative in being a measure of change; not a relationship such as that between past, present and future as we understand them; not any kind of entity, but essentially a psychological experience. By implication he goes farther: these are not his words, but time for an Aboriginal does not 'fly like an arrow'; again these are not his words, but time for an Aboriginal 'flies like a boomerang'; it curves and returns upon itself. With a sort of cosmic courtesy, it cycles and, because of that, it allows what to us are asymmetrical and irreversible temporal relations to become for Aborigines non-temporal and mutually compenetrative between past and present. It is therefore of no significance that Aborigines may seem ahistorical in outlook, and remember nothing farther away than the great-grandfather's day: the cosmos, as it were, remembers for them. The world of any Aboriginal community is saturated with memorial signs of things on the remembering of which human life depends. So that, for Elkin, The Dreaming as the condition or ground of existence, is timeless and cannot receive any change, which may help to explain the discovered tendency of Aboriginal society to accept only those new things that will fit the forms of permanence.

Elkin handles the Aboriginal categories of space and number in somewhat similar fashion. In essence, he regards the absence of measuring and numbering by units in linear order as 'a striking, if not the basic, difference in the epistemological concepts of Western and Aboriginal thought'. I will leave that very large proposition as stated, and to move on to his, to me, rather strange proposition that Aborigines were 'owned' by the territory which, in ordinary speech, we would say they 'owned'. He repeats the proposition in a number of ways: a man's country 'knew' him and gave him 'sustenance and life'; what we call 'possessions' or 'things' – the ground itself, symbolic sites, totems, totem places – are not 'things' but 'sacramental means through which man identifies himself with, and participates in, The Dreaming'.

Now, having written much about 'The Dreaming', and, in a sense having invented it, in that I was the first to write about it with a capital T and a capital D, I should perhaps be the last to say so, but The Dreaming is coming in for a lot of attributions that I think it should accept only under advisement. There is, for example, a distinctly zoological undertone to the idea of any person being 'owned' by a tract of country. This notion has entered into Australian law, at least as an *obiter dicta*, as an outcome of Mr Justice Blackburn's judgment in the Yirrkala land case, in which he used certain words to the effect that the members of certain clans were owned by the clan lands.

Having admitted – superfluously – as you will have noted, that I am no philosopher, I now admit, in supererogation, that I am no lawyer, but at the same time I insist that there is something wrong at the heart of this proposition. I argue that a 'property' relation is a direct relation between a person and an object only in an elliptical way. It is a relation between persons *in respect* of an object: and this is vastly different. It is at the least a triadic, not a dyadic relation. What we see in the Aboriginal world is a relationship between the members of a patrilineal local clan, or similar group, jointly and the whole world of other persons, single, joint, or common: a relationship expressed as a claim of right, with well-understood 'incidents', in respect of a finite territory, and all its symbols. It approximates to a covenanted relationship, entered into by, and multilaterally agreed to amongst, the ancestral founders of Aboriginal society, and raised by religious tradition to sacramental status. To speak of land 'knowing' or 'owning' anyone is to me a reversion to animatism.

I spoke earlier of the anthropological criticisms of the post-Socratic Western philosophical tradition. But even if we turn to the pre-Socratics we need to remember that they were already 'the heirs of a mature civilization and culture and to some extent (were) reactionaries against it. They revolted against the mythological, imaginative view of the universe and its origin, and endeavoured in a scientific, free and unprejudiced spirit to answer the problem in a rational way'.[16] There is clearly a risk of enormous anachronism even if we attempt no more than to look for similarities between their anti-mythological thought and the pre-philosophic thought we imagine we can intuit or deduce from Aboriginal religious thought and practice. Moreover, one is entitled to ask whether even the earliest Greek philosophers, from the very nature of their known interests, are likely to be helpful. They were in a sense physical philosophers, trying to discern a common hidden structure behind the outward appearance of the physical world. Their imagery was material, and so was their nomination of the substance common to all corporeal change – water, fire, air, and 'the boundless' – as the material principle of things. I would think that, if we accuse the Aborigines of philosophy, we cannot justly accuse them of hylozoism, of attributing life to matter, as did the Ionians. Nor, as I understand them, did the Aborigines puzzle over movement and change like the Greeks, or pursue knowledge of the cosmos for its own sake. I can see no evidence that they had conceived of an *Arche*, a material principle of all things, although their symbolism of water, air, fire and – dare I say? – the boundless Dreaming is well known to be richly developed. But it seems to me to be following a false scent to pore over the Aboriginal data looking for hints of a search for unity of substance in all material diversity, or for a hidden structure of reality behind physical diversity, or for a search for knowledge for its own sake. And lastly, I doubt if it could rightly be said that the Aborigines were, like the pre-Socratics, 'captivated by "movement" in the widest sense of the word: movement in the heavens, in the coming-to-be and passing-away of things of experience, in the incessant change of human life, individual and political'.[17]

Now, I do not deny the value even of distant analogy, but here are four good reasons for caution until whatever analogies we draw with Western philosophical thought are deepened and refined. There are other difficulties too, the greatest being the absence of a literate tradition, the fact that there was nothing to suggest the growth of a self-conscious intellectual detachment towards the myths – no Hesiod or Homer to winnow and organise the raw material, and, last but not least, except for a few specialists, our abysmal ignorance of the deeper semantics of Aboriginal languages, including the secret languages often used by ritualists.

But here I withdraw a pace or two. In their own way the Aborigines did try to catch hold of a hidden structure of things. I wrote elsewhere that they seemed fascinated almost to the point of obsession with 'vitality, fertility and growth', and that

> vitalistic things obtruded throughout the myths and rites – water, blood, fat, hair, excrements, the sex organs, semen, sexuality in all its phases,

> the quickening in the womb, child-spirits, mystical impregnation and reincarnation; the development of the body from birth to death, the transitions of the human spirit from before organic assumption until after physical dissolution; apparently animated phenomena such as green leaves, rain and the seasons, lightning, whirlwinds, shooting stars and the heavenly bodies; or things of unexplained origin, unusual appearance and giant size . . .[18]

To say so is not to rediscover the Tylorian *anima* or Marrett's animatism. But it is a topic for another occasion.

## NOTES

1 William James, *The Essential Writings*, edited by Bruce Wiltshire, Harper and Row, New York, 1971, p. 221.
2 E.A. Worms, 'Religion' in *Australian Aboriginal Studies*, 1963, p. 231.
3 W.E.H. Stanner, 'Religion, Totemism and Symbolism' in R.M. and C.H. Berndt (eds) *Aboriginal Man in Australia*, Angus and Robertson, Sydney, 1965, pp. 213, 215.
4 T.G.H. Strehlow, *Aranda Traditions*, Melbourne University Press, Melbourne, 1947; 'Personal Monototemism in a Polytotemic Community', in *Sonderdruck aus Festschrift fur Ad. E. Jensen*, 1964.
5 Strehlow, 'Personal Monototemism in a Polytotemic Community', p. 729.
6 Charles H. Eden, *The Fifth Continent*, Society for Promoting Christian Knowledge, London, 1877, pp. 69–70.
7 Eden, *The Fifth Continent*, pp. 69–70.
8 William James, *Essential Writings*, p. 241.
9 James Feibleman, *The Theory of Human Culture*, Humanities Press, New York, 1946.
10 L.R. Hiatt (ed.), *Australian Aboriginal Mythology*, Australian Institute of Aboriginal Studies, Canberra, 1975, introduction, p. 10.
11 Hiatt, *Australian Aboriginal Mythology*, p. 10. The quotation is from Róheim.
12 Anton Baumstark, *Comparative Liturgy*, Mowbray, London, 1958, p. l.
13 Stanner, 'Religion, Totemism and Symbolism', p. 235.
14 Edward A. Tiryakian, *Sociologism and Existentialism*, Prentice-Hall, Engelwood Cliffs, New Jersey, 1962, p. 3.
15 A.P. Elkin, 'Elements of Australian Aboriginal Philosophy', *Oceania* 40 (1969), pp. 85–98.
16 Ignatius Brady, *A History of Ancient Philosophy*, Bruce Publishing Co., Milwaukee, 1959, p. 31.
17 Brady, *A History of Ancient Philosophy*, p. 66.
18 Stanner, 'Religion, Totemism and Symbolism', p. 217.

CHAPTER TWO

# A Profile of Good and Bad in Australian Aboriginal Religion

*Ronald M. Berndt*

## I

My theme of' 'good' and 'bad' in Aboriginal religion is one which is close to all theological thinking. It is also one which, I believe, was implicit in some of Charles Strong's writings, as one would expect it to be.[1] Before I explore this issue, however, it is necessary to say something about Aboriginal religion in general terms so that my theme can be viewed in perspective.

Most of us have ideas about what constitutes religion, or *a* religion, even though we might be hesitant in articulating a definition which could fit a number of different religious orientations. Moreover, in view of the spate of material on Aboriginal society and culture emanating from varying sources, some of which may well be dubious, we might take the line of least resistance and read into what we hear about Aboriginal religion what we already know about our own or others.

That kind of approach is almost a time-honoured one. We like to clothe the strange or the unfamiliar with an identifiable mantle which provides an explanatory frame of reference in our own terms. Bringing alien things into our own experience and treating them in this way is a relatively common device. It enables us to rationalise them; and by finding basic similarities we can commence to use them, or express tolerance toward those who use them, or are of them. However, that process of transformation usually takes us a long way from their empirical reality and, in our particular case, from what Aboriginal religion means to traditionally-oriented people.

The search for meaning is central to systematic anthropological research; but methodological devices used in that process often remove it from the empirical situation. Consequently, the end product that tells us what particular religious phenomena mean to particular believers or practitioners can differ considerably from an explanation offered in more general terms. The process of interpretation can have its dangers. It can hide or, at best, overshadow what people have to say about their religion. To put this in another way, the understanding of Aboriginal religion has been greatly affected by theories about religion. That does not mean that interpretation is not a significant heuristic device. My much revered teacher, the late Professor A.P. Elkin, saw Aboriginal religion as concerning primarily the 'secret life of men'. Only grudgingly did he include women within the sacred dimension, and then only with particular limitations. In the third edition (1954) of his *Australian Aborigines* he wrote, of women, that 'they are in the "nave", and sometimes even in the "chancel" '.[2] Because he conceptually separated religion from everyday living and emphasised the idea of 'secrecy', his philosophical approach led him to think in mystical terms, a kind of oversanctification of belief and ritual. Elkin sought a methodological scheme in order to provide added meaning to his material on Aboriginal religion;[3] and that guided him toward paths which were vulnerable to criticism, as Stanner has quite rightly pointed out.[4]

Stanner himself, however, has not been immune to this. In his monograph 'On Aboriginal Religion', it is clear that various theories of religion have influenced considerably his own thinking about Aboriginal religion.[5] While I do not follow him in his delineation of ritual sacrifice in relation to initiation,[6] nor in his treatment of sacramentalism, his analysis of Murinbata religion was grounded in a firm belief in the continuous relevance of religion in everyday living.[7] He has probably influenced me, at least to some degree, in my own approach in *Australian Aboriginal Religion*[8] – of which he has been critical.

## II

Elkin and myself have been the only two Australian anthropologists so far who, in writing about Aboriginal religion, have been able to draw on firsthand knowledge of a fairly wide range of Aboriginal societies. Most other studies (for example, those by Warner, Strehlow and

Meggitt), including Stanner's, have focused on the religion of one particular Aboriginal society. It is well to remember that, traditionally, Aboriginal culture was not the same throughout the continent. Nor was there any central or federal authority. The picture was one of relatively independent sociocultural constellations, that interacted only within a certain regional range. The members of such constellations were jealous of their own internal integrity and proud of their own unique identity: differences and contrasts between them were important in helping to define that identity. It was not strictly possible to speak of one Aboriginal religion. There were, rather, many Aboriginal religions. We can identify basic similarities – notably, in the organisation of activities associated with ritual expressions; but differences between belief systems, in meaning and in symbolic interpretation, were quite crucial.

The social component, the social dimension of religion, must not be underestimated; but the question of mytho-ritual meaning is of fundamental significance. While religious knowledge was something which all members of a particular social group possessed in some degree, and was seen as being uniquely theirs, related to them and to them alone, some mytho-ritual complexes were much broader in perspective. Common threads of belief and practice did link or hold together large numbers of people belonging to different social units, although acknowledgement of similarity was not always made explicit. Even where it was, variation between one sociocultural constellation and the next was expected and 'normal'. It is only in recent years, with the growing interest in establishing an overall Aboriginal identity, that attempts are being made to play down differences and to highlight common elements.

The lineaments of all Aboriginal religion, looked at from outside, in overview, were basically alike. They rested on a three-fold set of relationships: between human beings themselves; between human beings and nature; and between human beings and their deities. This was articulated through what has been called in translation 'the Dreaming', a concept which was and is a key to the eternal verities of human living. Variously expressed, it provided a charter for the whole pattern of human existence. It was manifested through mythic characters, often in human form but often with shape-changing propensities. Their actions shaped the land and the environment we know today. Some were responsible for creating human beings and natural species and for introducing particular social orders. Some were more circumscribed in their actions and/or more localised. They humanised the world – the world of their believers and adherents.

Their adventures and travels usually concluded in either of two ways. One was transformation or metamorphosis: they finally changed their physical shape, adopting the physical forms we can see them in now. Or they moved out of one particular area into another; and within a certain range, their paths provided lines of communication and shared ritual linkages between neighbouring groups. In either case, they left behind them an essential quality which we can call a sacred power. Thus they continue to live on eternally in spiritual form, and to influence the actions of human beings. They also left tangible expressions of themselves throughout the countryside. Such places contain something of their spiritual essence. They sanctify the land, and are often focal points for ritual action.

These mythic beings, then, are not only intimately associated with the land. They are part of it. They are also directly related to living Aborigines. This linkage exists mainly through the ability of mythic beings to change their shape. For example, a particular spirit is mythically manifested through a particular creature. In fact, all such creatures today are a reflection of different spirits, and all are believed to contain the essential essence of the Dreaming. There may also be other correlations through which that spiritual essence is conveyed. Through conception or birth, every Aboriginal person is believed to have a similar linkage. A mythic symbol, in the form of a creature or some associated manifestation, animates a foetus, bringing with it a life-force emanating from the Dreaming. This symbol, or 'totem' as it is sometimes called, serves as an agent, a manifestation of that bond. In doing so, it underlines the belief that he, or she, has the *same* spiritual quality as a particular mythic being, and is closely identified with that being. In some areas, he or she is regarded as a living representation of a particular mythic character. Aboriginal men and women are identified through the myths, and identify themselves within these. Human beings are regarded as being part of nature, bound to it by strong emotional ties, sharing a common life-force.

This view emphasises the contemporary relevance of a *living* mythology which concerns everyday behaviour and thought. Mythology, whether or not it has a ritual expression or a ritual counterpart, is not so much a celebration of the past. It has to do with the present, and is a continuing force, adaptive to changing social circumstances. In brief, the structure of mythic events is believed to have been set once and for all at the very beginning of things, during the creative era. Those events have a continuing relevance to man. And mythic actions, shorn of their supernatural and magical elements, bear a close resemblance to those of traditionally-oriented Aborigines. Such myths are symbolic statements, believed to convey more than their bare story value. They are explanatory vehicles which are subject to interpretation. The events they portray provide guides to action, the good and the bad among them.

Traditional Aboriginal societies were examples of what have been called sacred societies. That is to say, religion was all-pervasive and permeated all aspects of social living. It is true that certain rituals or particular areas or sites were set apart, that access to them was restricted. Many of the great rituals, including their songs and the emblems which were used, were of a secret-sacred nature. There were rules governing the admission or exclusion of particular persons, both males and females. In general terms, the major religious rites were dominated by men, and women were more or less submissive supporters. Nevertheless, virtually everyone in a particular society was involved in some way. Aboriginal religion was marked, not so much by a visible demarcation between the sexes, as by complementarity between men and women. Socio-economic interdependence between men and women, whether young or old, made possible the holding of large ritual sequences. This did not invalidate or detract from the significance of the secret-sacred. Detailed religious knowledge was held by a selected few. Symbolic meanings and mytho-ritual interpretations were graded. There was scrupulous protection of emblems and other aspects from the uninitiated. Custodians of religious knowledge – the specialists, as it were – were fully-initiated older (not necessarily 'old') men. Nevertheless, the outlines of the great myths were known (*had* to be known) by all members of a particular society or group. Their more esoteric symbolic allusions, their more complex inner meanings, were the concern only of fully-initiated men.

Two points need to be made. One, Aboriginal religion concerned everyone within a community, in varying degrees. Two, Aboriginal religion in its mytho-ritual expression was intimately associated with everyday social living, with relations between the sexes, with the natural environment, and with food-collecting and hunting. And, *as* religion, it was concerned with the meaning of life, with the fundamental patterning of human existence, and with what we can call the moral universe.

## III

There are several ways in which we may look at this 'moral universe'. I shall approach the matter through the internal content of particular myths. Not all can be treated in this way, but many of them can.

Statements are made about what happened in the creative era – in that dimension of the Dreaming. Through some action on the part of a mythic being, a direction is taken which changes subsequent events; it has not only mythic but also continuing human implications. A simple example is one that tells how death came into the world. The reference is to physical death. There are many versions, from all over the continent. These are two very short ones.

> In a Maung version from western Arnhem Land,[9] Moon man quarrels with Spotted Possum, or Spotted Cat, who is mortally wounded. As Possum lies dying he says: 'All the people who come after me . . . will die forever!' Moon, however, replies: 'You should have let me speak first, because I won't die.' Because Possum spoke first, human beings die.
>
> In a similar myth from north-eastern Arnhem Land,[10] Moon man lives with his sister, Dugong. Because she is in pain after being severely bitten by leeches, she decides to leave her human form (that is, to die) and become a dugong. Moon, however, does not want to die. He says he will go into the sky: that he will die, but will come back alive. His sister replies: 'When I die, I won't come back, and you can pick up my bones.' That is how death came into the world.

In a different context, Stanner, on the basis of Murinbata mythology, writes of a 'wrongful turning of life'.[11] There is 'the persistent suggestion', he says, 'of many myths that there has been some kind of "immemorial misdirection" in human affairs, and that living men are committed to its consequences'. His example is that of the mythic woman, Mutingga, who swallows several children. As a result, she is killed, her belly opened up and the children removed alive. In the discussion of this myth, which concerns the rite of *punj*, Stanner observes, among a number of things, that Mutingga should not have died. However, she had 'gone wrong', and it was her own fault. As a result, men now have the bullroarer which 'stands for' or is symbolic of her. A parallel should not be drawn between this sequence of events and the disobedience of Adam and Eve. In the case of Adam and Eve, a contract was made, and the breaking of that contract brought sin into the world. The original mythic picture as far as Aboriginal Australia is concerned is different.

The Mutingga example is roughly similar to the Mara version of the Kunapipi myth.[12]

> Mumuna (the Mother), aided by her two daughters (the Mungamunga), entices men to their camp. During the night, when they are making love with the girls, she kills the men, then roasts them and swallows them whole. Afterwards she regurgitates them, expecting them to be revived by the bites of meat ants; but they are not. This performance is repeated again and again, until her daughters become worried about the death of so many men. In the meantime, however, relatives of the men have formed a search party and eventually discover what has been happening. Their leader, Eaglehawk, catches Mumuna in the act and kills her. Her death-cries enter every tree, and so does her blood. It is really the blood which contains the sound. Eaglehawk then cuts down a tree and makes a bullroarer. As he swings it, it 'turns into a mumuna'; its sound is that of the Mother as she died.

As with the Murinbata example, the Gunwinggu-speaking people of western Arnhem Land have myths in which the death of a mythic being brings about a ritual 'advantage'.[13]

> In one case, Lumaluma, the Whale, comes on two men incorrectly carrying out a sacred *maraiin* ritual.[14] He is enraged at this, and frightens them away. Then he finds their *maraiin* emblems, which represent various natural species. He spears each of the emblems in turn, calling its name: each takes its animal shape and returns to its natural habitat. He gathers up some of the other objects he finds and goes back to his home camp. The people are angry, and plan to hold another *maraiin* ritual. Against the advice of his relatives, Lumaluma attends, and is speared. Before he dies, he reveals all of his own emblems and the appropriate ritual that goes with them. After that, he goes down to the sea and 'turns himself' into a whale.

The problem here is one of interpretation. Do such examples represent 'an immemorial misdirection', as Stanner has put it? In our own work on the Gunwinggu, we commented briefly on this issue.[15] While an 'immemorial misdirection' can easily be seen to be relevant to myths about death coming to man, it is not particularly apparent in the others. Gunwinggu speakers would interpret such actions on the part of mythic beings as an exercise of 'free will'. Mythic beings, like human beings, can choose one course of action in contrast to another. The choice they make has consequences for themselves and for others, but does not necessarily commit them irrevocably. However, one consequence of the mythic action for human beings (as in the case of

Mutingga, Mumuna and Lumaluma) is ritual advantage. It results in the introduction of ritual which, supposedly, would not have come about without a wrong act taking place. Out of bad, comes something good. In the myth itself, no moral judgement is made: it is simply that this is the course of events which brings about ritual benefits – 'this is how it came about'. The comment by Stanner that Mutingga 'went wrong' can well be regarded as her having made a wrong choice, that it was her own fault, and need not have been. Among the Gunwinggu, there are other examples which underline the aspect of 'destiny' or of 'fate': that certain events occur which are beyond the control of a mythic being and, presumably, beyond the control of man.

## IV

Spirit characters most subject to this fatalistic complex are, in western Arnhem Land, called *djang* characters. Like the major mythic beings already mentioned, they move across the country and, in the process, they introduce changes in the local landscape and leave behind there supplies of natural species. The primary difference between them and the others is that they actually take a 'wrong turning', do something they should not have done and, importantly, recognise this. The suggestion is that, if only they had known that what they were doing would bring disaster on themselves and on others, they would have acted differently. Possession of that knowledge would have enabled them to make a choice between one course of action and another. However, the dice are loaded and, consequently, they are fated to 'go wrong' – nothing can be done about it, and they don't really resist their destiny!

> At Gudjegbin, a spirit man killed a wallaby, and he and his wife prepared an oven in which to cook it. Unfortunately, they have made their oven on taboo sandy ground. As the animal is cooking, its stomach bursts and the blood seeps into the sand. The noise and the smell of the blood attract two Rainbow Snakes (Ngalyod), who emerge from nearby rocks. They swallow the pair and then vomit them as rocks. The two characters in the story had 'made themselves wrong'.
>
> In another example, an orphan living at Ilngir, near the mouth of Cooper's Creek, cried continually. His mother's sister, Inimbu, offered him different kinds of food to keep him quiet, but he refused every one. Ngalyod, the Rainbow Snake, was disturbed by his crying. She came across the country toward the camp where the noise was coming from. She made the ground shake and made flood waters rise, foaming. And

> the cold wind was so bitter that all the camp fires died. Eventually, she surrounded all the people camped there and swallowed them, including the orphan. In a sequel to this, other people, on hearing of this, followed up Ngalyod and speared her so that she vomited all of them, still alive.

Such myths are very detailed and there are many variations on this particular theme.

> A common one is that an orphan is neglected, and not adequately fed. His brother is angry. To punish the whole camp, he deliberately breaks a taboo Ngalyod egg (sometimes a taboo stone) secreted in a tree. Ngalyod makes her appearance, bringing with her an intensely cold wind which 'turns' all the people into rock at Ganyulaidjgandi: 'they make themselves *djang*'. Something wrong had occurred; nothing could have been done to avert disaster.

And finally, among the many myths of this kind:

> A man named Gawariwari lives on wild honey which he collects. Since he eats only this, and is always collecting honey from trees, one of his arms remains raised in an upright position. He moves across the country, putting honey into his basket. He comes to a place named Gugulgoidj. Everywhere he looks, there is honey. From a large tree, however, comes the loud buzzing of bees. There is something different here, he thinks, and his body starts to tingle. He begins to worry. 'What am I going to do?' he asks. 'Perhaps I have spoilt this honey?' A storm breaks, and with the rain comes Ngalyod. Gawariwari cries out: 'I have spoilt myself. I had better run to Gulbalga!' But he can do nothing to save himself, there are too many Ngalyod waiting to swallow him. So he turns himself into a painting at Gulbalga rocks: he 'makes himself *djang*'.

The interpretation of such myths as these, which are part of the fabric of western Arnhem Land religion, requires the presentation of much more detail than I am able to include here. They are not typical of Aboriginal mythology as a whole and are quite distinctively Gunwinggu. Many characters set out in search of a country, a particular place (or a particular kind of place) where they are to become *djang*. They embark on their journey with that specific expectation – that they will be transformed, will put their spirits 'for ever', at their pre-defined destination. It is *within* that frame, and not outside it, that they take a course of action which leads to that denouement. If and when they 'do wrong', or 'go wrong', it is within the context of an already-shaped destiny.

The interplay of free will blocked, and inevitable disaster, constitutes a cultural emphasis which points up an essential conflict in human values. But the myths are much more than this. They symbolise a fundamental dilemma of man. While not necessarily undermining man's essential harmony with nature, they nevertheless indicate the presence of hostile forces which are not easily placated and which can be aroused inadvertently.

Ngalyod, the Rainbow Snake, is a key cathartic figure. Ngalyod (or other equivalent names) may be referred to as male or female, may be represented in multiple form, and may or may not have children. As the 'good Mother', in this region, she is an expression of human and environmental fertility and the sponsor of ritual which concerns the well-being of the society and its members. In her 'bad Mother' manifestation, she is fear-inspiring, easily angered and quick to respond to real or supposed transgressions. She is a living symbol of the balance between 'goodness' and 'badness', and of the view that wrong actions on the part of human beings (whether or not they are intentional) are to be expected and will not or cannot necessarily be prevented. This theme is at the root of questions about the destiny of man. While warnings are apparent in the myths, which make explicit what disasters can befall human beings, these disasters are not easy to evade and the results are inevitable.

Even in the context of the *djang* myths, therefore, it is not a case of an 'immemorial misdirection'. Mythically, each *djang*-transformation or 'turning' (that is, becoming something else) is a creative act in the overall process of humanising or spiritualising the natural world. Many *djang* centres are species-renewal sites, activated through particular rites. Many, of course, are not, and exist as *self-perpetuating* species-renewal sites. In that sense, out of a perceived wrong act, good emerges.

## V

This problem of 'good' and 'bad' was one that undoubtedly exercised the minds of Aborigines as they told their myths around camp fires or sang and danced them out on the ritual ground. Differences between good and bad actions were never in doubt. They were spelt out in considerable detail in the mythology which constituted the basis of their belief system, and were identified in everyday life.

> When a north-eastern Arnhem Lander of the *dua* moiety dies, his or her spirit is taken by Bunbalama (the Paddle Maker) in his canoe out to sea in the direction of Bralgu, the land of the dead. He or she transfers to the back of a porpoise, and goes on to Bralgu. There a *bilgbilg*, masked plover,

> warns Gringbilma, who is on the look-out for newly arrived spirits. The newcomer is asked where he comes from and who his relatives are, and then passes on to meet two old women named Yambiyambi and Lialugidj. He is told to drink unclean water from a well. As he bends forward, they look at his nasal septum. If it has been pierced properly and can be seen through, he is told not to drink, but to continue on to where the other Bralgu spirits are living. If not, Yambiyambi hits him on the head with her conch shell and the new spirit is killed for ever: he cannot join the other Bralgu spirits and will not be reincarnated as a human being – he simply disappears entirely.

There are several variations on this theme, in this area and in others.

> Among Gunwinggu speakers, for instance, a new spirit passes ill-intentioned guardians of the spirit world who attempt to do him harm. Escaping them, he continues on to the sea coast where he meets the Ferry Man, who takes him across by canoe to the land of the dead where he joins the other spirits. If the new spirit is a woman, the Ferry Man brings a new canoe, lifts her gently into it, and does not beat her as he does a male spirit.

In these accounts, a spirit of a newly dead person is not judged according to the good or bad behaviour of that person during his or her lifetime. The tests relate entirely to whether or not he or she had conformed with traditional custom, although there is preferential treatment for women in some cases. The journey to the land of the dead is supposedly fraught with difficulties which symbolise the vicissitudes experienced in life. On having reached the promised land, he or she joins the immortals, and may be reborn. This absence of accountability to mythic beings for what a person has or has not done during his or her lifetime, emphasises a basic Aboriginal view toward such issues.

Aboriginal mythology is abundantly supplied with what can be described as 'good and bad examples'.[16] The question really is, how should we interpret these? If we accept the premise that myths are a kind of mirror of reality (although never an exact mirror), that they reflect to some degree contemporary living, and that they are symbolic statements about these things – then, we can make a little headway in interpreting them. Radcliffe-Brown once wrote about the cosmos being ruled by law, that men and women ought to observe the rules of behaviour – but that 'there are irregularities in human society and in nature'.[17] Stanner, speaking of myths, also suggested that they 'are a sort of statement about the whole reality, a declaration about the penalties of private will, and by implication a thesis on the spoiling of possible unity'.[18] I would agree with the first part of this, but not necessarily with the implication. It was with a different interpretation that I was concerned in my paper on 'Traditional morality as expressed through the medium of an Australian Aboriginal religion'.[19]

In brief, the 'irregularities of human society and in nature' constitute part of a total system and are written into it as part of the condition of social living. Consequently, they are *part of that unity*. Hiatt misunderstood this point when he wrote that if a myth merely describes the good and evil that people do, then either it is a charter for both good and evil or not a charter at all'.[20] The issue is not as simple as this. In the Western Desert, the great mytho-ritual religious cycle of the *dingari* expresses in its patterning a series of mythic incidents, commenting on the difficulties experienced in Desert living at both the social and environmental levels.[21] These conceptually provide two complementary orientations, in which particular circumstances are regarded as being good or bad, as the case may be. While the seasons remain good, people (mythic or otherwise) are able to achieve reasonable personal satisfaction. Bad seasons can bring hunger, thirst and even tragedy. In social living, breaches of the peace occur, which may be occasioned by fear, jealousy, quarrelling, trickery, theft, seduction, murder and so on. These infiltrate the ethical system as such. In this way, the *dingari* provides a yardstick against which both moral and immoral actions are conceived of as a natural condition of man. Each incident categorised as being bad, or immoral, is resolved in some way which permits a return to the status quo. The resolution may not at all times appear to be of a kind we would 'naturally' expect. After all, we are dealing with different assumptions about law and order and the moral universe. Nevertheless, an act adjudged 'bad' follows its own course, which is likely to bring disaster or punishment on the wrongdoer. That course of action is spelt out in the myth, and is not simply assumed or left unrecorded.

I shall give two examples, very much summarised:

1 Ngadjinaulweru, an old man, makes a small boy, Mudila, carry a heavy load of boomerangs without giving him food. While he is out cutting more wood for boomerangs, Mudila obtains meat himself and cooks it. However, he eats this alone and hides the fire. Ngadjinaulweru returns hungry and cold. In the night, Mudila escapes with his fire. The old man tracks him down, but is tricked by the boy and drowns in a creek, where he remains. The boy goes into a hole, where he also remains. (These are their Dreaming sites, near a big hill on the Canning Stock Route.)

2 Gadadjilga, a mythic lizard man, seduces a taboo relative (one of the Ganabuda mythic women). In turn he is killed by the other Ganabuda women at Djawuldjawul soak, near Lake White.[22]

Such examples can be multiplied, within differing contexts and in relation to different reprehensible acts. What must be kept in mind is that such examples are mythically framed, are religious, and may be re-enacted in ritual. They reflect, as Stanner mentions, 'much of the "human-all-too-human" character of man'.[23]

Myth, as to some extent a reflection of reality – and Western Desert mythology mirrors this reasonably well – demonstrates this essential character of man. Moreover, because such myths belong to the Dreaming, as do all of those I have noted here, they are part of the sacred-past-in-the-present. In other words, these myths and the religious system into which they fit, concern issues relevant to the welfare of man. If we think of some of these as bizarre, or even as fantastic (as Hiatt seems to think some of them are), that is not really the point.[24] They are symbolic statements, sufficiently flexible to meet the demands of changing events within their own universe of experience. In another sense, they explore the vagaries of human thought, which is not necessarily systematic at all times and does not always identify the implications of specific acts.

In such a body of mythology, relevant to a particular religious expression such as the *dingari*, we are presented with a moral system which portrays the actions of mythic beings who are themselves deities. The lesson driven home is that wrong-doing brings its own punishment in this life, not in the next. In the Bralgu case, where a new spirit is finally 'killed' if his or her nasal septum is not pierced, this is not punishment for doing wrong to others. He or she is being punished for not conforming with the cultural norm. In ordinary circumstances, everyone *would* have their nasal septums pierced, so that the situation is in a sense unreal. The myths I have just discussed are more down-to-earth. What they are saying is that there are things which can and do happen in the ordinary process of social living. They may be good or they may be bad, and they happened to mythic beings; it is therefore likely they will happen to human beings. They are part of an inevitable and irreversible frame of existence – when bad actions affect, harmfully, other persons, some form of punishment is bound to result. The good is conceived as co-existing with the bad.

Supernatural intervention is not really envisaged – except in the case of specific ritual infringements, where sanctions are imposed, through human agents. Generally, a deity does not intervene in the affairs of man unless induced to do so. People themselves must take some initiative, or make some move. Ritual activity is the normal channel through which man communicates with his deities. Intrusion into a taboo area, or contravening some rule directly associated with a mythic being, automatically triggers off a ritual response, which arouses the deity. In the *djang* examples, we saw that cooking on sandy ground, breaking a Rainbow's egg, repeated crying on the part of a child, and so on, can bring – or summon – the Rainbow Snake. The breaking of a taboo is in itself a kind of ritual, in reverse, which brings about what can be called divine punishment.

In ordinary circumstances, human beings must work quite hard to gain a livelihood directly from their environment. But, in Aboriginal belief, this kind of hard work is not enough. For the seasons to come and go in an orderly fashion, for the species to be regularly renewed, ritual must be performed. Human beings must play their part. The three-sided relationship I mentioned before, between people and natural environment and deities, was seen as one of interdependence, of working in conjunction with one another; but it called for a concerted effort on the part of human beings. I use the word 'conjunction' in this context, rather than 'harmony', for a particular reason. It is not so much that Aboriginal creative beings made people in their own image (or vice versa) – although many of them did so, as in the case of the great Gadjari, the Djanggau (Djanggawul) and Waramurungoindju, to mention only three. Remember that Aborigines in many areas, particularly in the Western Desert, through birth or conception, have within them a part of, or are manifestations of, particular mythic beings.[25]

There is, however, a basic dilemma here – not necessarily seen as such by those Aborigines involved in traditional situations. On one hand, myths purport to show a range of possible mythic and human action. Superficially, a range of choices is presented for inspection. It is not so much the 'good' which is emphasised. That is taken for granted. But the 'bad' receives much more attention – as it should, because through that device its inevitable, harmful repercussions are highlighted. On the other hand, there is the question of destiny, which removes free choice, or severely limits it. Once someone has taken a 'wrong turning', the process is irreversible. *Djang* myths demonstrate this aspect. So, in a sense, do those from the Western Desert where wrong actions speak for themselves. The dilemma is not resolved by saying, as do these myths, that good and bad acts are part of the natural order of living. Or, is it saying quite simply and unequivocally that human beings are innately fallible? One point, however, enhances the view that the moral order of Aboriginal man consists of a mixture of both good and bad because this is also the state of nature, of which man is an integral part.

'Evil' is, on the whole, too strong a word for the kind of concept we have here. 'Bad' is more appropriate. As we have seen, good and bad were not polarised as two sharply opposed forces, or entities. Perhaps such a stark crystallisation of opposites, a confrontation of two monolithic concepts or symbolic figures, would not have suited Aboriginal perspectives. That approach possibly sits better in the framework of a religion which emphasises a single supreme deity, or a struggle for supremacy between two key deities. In this respect, some people have hesitated to use the term deity for the supernatural beings, even the main creative beings, of Aboriginal religions; but I do not want to go into the matter of terminology here. They have enough of the attributes of beings usually called deities, in their activities *and*, particularly, in the attitudes of believers toward them, to warrant that label.

It is not that Aborigines did not recognise two-fold contrasts and oppositions. Their social structures are built up almost on a basis of such divisions, and not only the two-fold moiety categorisations that were (and still are) fundamental in so many areas. Structural analysis of Aboriginal myths is an especially intriguing and absorbing field of study because of its contrasting features. The point is that in all these fields there is a complex intermeshing or cross-cutting of contrasts, of opposites and oppositions and mediators. There seems to be no room for a massive confrontation which would subsume or override or discourage mediation. Or, to change the analogy, in myth there is not a continuing struggle between the forces of good and the forces of evil, or between good forces supporting God and bad forces aligned with the Devil. In religious statements, in myth, as in social structure, the contrasts are not cumulative. The picture is more muted. The 'essence' of good and bad is there, but the drama is not presented in terms of a pre-defined moral formula. Just as people traditionally, in their socioeconomic activities, had to contribute a fair amount of work and not wait for others to do it, so they did not get all of their myth-interpretations ready-made. Something was left to them, to put the implications together in the course of their own lives.

## VI

It is the intimate relationship between human beings and their natural environment which distinguishes Aboriginal religion from so many others. Aboriginal religion was, and is, concerned with physical and spiritual survival. These imperatives are enunciated within the mythological context of the Dreaming; and they pervade all aspects of social living. Aboriginal religion is a total way of life; and the transcendental is viewed as a necessary component, inseparable from ordinary living.[26]

While myths are receptive to change, and can be variously interpreted as the occasion demands, they also reflect specific circumstances relating to Aboriginal traditional social living and, as I have said, are deeply rooted in the natural environment. Not only are the deities 'of the land', a land which they moulded and humanised. Many of them have the potential to take other shapes – perhaps human, perhaps animal, bird and so on. The land is a living and tangible expression of their presence within it; and they are represented and symbolised by virtually everything within it. Aboriginal people were traditionally in harmony with this view, identifying personally within that patterning, identifying with their gods in either their good or their bad manifestations.

In such circumstances, the changes which have been wrought by alien intrusion were more than merely damaging in socio-personal terms. They were a deliberate and thoughtless erosion of the Aborigines' emotional and affective life, an erosion which was even more far-reachingly significant to their welfare than the senseless killings and maltreatment which have marked the greater part of their contact with Europeans. Missionaries, who were on the scene from the earliest period of European settlement, were mostly ignorant of the tenets of Aboriginal religion. Unfortunately, many have remained so. In a sense, they were blinded by their own religion, just as Aborigines were. Any attempt at rapprochement led only so far. With Aborigines, it was not simply a matter of changing their belief system. It meant (or would have meant) changing virtually every aspect of their very being. However, since all religions have a measure of commonality, it would conceivably have been possible to establish a unity of interest, whereby Aboriginal religious views could have been taken into account. This happened only rather late in the day. By ignoring Aboriginal religion, earlier missionaries undermined the essential ingredients of religiosity which were there, and in doing so hastened the downhill plunge toward increasing secularisation. A parallel to that course can perhaps be found in the fatalistic idea of a 'wrong turning' which led to inevitable destruction – except that, as far as the *djang* are concerned, the context was different, and so were the results.

The tide was stemmed to some extent, but not for all Aborigines. Many sociocultural systems were totally destroyed – often along with all or most of their members. Nevertheless, in a number of other areas the mytho-ritual orientations continue to exist, although mostly in a modified or reconstructed form.

There are a few, very few examples where genuine attempts were made by Aborigines themselves to combine both Aboriginal and Christian elements. The Elcho Island adjustment movement, in north-eastern Arnhem Land, is a case in point, where a memorial composed of sacred emblems was erected.[27] Among them was one emblem, primarily concerned with local mythology, which had at its apex a Christian cross. I shall not attempt to discuss this innovative approach here, except to say that it was mainly politico-religious and symbolised possibilities which were unfulfilled, and which received a considerable set-back in the development of bauxite mining on the Gove peninsula. Another marked innovation was the introduction of two large panels in the Yirrkalla Methodist church.[28] These depicted incidents from the great *dua* and *yiridja* moiety mythic epics of north-eastern Arnhem Land. However, the abiding presence of these deities (manifested through the paintings) played no part in the church service as such: they simply became part of the local congregation.

The background to both of these examples was the favourable climate of Mission opinion. The Methodist Overseas Mission, on all its stations along the Arnhem Land coast, had a policy or an ideal of 'keeping what's best in the Aboriginal culture'. Not all of the individual missionaries were equally enthusiastic about this, and there were difficulties in translating it into practice. But it made a place for Aboriginal *culture* in the new regime, in suggesting that the Aboriginal creative beings were equivalent (in one respect) to the prophets of the Old Testament, who preceded the coming of Christ and the changes and revelations that came with Him. This Mission view also made a place for Aboriginal *people* of the past: the argument went that they could not be condemned to hell because they had died before the Christian message came to them. The enlightened Methodist approach was in marked contrast to that of some other Christian missions working among Aborigines, even until quite recently.

Even more destructive of Aboriginal religion was alienation of the land. In some regions, as in the Western Desert and eastern Arnhem Land, Aborigines had more opportunity to continue their normal associations with their own territories. Of course, this was not always the case. Inroads were made and continue to be made in varying directions that tend to undermine traditional religion, even in its present, modified forms. The increasing presence of Europeans and of mining is perhaps the most conspicuous and devastating in this respect. Nevertheless, even when Aborigines came into mission settlements they did not lose sight of their own country, and their emotional attachment toward this did not diminish. Recent movements toward decentralisation (in regard to the 'homeland' movements, as they are called) offer opportunities to take up at least some of the threads which in the immediate past have frayed or become slack. Some threads have, however, been entirely broken. In the pastoral areas of the north, in the Northern Territory and in the Kimberleys, traditional religion has certainly not remained intact. But a fair amount has survived, to serve as a refuge to which its adherents could, and still can, escape from the exigencies of an unsympathetic and demanding situation which remained entirely outside their control.

The picture of contemporary traditional Aboriginal religion, in areas where it is still a living reality, is one of a people's reliance on its basic tenets and adherence to its local manifestations. The mythological content remains structurally unimpaired, except for the omission of particular repertoires which are not handed on owing to inherent difficulties of oral transmission in the new situation. Belief remains relatively firm. The word 'relatively' is crucial here, because far-reaching changes have occurred in interpretation and symbolic allusion. Mainly, these changes have been brought about through two developments.

One is an upsurge of interest, not just in finding Aboriginal identity, but in strengthening and ratifying it. Real socio-personal identity, as we have seen, rests in the Dreaming. We could therefore expect religious expressions to receive some attention, and even some refurbishing. The other source of pressure toward change is the recent interest in land rights claims. Some Aborigines see in these an opportunity, not only to regain their own home lands, but also to revivify their religion. A great deal has been made of the political aspects of this struggle, but it really goes much deeper. Possession of land means in effect a continued commitment to traditional religion, whatever form that may take in such changed circumstances. It means, too, a measure of emotional security. These two aspects dominate Aboriginal opinion today.

Both these emphases have led either to an enhancement or to a revival of religious activity. They have led also, as I have already indicated, to many changes. In the Western Desert, for instance, there is a strengthening and a widening of the sphere categorised as being secret-sacred. Some of these changes concern aspects which were traditionally much more flexible. To take one point, the exclusion of women is more apparent today than it was previously. This is also the case with certain rituals, and the emblems and designs used in them. Many of these a few years ago were ordinarily sacred, or open-sacred; now they are regarded as *secret*-sacred.

The theme of exclusion-inclusion has always been a marked feature of Aboriginal ritual life. In my view, this has militated against its more adaptive potentialities. That aside, the strengthening of the secret-sacred dimension is also a device through which 'outsiders' may be excluded and Aboriginality enhanced. In contrast to this is an example from north-eastern Arnhem Land. While retaining sections of the secret-sacred, religious leaders there have relaxed some of the rules of restriction so that parts of the most important rituals may be performed publicly. As a consequence of this, overall religious commitment has been immeasurably widened.[29] In the Kimberley region of Western Australia, religious revival has taken the direction of encouraging large initiatory meetings which attract members of surrounding communities as well as others from far distant places.

Land, and what it means in socio-personal terms, continues to remain significant. When land is alienated, its natural resources depleted, its physiographic features destroyed, this irrevocably harms not only the trappings of belief but, without doubt, traditional religion as such.

In a film produced in 1978, *Walya Ngamardiki – the Land, My Mother*, the creative Mother Waramurungoindju of western Arnhem Land is represented in the shape of a young Aboriginal woman. This imagery brings together three elements: land, symbols, and human figure – specifically, a female human figure. One message it conveys is the importance of the land for Aboriginal people, not only now but for future generations (the young, potentially-fertile-mother aspect). The other is the mythic substantiation of land not simply a generalised relevance, but a specific and a direct local one. Land rights submissions to the Northern and Central Land Councils in the Northern Territory are framed, at one level, in terms of hereditary occupation by particular Aborigines in regard to particular stretches of country. At another and more fundamental level, ownership and possession of land are emphasised through mythic and ritual affiliation. It is myth, sometimes with associated ritual, sometimes in the form of what Stanner has called 'riteless myths', which provides the charter of ownership and constitutes its deeds of possession.

Thus the deities themselves are brought into the harsh light of a court of law, and paraded for the public scrutiny of unbelievers. While their role has changed in recent years, it has not changed in relation to their own land. They continue to justify and to substantiate the rights of their human representatives to hold that land.

Traditionally, of course, there were never any doubts concerning who held that land, in the name or names of the mythic beings. Land was taken for granted. While ownership was thrown into doubt from earliest European settlement, there was no doubt among the Aborigines themselves. The fact that some of these lands are being legally recovered today, simply fulfils the promise of the eternal Dreaming.

Current developments emphasise the fact that Aboriginal religion is vitally concerned with all aspects of social living. Metaphorically, the deities need to display themselves in the service of man and of themselves: that their 'presence' should be sought, and found necessary, in a mundane court of law is not incongruous.

However, we have seen that mythic beings were not, and are not necessarily all-powerful. In many cases, as their mythology reveals, they were and are just as vulnerable to disadvantageous circumstances as are their human counterparts, beset by the forces of good and bad as all of us are. Circumstances were and are often beyond their control, as they are beyond ours. The 'human, all too human' quality of the deities underlines the fallibility of them and of man. The good does not necessarily triumph. The bad may well do so – since, after all, it is part of man's expectation of living.

There are converse parallels we might make, too, concerning the powerful and catastrophic personality of one side of the great Ngalyod, the Rainbow Snake of western Arnhem Land. Those parallels no doubt have been made by Aborigines themselves and will continue to be made – but I shall not spell them out here.

In spite of that, in the face of overwhelming vicissitudes experienced by Aborigines throughout this continent, and wherever Aboriginal religion prevails, the deities, so many Aborigines still believe, will continue to live spiritually.

Provided faith sustains them, Aborigines may win out in this life, not necessarily in the next. But the trend toward secularisation is not a figment of the imagination. It is a reality, a powerful reality, facing all Aborigines today, as it faces us. Could it be that Stanner's 'immemorial misdirection' has already taken place?

NOTES

1 C.R. Badger, *The Reverend Charles Strong and the Australian Church*, Abacada Press, Melbourne, 1971.
2 A.P. Elkin, *The Australian Aborigines*, Angus and Robertson, Sydney, (1938) 1974, p. 213.
3 A.P. Elkin, 'Elements of Australian Aboriginal Philosophy, *Oceania* 40 (1969).
4 W.E.H. Stanner, 'Some Aspects of Aboriginal Religion', Charles Strong Memorial Trust Lecture, see Chapter 1 above.
5 W.E.H. Stanner, 'On Aboriginal Religion', *Oceania* 30 (2 and 4), 31 (2 and 4) and 32 (2), (1959–61).
6 W.E.H. Stanner, 'On Aboriginal Religion, I. The lineaments of sacrifice', *Oceania* 30 (1959), pp. 109–10.
7 W.E.H. Stanner, 'On Aboriginal Religion, II. Sacramentalism, rite and myth', *Oceania* 30 (1960), p. 278.
8 R.M. Berndt, *Australian Aboriginal Religion* (Four fascicles), Brill, Leiden, 1974.
9 R.M. and C.H. Berndt, *The World of the First Australians*, Ure Smith, Sydney, (1st ed., 1964) 1977, p. 397.
10 R.M. Berndt, 'A Wonguri-Mandjikai song cycle of the Moon-Bone', *Oceania* 19, no. 1 (1948), pp. 19–20.
11 Stanner, 'On Aboriginal Religion, II. Sacramentalism, rite and myth', pp. 260–65.
12 R.M. Berndt, *Kunapipi*, Cheshire, Melbourne, 1951, pp. 149–52.
13 Stanner, 'On Aboriginal Religion, II. Sacramentalism, rite and myth', p. 265.
14 R.M. and C.H. Berndt, *Man, Land and Myth in North Australia: the Gunwinggu People*, Ure Smith, Sydney, 1970, pp. 121–22.
15 Berndt and Berndt, *Man, Land and Myth in North Australia.*, pp. 229–33.
16 Berndt and Berndt, *Man, Land and Myth in North Australia.*, pp. 27–29.
17 A.R. Radcliffe-Brown, *Structure and Function in Primitive Society*, Cohen and West, London, 1952, p. 166.

18 Stanner, 'On Aboriginal Religion, II. Sacramentalism, rite and myth', p. 266.
19 R.M. Berndt, 'Traditional morality as expressed through the medium of an Australian Aboriginal religion' in R.M. Berndt (ed.) *Australian Aboriginal Anthropology*, University of Western Australia, for the Australian Institute of Aboriginal Studies, Canberra, 1970, pp. 216–47.
20 L.R. Hiatt (ed.), *Australian Aboriginal Mythology*, Australian Institute of Aboriginal Studies, Canberra, 1975, pp. 6–7.
21 R.M. Berndt, 'Traditional morality'.
22 R.M. Berndt, 'Traditional morality', pp. 224–5; R.M. Berndt, 'The Walmadjeri-Gugadja' in M.G. Bicchieri (ed.), *Hunters and Gatherers Today*, Holt, Rinehart and Winston, New York, 1972, pp. 207–9.
23 W.E.H. Stanner, 'Religion, totemism, and symbolism' in R.M Berndt and C.H. Berndt (eds) *Aboriginal Man in Australia*, Angus and Robertson, Sydney, 1965, p. 218.
24 Hiatt, *Australian Aboriginal Mythology*, p. 7.
25 R.M. Berndt, *Australian Aboriginal Religion*, fasc. 1, p. 10.
26 R.M. Berndt, *Australian Aboriginal Religion*, fasc. 4, p. 28.
27 R.M. Berndt, *An Adjustment Movement in Arnhem Land*, Cahiers de l'Homme, Paris and Mouton, The Hague, 1962.
28 A.E. Wells, *This their Dreaming*, University of Queensland, St Lucia, 1971.
29 R.M. Berndt, 'Looking back into the present: a changing panorama in eastern Arnhem Land, *Anthropological Forum* 4, no. 3 (1978–79).

CHAPTER THREE

# Aboriginal Women and the Religious Experience[1]

*Diane Bell*

In giving the Charles Strong Memorial Trust Inaugural Lecture in 1976, Professor Stanner discussed what he called the 'tetrad' of Aboriginal religion: living people, their countries, their totems and their ancestors.[2] With the elegance and insight characteristic of Stanner's writing on religion, he contended that although there may still be some who question the rightness of including Aboriginal beliefs, acts and objects within the scholarly scope of comparative religion, the intellectual requirements can be, and long ago have been, amply satisfied. It was a theme to which he had turned in 1962 in his essay 'Religion, Totemism and Symbolism',[3] and one which, for my topic, 'Aboriginal Women and the Religious Experience', is particularly apposite.

Reading Stanner had been one of the delights of my undergraduate career. His Boyer Lectures, 'After the Dreaming',[4] set me thinking about the nature of Aboriginal society; his monograph, *On Aboriginal Religion*,[5] directed my attention to the beauty, complexity and sheer poetry of Aboriginal belief systems; his portrait of 'Durmugam: a Nangiomeri'[6] brought to the arid wastes of anthropological theory, the intimacy and immediacy of the lives of the people who become the basis of our studies. But it was not until 1976, when I took up a postgraduate scholarship at the Australian National University, where Stanner was Emeritus Professor, that I met him. I sought his advice on the project I was about to undertake in Central Australia: a study of Aboriginal women's ritual life. While at that stage my understanding necessarily was derived from the classic desert ethnographies of Spencer and Gillen, Meggitt, Munn and Strehlow,[7] my questions were generated by my intuition that a feminist critique could lead to deeper understandings of Aboriginal women's lives and Aboriginal society, just as feminist social scientists had shown was possible in other societies.[8] According to desert ethnographers, Aboriginal women were deemed to be of lesser cultural importance than men, but then, from other sources, I knew that desert women had a separate and secret ritual life.[9] How, I wondered, did women perceive their role? Did they endorse a derogatory self-image or did they nurture a more sustaining one? Did they merely submit to male authority or did they have an authority base of their own? Were men the only guardians of religious Law, or did women, too, share in that body of culturally valued knowledge?

Many saw me as an angry young woman, but Stanner smiled conspiratorially and, with reference to his Daly River material, said, 'You know I always checked my work with one old lady'. He tugged my long hair and added, 'That won't last long'. It was not the problem of caring for long hair to which he referred but rather the Aboriginal practice of cutting one's hair on the death of close relatives. Because I wanted to work on ritual he knew I would need to participate in the ceremonial life of women and that, in so doing, I might well be drawn into a mourning ceremony. For eighteen months I lived in an Aboriginal community,[10] where I was incorporated in the kinship system and, as a classificatory mother, sister and mother-in-law to various young men, participated in their initiations; where as an older woman with two children – a son who was seen to be nearing the age of initiation and a daughter approaching marriageable age – I was admitted into the ritual world of women and participated in many women's ceremonies. When I returned to Canberra I was able to discuss my ethnographic understandings of desert society with Stanner anew. We argued long and furiously. On some issues there was no resolution: our fieldwork experience was undertaken in such different regions and under such different circumstances.

Then, in 1981, as anthropologist to the newly formed Aboriginal Sacred Sites Protection Authority in Darwin,[11] I had the opportunity to work with women of the Daly River and to participate in a closed and secret women's ceremony. Although I could not discuss the content of the rite with Stanner, I desperately wanted to explore with him the implications of the structure of the ceremony and my analysis of its import, for his analysis of women's role and status. But Stanner died in October 1981. I was working on the Daly River Land Claim[12] with people who had known him. We heard the news as we swam at the crossing where he had forded the river decades before.

Let me then, by way of tribute to the 'old man' – a term of respect in Aboriginal society – develop, with reference to Aboriginal women and approaches to the study of their religious beliefs and practices, the theme of his earlier essay and lecture. Beginning with Tylor's observation that 'a once-established opinion, however delusive, can hold its own from age to age', Stanner traced the gradual awakening of scholars to the intricacies of Aboriginal religion.[13] If, he argued, we looked beyond the symbol to the symbolised, we would find that the end of Aboriginal religion was, in Confucian terms, 'to unite hearts and establish order'.[14] However, Stanner pointed out, the myopia of early observers had restricted the study of religion. Of people such as David Collins, the Reverend J.D. Woods, Bishop Salvado, A.A.C. Le Souef, all of whom held, in one form or another, that Aborigines were devoid of religious susceptibilities, Stanner wrote:

> It should not be supposed that they lacked information, learning or humanism. For the most part they were knowledgeable, serious-minded men . . . but they were very sure of their vision. They were genuinely unable to see, let alone credit, the facts that have convinced modern anthropologists that Aborigines are a deeply religious people. That blindness is an important part of our study. It profoundly affected European conduct towards Aborigines.[15]

A host of skilled ethnographers have done much to correct the faulty vision: shafts of bright light have illuminated important aspects of Aboriginal religion such as totemism, Dreaming and cultural symbolism; regional cults and initiation practices.[16] But when we look for expositions of Aboriginal women and their religious life we find not 'that blindness' but a blinkered approach which nonetheless has ramifications for 'European conduct towards Aborigines'. Like the observers of yore, we find a surety of vision when it comes to Aboriginal women's place in society. It would seem that before Aboriginal women's religious life can be recognised, women themselves must first be reinstated as full members of their society. It is as if the white male observers' perception of older Aboriginal women as physically unattractive, has prevented any consideration of their cultural worth. One of the earliest observations is from Peron, a member of Baudin's expedition of 1801–1804, who was repelled by the ugliness of Aboriginal woman. He wrote:

> She was uncommonly lean and scraggy, and her breasts hung down almost to her thighs. The most extreme dirtiness added to her natural deformity.[17]

This response persists. Hart and Pilling write of older Tiwi women as 'ancient hags'.[18] Yet it is these women who are the repositories of knowledge, who in their own domain, the single women's camp, an area taboo to men, discuss important ritual concerns. Meggitt characterises these camps as 'hot beds of gossip'.[19]

Unchallenged by the argument that the impact of changes wrought by the shift from a hunter-gatherer mode of subsistence to a sedentary lifestyle on missions, settlements, cattle stations and in the towns, may have implications for women's status,[20] male dominance is presented as a timeless, enduring reality. Unshaken by the work of Hamilton and Goodale[21] on women's important role in marriage arrangements, we still read of women as the pawns in the games of the male polygynous gerontocracy.[22] Unmoved by the in-depth studies of Phyllis Kaberry in the Kimberleys in the 1930s;[23] Catherine Berndt in South Australia, Western Australia and the Northern Territory from the 1940s onwards,[24] and Jane Goodale with Tiwi on Melville Island in the 1950s,[25] in all of whose work there is ample documentation of the religious character of women's ceremonies, the concept of Aboriginal woman as the profane and excluded persists. Feared for her life-giving powers and constrained by a hearth-centric worldview; the substance of symbols but never the creator of her own social reality; Aboriginal woman's views are dismissed as peripheral to an understanding of Aboriginal society.

In 1937, in introducing his reader to the totemic beliefs and practices of Murngin of north-east Arnhemland, Lloyd Warner wrote of women, 'Little sacred progress is made during her lifetime'.[26] In a similar mode but 35 years later, Ken Maddock generalised that:

> . . . men's cults, despite their secret core, require the active participation of the community at large . . . [and] express broad cohesive and impersonal themes such as fertility and continuity of nature, the regularity of society and the creation of the world. Women's cults are centred upon narrow, divisive and personal interests such as love-magic and female reactions to physiological crises. It is in keeping with the generality of male-dominated religion that men's cults are enacted on a greater scale and with more elaborate symbolism than the women's.[27]

Bern, in basic agreement with Maddock and Warner, stated 'Aboriginal religion is, par excellence, the business of men'.[28] He has argued that although there exists the potential for women 'to construct a counter consciousness to challenge the mature male ideological and political hegemony', women's own autonomous religious life is not one of these contexts because the relevance of women's rituals is for them alone.[29]

On the basis of fieldwork spanning six years, mostly in Central Australian communities with Warlpiri, Warumungu, Alyawarra, Kaytej, Warlmanpa and Anmatjirra speakers, but also in communities close to those in which Warner, Bern and Maddock worked in the Roper River area and Arnhem Land, I would paint a quite different picture of women's religious life.[30]

My documentation and analysis of women's world suggests that in ritual women emphasise their role as nurturers of people, land and relationships. Their responsibility to maintain harmoniously this complex of relationships between the living and the land is manifest in the intertwining of the ritual foci of health and emotional management. Through their *yawulyu*[31] (land based ceremonies) they nurture land, through their health and curing rituals they resolve conflict and restore social harmony and through *yilpinji* (love rituals) they manage emotions. In *yilpinji*, as in their health-oriented *yawulyu*, women seek to resolve and to explore the conflicts and tensions which beset their communities. In centres of population concentration where Aborigines now live, jealous fights, accusations of infidelity and illicit affairs occur on a scale impossible a century ago when people lived in small mobile bands. Thus today, women's role in the domain of emotional management is, like their role in the maintenance of health and harmony, truly awesome.[32]

In women's rituals the major themes of land, love and health fuse in the nurturance motif which encapsulates the growing up of people and land and the maintenance of the complex of land/people relationships. When women hold aloft their sacred boards on which are painted ideational maps of their country, when they dance hands cupped upwards, they state their intention and responsibility to grow up country and kin. To Aboriginal women, as the living descendants of the Dreamtime, the physical acts of giving birth and of lactation are important but are considered to be one individual moment in a much larger design. Their wide-ranging and broadly-based concept of nurturance is modelled on the Dreamtime experience, itself one all-creative force. When women rub their bodies with fat in preparation for the application of body designs which, like the boards, symbolically

Alyawarra women, wearing the design for their country, Erulja, give evidence in the Alyawarra and Anmatjirra Claim to the Utopia pastoral lease, 1979.

encode information about sites, dreamings and estates, when they retrace in song and dance the travels of the mythological heroes, they become as the ancestors themselves. Through ritual re-enactment women establish direct contact with the past, make manifest its meaning and thereby shape their worlds. The past is encapsulated in the present: the present permeates the past.

Variously discussed in terms of the Dreamtime, or Dreaming, Aboriginal religion for desert people is the moral code which informs and unites all life under one Law, the *jukurrpa*. It was in the Dreamtime that the code was made known by the ancestral beings whose tracks criss-crossed the land. The ancestral activity gave form and meaning to the land for the maintenance of which, living men and women, as the direct descendants of the *jukurrpa*, are today responsible.

The body of knowledge and beliefs about the ancestral travels is shared jointly as a sacred trust by men and women, each of whom has distinct responsibilities for the ritual maintenance of this heritage. Both have sacred boards, both know songs and paint designs which encode the knowledge of the Dreamtime. How each sex then fleshes out this common core of beliefs and knowledge is dependent upon their perception of their role and their contribution to society. Men's roles and perceptions have been well documented: women's are rather less well known.

The structuring principles of women's rituals, their content and focus on the maintenance of social harmony, link the ritual worlds of men and women. In both sets of rituals there is celebration of the central values of the society. Women and men alike trace their descent from the Dreamtime through two distinct lines of descent. From one's father and father's father a person has the rights and responsibilities of *kirda*; through one's mother and mother's father those of *kurdungurlu*. From one's mother's mother one also enjoys a special relationship to what is called one's *jaja* (granny) country. Other interests in land are stated in terms of conception Dreamings, residence, marriage, place of death and burial. Through these overlapping and interlocking modes of expressing how one is 'of the land', Central Australian men and women locate themselves within the ancestral design. In ceremony, visits to country and decision-making, the complementarity and interdependence of men's and women's worlds are evident.

As we move further north the terms of course change. In the Roper River area one speaks of *minirringki*, *jungkayi* and *dalyin*, but the multiplicity of ways of tracing a relationship to land remains a salient feature of the culture. For the benefit of those who may be unfamiliar with the disputes concerning local and social organisation and land tenure systems in Australia, let me explain. Woman's relationship to land and to the ancestors is often explained as derivative of her relationship to someone else, for example, her husband or her father, but not as the mirror image of the male system. In the literature there has also been a stress on patrilineal descent as the basis of group membership. However, evidence forthcoming in land claims where Aboriginal witnesses provide direct statements concerning land, supports the position I have outlined here.[33]

Under the Law men and women have distinctive roles to play and each has recourse to certain checks and balances in social, economic and ritual domains, which ensure that neither sex can enjoy unrivalled supremacy over the other. Men and women alike are dedicated to observing the Law which orders their lives into complementary but distinct fields of action and thought: in separation lies the basis of a common association that underwrites domains of existence. Men stress their creative power, women their role as nurturers, but each is united in their common purposes – the maintenance of their society in accordance with the Dreamtime Law. Ritual allows both men and women to demonstrate their commitment to the long-established code of the Dreaming in a manner which is peculiarly male or female.

Ceremonies may be classified as those staged by women which are secret and closed to men, those in which men and women participate, and those staged by men which are closed and secret to women. Most analyses begin from within the latter. If, however, we begin from within woman's ceremonial world and explore her ritual domain, we find that women see their lives as underwritten by their independence and autonomy of action. These self-evaluations are not easily dismissed, for they are legitimated by women's direct access to the *jukurrpa*. A further symbol of women's independence is the *jilimi*, or single women's camp, which has as its residential core the older and respected ritual leaders and their dependent female relatives. During the day it is the focal point of women's activities, during the evenings it provides a refuge. Like the women's ceremonial ground this area is taboo to men.

Obviously if women held they were independent while men insisted that women were subservient and the male claims were backed in terms of their control over women's domain, then we could suggest that women were not facing the harsh reality of life and that they were using ritual as an escape mechanism. I have found this line of analysis hard to sustain because, in my experience, women's ceremonies are respected by men. In the rituals jointly staged by men and women where interdependence is apparent, each brings to bear the knowledge that he or she is the proud descendant of a jointly shared spiritual heritage. Finally, in the rituals associated with male initiation, an occasion when male control of women is said to be writ large, women engage in key decision-making which affects both ritual procedure and the aftermath of initiation. Furthermore, while men are engaged in their initiation business at their ceremonial ground, women are similarly engaged in ceremonies at their ground.[34] These rituals celebrate their ongoing role as nurturer of people, relationships and land. When we focus on the world of men and treat women's rituals as a subset, we blur the playing out of independence and interdependence of the sexes in the spiritual domain.

In ritual the Law is made known in a highly stylised and emotionally charged manner: the separation of the sexes, so evident in daily activities, reaches its zenith. Ritual activity may therefore be considered as an important barometer of male-female relations, for it provides, as it were, an arena in which the values of the society are writ large, where the sex division of labour is starkly drawn and explored by the participants. In ritual I found both men and women clearly stating their perception of their role, their relationship to the opposite sex and their relationship to the Dreamtime whence all legitimate authority and power once flowed. However, while women and men today, as in the past, maintain separate spheres of interaction, the evaluations of their respective roles and their opportunities to achieve status have altered fundamentally during a century of white intrusion into Central Australia.

How then are we to balance my statements concerning women's religious experience with those which cast women as outsiders? How are we to find a way of analysing male and female domains which does not distort women's contribution to the maintenance of religious values in Aboriginal society? Questions concerning religion are inexorably tied to those concerning gender values and women's role and status in Aboriginal society. To probe one is to find answers to the other. Let us then examine the factors which have distorted our vision of women in Aboriginal society.

At the most obvious level, because of the sex segregated nature of Aboriginal society, it is extremely inappropriate (and in terms of in-depth fieldwork unproductive) to attempt to work equally with men and women. Usually one is identified with members of one's own sex and is able to move freely within that sphere. It follows that women can most easily be studied by another woman, but funding more female field-workers will not necessarily ensure that women's perceptions are explored. There have been women in the field, for example Ursula McConnel and Nancy Munn, both of whom worked on Aboriginal religion but neither of whom found women to be critical to their study.[35]

Fortunately for my study, women considered my position agreeable for one who sought ritual instruction. As a divorced woman in receipt of a government pension (pensioners are important people in Aboriginal communities) I was in a similar position to the ritual bosses with whom I worked: I was economically and emotionally independent of men. Aboriginal women often worry that white women, if allowed access to their secrets, might discuss the same with their husbands, but I was classified as a widow and considered to be safe. Further, the social status I enjoyed by virtue of my two outgoing and energetic children, allowed me access to the world of adult women. Ritual knowledge resides with the older women who, once freed from the immediate responsibilities of child care, devote their time and energies to upholding and transmitting their spiritual heritage to successive generations.

At another level, if we step back from the field situation, we find that the theoretical preoccupations, research design and the nature of the discipline in Australia have all conspired to relegate women to a position of marginality within Aboriginal society and within the discipline. Let me explain. Aboriginal society was not systematically studied until two Oxford scholars, Baldwin Spencer and W.E. Roth, began their scientific work in Australia during the late nineteenth century. Hitherto data had been drawn from the casual observations of early explorers and settlers. Well-educated professional men who dabbled in anthropology collated and compiled this information. Even when detailed research began, the methodology was more of an armchair variety where speculation abounds: intensive participant-observation fieldwork which may have highlighted women's activities, and which has come to characterise the practice of anthropology, was not undertaken. Once again, let me draw a parallel with Stanner's theme. Although he was writing of religion as a male prerogative, his observation applied equally well to studies of women.

> Contemporary study is weakened by the fact that there is so much bias in the old printed record. One cannot turn very hopefully to it for test or confirmation of new insights. For so much of the information was the product of minds caught up with special pleading of one kind or another.[36]

Of course Spencer and Roth were men of the Victorian era and their own model of femininity is evident in their notes and in their published work. It was a model wherein their own social order was the epitome of all civilisation, a characteristic of which was the domestication of female sexuality.[37] All other sexual values and sexual orders were held to be primitive, lacking the hallmark of civilisation. Such an analysis obviously has attractions because 50 years later Evans-Pritchard was still extolling the virtues of Victorian womanhood as a standard against which to measure the position of women in other societies.[38] It is little wonder then that the independent and, to the Victorian eye, wilful ways of Aboriginal woman, received scant recognition in the ethnological debates. In behaving in such an untamed fashion she was merely demonstrating her uncivilised and uncultured primitiveness.

Australian anthropology bears very much the stamp of British anthropology. The founder and first Professor of Anthropology in Sydney, Radcliffe-Brown, was a student of Rivers and influenced by Durkheim. For these men, women's opinions, values and activities were not critical to an understanding of society. No matter how stridently or positively women asserted that they shared the spiritual heritage of their society, they remained mute or socially disruptive in analyses based on the Durkheimian sacred-profane dichotomy.

In summary then, the tendency has been for male fieldworkers to study male institutions and subsequently to offer analyses which purport to examine the totality of Aboriginal society. Evaluation of female institutions has too often been based on male informants' opinions, refracted through the eyes of male ethnographers and explained by means of the concepts of male-oriented anthropology. Thus statements concerning the role and status of women are formulated within a context of a public male ideology, which means that only rarely can they be reconciled with the behavioural patterns of Aboriginal women in their society.

Why have practitioners felt so secure with this approach? I suggest we delve deeper and look at the way in which male-female relations have been conceptualised. This aspect of the problem has been tackled from within three different frameworks, each of which has generated different questions and thus produced different answers. The first, which I call 'Man Equals Culture', is the most consistently worked out and certainly the most popular. The second, an 'Anthropology of Women Approach', presents an ethnographic challenge to the first, but may be easily dismissed or subsumed. The third, which I call 'Towards a Feminist Perspective', is the only real challenge to the first. It brings to bear on the problem of women the burgeoning corpus of feminist scholarship, but so far it has produced more questions than answers.

These three organisational frameworks are akin to Kuhn's notion of a 'paradigm' which predicts a problem or set of related problems that the community of practitioners then sets out to resolve.[39] But, as Kuhn makes clear, one cannot move easily from within one version of the paradigm to work within another, as to do so involves something of the magnitude of a Gestalt switch. Although the various practitioners of one paradigm may use the same vocabulary, the conceptual baggage which adheres to a term varies radically between paradigms. For example, if religion is defined as the sacred domain controlled by men, then it is difficult to document the activities of women as anything other than profane. However, if religion is defined in terms of a commonly held set of values, beliefs and practices, both men and women may then be depicted as sharing in religious experiences.

Within the 'Man Equals Culture' paradigm, the problem has been to find a suitable characterisation of woman's role and status in terms of her lack of control over her own life. Armed with a diverse theoretical weaponry, such as Marxian class analysis, Lévi-Straussian structuralism and Durkheimian dualism, the practitioners have sought to explain women's secondary position in terms of economic markers, in the realm of symbolism, social organisation and kinship. I have already discussed Warner, Maddock and Bern but not Geza Róheim, who undertook fieldwork in Central Australia in 1927 and wrote specifically of Aboriginal women.

Women, Róheim contended, had no religion, no corporate ceremonial life, only magic. Róheim asked two important questions of woman: 1) What sort of person is she? and 2) What are her work, her plays, her interest in everyday life, her passions, anxieties and pleasures?[40] His study was restricted by the form of these questions and by his Freudian approach. Róheim's particular version of the psychoanalytic approach, although crude, has provided insights which have been refined and were popular again in the 1970s.

Shulamith Firestone has argued that, in the Victorian era, Freudianism was a more palatable doctrine than feminism because it supported the status quo and the integrity of the family.[41] Women who did not conform were simply deviants. It is tempting to run the same argument in the 1970s, when feminism poses a threat to male hegemony in many domains and seeks more wide-ranging concessions than simply the right to vote. In a similar vein, Stanner suggests we may find a link between the blindness of which he writes and the struggle over ritualism within the Christian church between the years 1850 and 1920.[42]

Perhaps the most sophisticated and well-worked analysis of the adherents to the 'Man Equals Culture' paradigm is a symbolic analysis of Nancy Munn.[43] Like Róheim, Munn takes the male-female opposition to be a fundamental starting point in an analysis of Aboriginal society, but Munn's concern is with the sociocultural order, whereas Róheim's is with the individual psyche. As a woman, Munn certainly had access to the world of women, but her focus is the ritual symbolism of men and her valued informants male, because in Nancy Munn's analysis men control the keys to cosmic order.

From within the second paradigm the practitioners, such as Kaberry, Berndt and Goodale, begin with the assumption that women also have rights, opinions and values and that these are not exactly coincidental with those of the men. This type of research makes a chink in the doctrine of male dominance. It becomes apparent that it is not as complete as we once thought; nevertheless, as long as we insert certain qualifications, the model will more or less suffice and the data on women will illuminate the institutions of marriage, kinship, social structure and so on.

For example, in her extremely detailed and rich portrait of Aboriginal women, Phyllis Kaberry was able to challenge several of Róheim's grosser misconceptions about the function of women's religious life; to offer a counter to Warner's assertion that women make little sacred progress;[44] and finally, to depict Aboriginal woman as:

> A complex social personality having her own prerogatives, duties, problems, beliefs, rituals and points of view, making the adjustments that the social, local and totemic organisations require of her and at the same time exercising a certain freedom of choice in matters affecting her own interests and desires.[45]

Yet, many of Kaberry's most important observations concerning the nature of women's ceremonies have not been fully explored. Kaberry's critically important observation that men represent the uninitiated at women's ceremonies remains buried beneath a pile of studies of secret male cults, totemism and kinship which assume that the male view is the only important perspective.[46] We could suggest that supported by Elkin 'to tackle through women the problems of kinship, totemism, social organisation in general and the religion', Phillis Kaberry found her answers in those anthropological ways of looking at the world and of other cultures which were developed by men of the structural-functional school. Men were located at the centre of social action in such approaches.

Catherine Berndt, who has undertaken fieldwork in many different parts of Aboriginal Australia, proposed a model of the relationship between the sexes in terms of domestic, economic and religious domains within which the links of marriage and descent and the relations of dominance and authority are articulated.[47] This organisational device allows Berndt to discuss the inter-penetration of the spheres of male and female action. Berndt emphasises woman's importance as an economic producer and the brakes which women may thus apply to male ritual activity.[48] A question mark remains though in respect of the relationship between male and female ritual domains.

Jane Goodale claims that her work is mainly descriptive and limited to the Tiwi,[49] but comparison with mainland Aboriginal studies is enlightening. The nature of Goodale's debate with Hart and Pilling over marriage arrangements is reminiscent of Kaberry's challenges to

Warner and Róheim. Both Kaberry and Goodale went into the field to study women, both worked mainly with women informants and stressed women's importance, equality in some fields and near equality in others, in their depiction of women's role and status.

Like Kaberry, Goodale chose to organise her data within a life-cycle framework which, while providing a sympathetic portrait of women's lives, allows one to sidestep certain critical issues concerning the way in which men evaluate women's activities. Goodale however does tackle this problem in her final chapter where she sets out the differences between male and female worldviews. Tiwi women are unusual in that they are initiated at the same ceremonies as are the males, pass through the same formal procedures and are not excluded at any stage during the ceremony. But Tiwi women, like the women of Kaberry's study, are substantially economically independent, while being ritually dependent. Goodale states:

> Opportunities for males to express their individual qualities, and thereby gain prestige, appear to be more obvious and variable than those granted to females . . . Women are not expected to be innovators or creators – they do not even create 'life'.[50]

The women who have published in-depth studies of women have been, I suggest, constrained by the theoretical perspectives developed to focus on men as the leading and most interesting social actors. There was little impetus from within Australia to develop frameworks within which women were deemed of anthropological interest as social actors. While Elkin was encouraging women to document the lives of Aboriginal women, male fieldworkers who thanked 'my wife who collected material from the women' were laying the foundations for future research in Australia.

Like Kaberry's portrait of Aboriginal women, which concludes with questions concerning the nature of the relationship between men's and women's ceremonies, so with Berndt and Goodale. There are questions yet to be asked, answers yet to be given. The lack of dynamic models for analysing women's activities is a handicap. The Durkheimian yoke of women's profanity and the structural-functionalist equilibrium model wherein women are wives, mothers and sisters, weigh heavily on female-oriented research in Australia.

We then come to the third paradigm, that of feminist social scientists, who question the origins and mechanisms of the all-pervasive and hitherto persuasive cultural dogma of male dominance.

Perhaps, they suggest, it is not an enduring, timeless constant which regulates male-female in Aboriginal society. As yet this framework has produced more questions than answers and in the Kuhnian sense we are still at the stage of having too many anomalies to be satisfied with earlier paradigms but not yet a sufficiently elegant structure within which to analyse our new data. The old paradigm is under threat and an anthropology of women is not a satisfying alternative.

Stanner spoke of 'mystery mongering', and cautioned that we need not only to shake off the 'narrow scholarly preoccupations', but we need also 'to grub out the roots':[51] also sound advice for a study of women's lives. In seeking a clearer vision, I suggest we need to explore the possibility that qualitative changes in the relation between the sexes may have occurred during the past century. We cannot begin with a static model of male-female; we know too little of the women's lives, past and present, to argue for male dominance as an enduring, timeless reality. We need to be clear regarding the nature of woman's contribution to her society, her rights and responsibilities, before we endorse one particular model of male-female as an accurate gloss on gender relations. The recognition that male-female relations are not rigidly fixed and that women may develop their own power base, leads us to an analysis of the power differentials in Aboriginal society. Feminists have indicated important areas of inquiry but the extreme separation of the sexes in desert society represents an analytic challenge which I suggest is best met in the first instance by increasing our ethnographic understanding of women's domain.

Isobel White, in an exploration of sexual antagonism as symbolised in the male myths of Central Australia, argues that the values celebrated are those of a male- dominated society.[52] Men, White contends, see women as sex objects. Turning to her own fieldwork material from South Australia, she proposes that women see men as sexual conquerors to whom they submit, but not without a show of resistance. While I endorse White's analysis of Central Australian myths as exploring unresolved tensions inherent in male-female relations in Aboriginal society, I suggest that she has articulated a male value system which is not necessarily endorsed by women in Central Australia. The extreme separation of the sexes in everyday life in the desert is a phenomenon which myths also explore. It is therefore all the more important to examine women's myths from this area before endorsing one sex as controlling a mythological charter of values for all members of the society. I would suggest that in their myths women argue for the extreme flexibility of gender relations. The tension is not resolved, even in the myths.[53]

Writing of male-female tensions in the eastern portion of the Western Desert of South Australia, Annette Hamilton has suggested that women's secret ritual life represented a serious challenge to 'consolidation of male dominance', not because of any 'coherent ideological opposition expressed within it', but because its 'mode of organisation provides a structural impediment'.[54] Underlying the contrast between the sexes Hamilton argues there is:

> A well developed organisation that can best be understood as a dual society . . . I suggest that these two systems are, in the Western Desert as a whole, in a situation of dynamic disequilibrium whereby the male domain is intruding into the women's through ritual transformations and through the strengthening of male links between generations as a result of changes in the system of kinship and marriage.[55]

Hamilton argues that at the time of the arrival of whites, the whole of the Western Desert cultural area was in a state of transition. She suggests possible trajectories along which transformations can be traced and concludes that 'patrilineal descent has transcended the previous form of symbolic ancestor-based descent'.[56] It is in the shattering of the ritually maintained nexus of land as resource and land as spiritual essence that I have located a shift from female autonomy to male control, from an independent producer to one dependent on social security.[57] Thus while Hamilton and I are concerned to explore the changing nature of the relations between the sexes from an historical perspective, we have focused from rather differing conceptions of time and place and upon different institutions and sets of relationships.

To infiltrate women's autonomous ritual world in the Western Desert men need to undermine the mother/daughter tie because endogamous generation moieties organise ritual life. However ritual organisation in Central Australia emphasises the relation of person to place in terms of two distinct and complementary lines of descent – one through the father's patriline (*kirda*) and the other through the mother's patriline (*kurdungurlu*). Furthermore, Central Australian women have a wide range of ritual items which symbolise their relation to land and the *jukurrpa*.

Population-intensive settlement life has allowed women to consolidate these relationships and to forge, through ritual, new links with other women. But, while women today have increased opportunities to stage rituals, the range of rituals is restricted and women's independence eroded. Increased ritual activity has therefore not necessarily been accompanied by an increase in women's overall status.[58] We need to look to the way in which male and female roles are construed within the wider society of Central Australia in order to understand shifts in the locus of ritual power. Then we can argue that women's ability to stage closed sex-specific rituals constitutes a continuing and potent element of gender relations in Central Australia.

For Central Australia I have argued that men's and women's ritual worlds draw on a common spiritual heritage and that women's contribution to the religious life is not subsumed by the male practice. What then of other ethnographic areas? What of the regional cults of Kunapipi and Yabaduruwa? We have in the studies of Maddock, Bern, Elkin and Berndt, fine-grain ethnographic descriptions and analyses of male-controlled activities.[59] Women, we read, are necessary but their role is supportive: they cook; they are drawn to the verge of knowing men's secrets but their own participation is limited.[60] But what of women's own ceremonies? None of the above has suggested the possibility that women may have regional cults.[61]

In July 1981 I was able to record and participate in a *jarada*, a closed women's ceremony held at Nutwood Downs (in the Roper River area) which women from far-flung communities attended.[62] In song and dance, in gesture and design, the assembled women celebrated the travels of the Munga Munga ancestral women who pioneered the country from Tennant Creek to Arnhem Land. They scattered across the Barkly Tablelands; they travelled from Macarthur River and from the junction of the Wilton and Roper Rivers to a site on Hodgson River and thence to Nutwood Downs, where their tracks divide, one following the 'road' to Alice Springs, the other to a site on Brunette Downs. The Munga Munga assumed different forms, met with, crossed over, absorbed and transformed the essence of other ancestors; their influence infused country with the spiritual essence of women.

In the Munga Munga ceremony I saw (and was later able to discuss on several occasions with women who had participated), it was apparent in song and dance that they were retracing the extensive travels of the Munga Munga. In this way they provided a graphic representation of the links forged between groups in the Dreamtime. Within the context of this overarching responsibility for the Dreaming, women also stated their responsibility for particular tracts of land

and emphasised certain themes and, as with Central Australian women, emotional management and health were the principal ones.

At one level women gave form to a generalised notion of their responsibility for land, its Dreamings and sites, in expressions such as 'we must hold up that country', 'not lose him', but at another level the ceremony allowed certain divisions of labour for responsibility for country to be played out. (Those who traced their relationship from their father and father's father as *minirringki* and from their mother and mother's father as *jungkayi*, and from their mother's mother as *dalyin*, each had a particular role). In the dancing the women marked out the extent of the country of each language group.

Unfortunately I cannot go into details here but suffice it to say that in the Munga Munga ceremony women demonstrated their rights and responsibilities in land in both a generalised and particularistic fashion. Men were rigidly excluded from the ceremony but at the conclusion of the activity on the women's ground, they entered the main camp where the men had been sitting quietly. A gift exchange between men and women then took place. In this way the interdependence of men and women's worlds was celebrated. More work is necessary on the Munga Munga cult before we can discuss women's ceremonies in the area as dealing with 'personal reactions to physiological stress'. More work is necessary to show the structural continuities from desert to the riverine regions.

In Central Australia women celebrate their relation to land in *yawulyu* which focus on specific sites and dreamings. As we move further north, *yilpinji* is often equated with *jarada*. Elements of *yawulyu* have been incorporated in some *jarada* ceremonies in the riverine areas (for example in the Victoria River Downs region), but the distinguishing feature of *jarada* in the Roper River region remains the universality and pervasiveness of the Munga Munga in providing the mythological charter for all women's ceremonial activity. This includes women's participation in men's ceremonies.

In his lecture, Stanner set out the positive characteristics of Aboriginal religion, all of which stressed male practices and beliefs.[63] However, I would suggest that this summary could have been generated by a study of the ceremonial life of women. But Stanner was very sure of his vision. He wrote:

> Almost universally the evaluation of women was low in respect of their personal as distinct from their functional worth. They were usually held in low regard ritually, too, but not in all circumstances. Their

> blood-making and child-giving powers were thought both mysterious and dangerous, but there was nothing elevated in their sex or marriage.[64]

While there are wide-ranging regional variations in the organisation, thematic emphasis and form of women's ceremonies, as a guide to future research let me, in conclusion, generalise concerning the structure of women's religious life and consequences for approaches to this study.

1. Women trace their rights and responsibilities for the maintenance of their religious heritage to the past in diverse ways. In each region women's ritual roles appear to be the structural equivalents of men's. However we need to undertake regional studies before attempting wider generalisation.

2. In secret rituals which are closed to men, women celebrate their relations to the land, its sites and its dreamings. In ritual their lives and those of the ancestors fuse. Their focus on health, emotional management, resolution of conflict, benefits the whole of society, not just women.

3. In women's ceremonies the dominant theme is that of woman the nurturer. The mode of expressing this varies from the symbolic representations in the desert to the more direct physical representations in the lush north.

4. Analysis of women's role and status and gender values must be within a framework which allows for the dynamic intertwining of the sexual politics of Aboriginal society and the impact of social change.

5. Studies of women's ritual life are best undertaken by women field-workers who are accepted by Aboriginal women. 'Don't send girls on a woman's errand', older women have told me. Studies should also be by women who respect the Aboriginal women's code of secrecy.

6. Certain information concerning Aboriginal women's ritual lives is communicated through ceremonial activity. It is therefore necessary to observe and if possible to participate in ceremonies if one is to gain access to women's understanding of their religious life. Women do not verbalise their intense and complex spiritual attachment to land and to the ancestors, but rather answer questions concerning the *jukurrpa* in action.

'Is women's liberation really relevant to Aboriginal society?' I am often asked. 'Aren't you imposing your ideas on another value system?' This would be true if I were working with the Western women's concept of liberation, but in different societies, different issues are stressed. The desire of feminists in white Australian society to break down sex-role stereotyping to achieve social equality by men was viewed by my Aboriginal women friends as yet another cross which white women had to bear. They often sympathised with the lot of the white wife and mother. 'Poor thing, stuck inside all day, like a prisoner', they would comment. For themselves they sought to have their distinctively female contribution to their society recognised and accorded the value which it had in the past when they were critical to group survival. The role they wished to see recognised was not one of dependence or subjugation as wives and mothers, but a role of independence, responsibility, dignity and authority wherein they were enhanced as women, as members of their society, as daughters of the dreaming. It is this which I take to be the basis of 'liberation' in their society.

Within the context of Aboriginal society the maintenance of male-female relations entailed an ongoing dialogue based on an interplay and exchange between the sexes. This allowed women to participate actively in the construction of the cultural evaluations of their role in their society. But today, as members of a colonial frontier society, Aboriginal women no longer participate so predominantly in this process. The loss of land over which to forage constitutes more than an economic loss, for it is from the land that Aboriginal people draw not only their livelihood but also their very being. Today women are constrained and defined by the male dominated frontier society as the female sex, a necessarily dependent sex. No longer are women treated solely as members of Aboriginal society. The interrelations between the sexes are thus no longer shaped first by the set of male-female relations of Aboriginal society but also by the new forces of the wider colonial society.

In Northern Australia the incoming whites have brought new ideas and resources. These have been differently exploited by Aboriginal men and women. Women were disadvantaged from the onset because the male bias of frontier society immediately relegated them to the role of domestic worker or sex object. Men have been able to take real political advantage of certain aspects of frontier society, while Aboriginal women have been seen by whites as peripheral to the political process.[65] Women's separateness has come to mean their exclusion from the white male dominated domains whence new sources of power and influence now flow. There was no place within the colonial order for the independent Aboriginal woman who, once deprived of her land, quickly became dependent on rations and social security.

In land claim hearings Aboriginal women are speaking of their spiritual heritage, of their rights and responsibilities in land. The impact is profound. As one witness, Mollie Nungarrayi, said in the Kaytej, Warlpiri and Warlmanpa land claim:

> My father was *kurdungurlu* for that place. It was his to look after. He looked after the two places, Waake and Wakulpu and then I lost him; he passed away. Now it is up to me looking after my own country, Jarra Jarra and also Waake and Wakulpu. As my father could not go on to that country so from when I was a young girl I kept on doing the *yawulyu* [women's ceremonies], looking after the country . . . My sisters, Mona and Nancy, they are looking after that country too . . . we do that *yawulyu* for Wakulpu all the time . . . for fruit . . . so it will grow up well so that we can make it green so that we hold the Law forever. My father instructed me to hold it always this way so I go on holding *yawulyu* for that country. Sometimes we dance, man and woman together. For Wakulpu. So we can 'catch him up', 'hold him up'.[66]

Perhaps the Reverend Charles Strong may have championed these women had he been aware of the nature of their values.[67] Certainly his view that religion should be regarded as the spirit of life rather than a formal theological creed, would have been intelligible to Aboriginal women.

## AFTERWORD

In 1980, when I delivered this lecture, it caused quite a stir. My monograph *Daughters of the Dreaming* (1983) was yet to appear, and while the women's movement and Aboriginal land rights movement had sensitised the public to the need for a more subtle understanding of the dynamics of contemporary Aboriginal religion and gender relations, feminist analyses were resisted as mischievous interventions. Fourteen years later, despite many publications by fine anthropologists, much Aboriginal evidence in numerous land claims, the emergence of strong and articulate Aboriginal voices in the academy, the courts, media and politics, there is still widespread misunderstanding and ignorance regarding the bases of Aboriginal religion and Aboriginal relationships to land. If I were delivering this lecture today I would address this reluctance to be enlightened, the willingness to be comforted by old colonial myths of the 'lesser-than-rational' behaviour of indigenous peoples, and the more recent wave of New Age writings which appropriate Aboriginal beliefs and market homogenised, historical, romanticised accounts of Aboriginal spirituality.

From the mid 1970s through to the mid 1980s, I was heavily involved in applied anthropology and am pleased to note that in thirteen of the fourteen odd cases for which I prepared submissions and gave expert witness testimony, the claimants were successful and those tracts of land are now under Aboriginal control, or the accused were acquitted. Almost invariably special pleading was necessary to make it possible for Aboriginal women to be heard in court, and while considerable advances have been achieved, women still experience difficulty in bringing claims that rely on knowledge that is privileged on the basis of gender and seniority. My more recent research on such matters has turned to the issue of epistemologies and in particular the work of feminist philosophers of science. I have taken up these questions in the Epilogue of the new edition of *Daughters of the Dreaming* (1993).

In the Charles Strong lecture I concluded with a 'guide to future research'. That guide did in fact prove helpful as I continued research in Aboriginal communities and more recently with Native American peoples in the USA. I have been able to fill in a number of gaps in the literature and pose more questions for research with indigenous peoples, explore regional models, and address current concerns about the environment, the ethics of research, and human rights.[68]

## NOTES

1 I am grateful to the publishers of my book, *Daughters of the Dreaming*, for permission to reprint material – McPhee Gribble, Melbourne, who published the first edition in 1983, and Allen and Unwin, Sydney, who published the second edition in 1993.

2 Professor Stanner's Charles Strong Memorial Lecture, 'Some Aspects of Aboriginal Religion', is reprinted in Chapter 1, above.

3 W.E.H. Stanner, 'Religion, Totemism and Symbolism' (1962), in W.E.H. Stanner, *White Man Got No Dreaming*, Australian National University (ANU) Press, Canberra, 1979, pp. 106–143.

4 W.E.H. Stanner, 'After the Dreaming' 1968, in *White Man Got No Dreaming*, pp. 198–248.

5 W.E.H. Stanner, *On Aboriginal Religion*, Oceania Monographs, No. 11, University of Sydney, Sydney, 1966.

6 W.E.H. Stanner, 'Durmugam: A Nangiomeri' 1959, in *White Man Got No Dreaming*, pp. 67–105.
7 Baldwin Spencer and F.J. Gillen, *The Native Tribes of Central Australia*, Macmillan, London, 1899; M.J. Meggitt, *Desert People*, Angus and Robertson, Sydney, 1962; T.G.H. Strehlow, *Songs of Central Australia*, Angus and Robertson, Sydney, 1971; Nancy D. Munn, *Walbiri Iconography*, Cornell University Press, Ithaca and London, 1973.
8 See Michelle Rosaldo and Louise Lamphere, *Woman, Culture and Society*, Stanford University Press, Stanford, 1974; Eleanor Leacock, 'Women's Status in Egalitarian Society: Implications for Social Evolution', *Current Anthropology* 19 (1978), pp. 247–255.
9 C.H. Berndt, 'Women's Changing Ceremonies in Northern Australia', *L'Homme* 1 (1950), pp. 1–87; Catherine J. Ellis, 'The Role of the Ethnomusicologist in the Study of Andaringa Women's Ceremonies', *Miscellanea Musicologica: Adelaide Studies of Musicology* 5 (1970), pp. 76–212; Isobel M. White, 'Sexual Conquest and Submission in Aboriginal Myths' in L.R. Hiatt (ed.), *Australian Aboriginal Mythology*, Australian Institute of Aboriginal Studies, Canberra, 1975, pp. 123–142.
10 From August 1976 to January 1978, I undertook fieldwork at Warrabri, 375 km north of Alice Springs, Northern Territory. At that time it was a government settlement but with the passage of the Aboriginal Land Rights (NT) Act, 1976, it has become Aboriginal land (see below, note 12). In 1977 it was home to approximately 700 Aborigines (Warlpiri, Warumungu, Alyawarra, Kaytej) and 70 whites.
11 This authority was a statutory body established under Northern Territory legislation, the Sacred Sites Act, 1978, which was reciprocal legislation to the Federal Land Rights Act. In 1981 I was employed to respond to requests from Aborigines for site protection throughout the Northern Territory.
12 Under the Aboriginal Land Rights (NT) Act, 1976, Aborigines may bring claims to unalienated Crown land or land in which all interests other than those held by the Crown are held by or on behalf of Aborigines. Certain reserve lands, described in Schedules 1, 2 and 3, were also made Aboriginal land. Title to successfully claimed land is held by a Land Trust established for that purpose. Anthropologists assist in the preparation, hearing and assessing of evidence brought on behalf of the traditional owners. In the Daly River claim, I was engaged by the Northern Land Council, to prepare a submission regarding women's interests in the claim area. See Diane Bell, 'Daly River (Malak Malak) Land Claim: Women's Interests', (Exhibit 8) Darwin, Northern Land Council, 1981, pp. 1–33.
13 Stanner, *White Man Got No Dreaming*, p. 106.
14 Stanner, *White Man Got No Dreaming*, p. 143.
15 Stanner, *White Man Got No Dreaming*, p. 108.
16 A.P. Elkin, 'Studies in Australian Totemism', *Oceania* 4 (1933), pp. 113–131; W.L. Warner, *A Black Civilization*, Harper, New York, 1937; Ursula McConnel, *Myths of Mungkan*, Melbourne University Press, Melbourne, 1957; R.M. Berndt, *Kunapipi*, Cheshire, Melbourne, 1951; Strehlow, *Songs of Central Australia*; Munn, *Walbiri Iconography*.

17 M.F. Peron, *A Voyage of Discovery to the Southern Hemisphere*, London, 1809, pp. 67–68.
18 C.W.M. Hart and Arnold R. Pilling, *The Tiwi of North Australia*, Holt Rinehart and Winston, New York, 1960, p. 14.
19 Meggitt, *Desert People*, p. 236.
20 Annette Hamilton, 'Aboriginal Women: The Means of Production', in Jan Mercer (ed.) *The Other Half*, Penguin, Harmondsworth, 1975, pp. 167–179; Diane E. Barwick, 'And the Lubras are Ladies Now' in Fay Gale (ed.) *Women's Role in Aboriginal Society*, Australian Institute for Aboriginal Studies, Canberra, 1970, pp. 31–38; Marie Reay, 'Aboriginal and White Australian Family Structure: An Inquiry Into Assimilation Trends', *Sociological Review* n.s. 11 (1963), pp. 19–47; Diane Bell, 'Desert Politics: Choices in the "Marriage Market"' in Mona Etienne and Eleanor Leacock (eds) *Women and Colonization*, Praeger, New York, 1980, pp. 239–269.
21 Annette Hamilton, 'The Role of Women in Aboriginal Marriage Arrangements', in Fay Gale (ed.) *Women's Role in Aboriginal Society*, Australian Institute for Aboriginal Studies, Canberra, 1970, pp. 17–20; Jane C. Goodale, *Tiwi Wives*, University of Washington Press, Seattle, 1971; see also Bell, 'Desert Politics'.
22 L.R. Hiatt, *Kinship and Conflict*, ANU Press, Canberra, 1965.
23 Phyllis M. Kaberry, *Aboriginal Women, Sacred and Profane*, Routledge, London, 1939.
24 C.H. Berndt, 'Women's Changing Ceremonies in Northern Australia'; 'Women and the "Secret Life"' in R.M. Berndt and C.H. Berndt (eds) *Aboriginal Man in Australia*, Angus and Robertson, Sydney, 1965, pp. 236–282; 'Digging Sticks and Spears, or, the Two-Sex Model', in Gale (ed.) *Women's Role in Aboriginal Society*, pp. 39–48.
25 Goodale, *Tiwi Wives*.
26 Warner, *A Black Civilization*, p. 6.
27 Kenneth Maddock, *The Australian Aborigines: A Portrait of Their Society*, Allen Lane, London, 1972, p. 155.
28 John Bern, 'Politics in the Conduct of a Secret Male Ceremony', *Journal of Anthropological Research* 35 (1979), p. 47.
29 John Bern, 'Ideology and Domination', *Oceania* 50 (1979), p. 129.
30 In my work as consultant to Central Land Council, Northern Land Council, the Aboriginal Land Commissioner and in various projects concerning land rights, site registration and law reform, I have been able to complement and extend my original fieldwork (see above, note 10). See Diane Bell and Pam Ditton, *Law: the Old and New*, Aboriginal History, Canberra, 1980. Other information is in submissions to land claim hearings and reports to the Aboriginal Sacred Sites Protection Authority (see note 11).
31 Throughout I have used the orthography of the Warlpiri bilingual program Yuendumu, NT. With the exception of the terms from the Roper River, all other terms are in Warlpiri and are well known throughout Central Australia.
32 See Diane Bell, *Daughters of the Dreaming*, McPhee Gribble, Melbourne, 1983 and Allen and Unwin, Sydney, 1993.

33 See Diane Bell, 'Statement to the Kaytej, Walpiri and Warlmanpa Land Claim', Exhibit 48, 1982; Kenneth Maddock, *Anthropology, Law and the Definition of Australian Aboriginal Rights to Land*, Institute of Folklore, Catholic University, Nijmegen, 1980.
34 See Bell, *Daughters of the Dreaming.*
35 McConnel, *Myths of Mungkan*, Munn, *Warlbiri Iconography*.
36 Stanner, *White Man Got No Dreaming*, p. 123.
37 Elizabeth Fee, 'The Sexual Politics of Victorian Social Anthropology' in Mary S. Hartmann and Lois Banner (eds) *Clio's Consciousness Raised*, Harper and Row, New York, 1974, p. 101.
38 E.E. Evans-Pritchard, *The Position of Women in Primitive Societies and Other Essays in Social Anthropology*, Faber and Faber, London, 1965, pp. 37–58.
39 Thomas S. Kuhn, *The Structure of Scientific Revolutions*, University of Chicago Press, Chicago, 1970, p. 43ff.
40 Geza Róheim, 'Women and Their Life in Central Australia', *Royal Anthropological Institute Journal* 63 (1933), pp. 207–265.
41 Shulamith Firestone, *The Dialectic of Sex*, Jonathan Cape, Great Britain, 1971, pp. 46–72.
42 Stanner, *White Man Got No Dreaming*, pp. 108–109.
43 Munn, *Walbiri Iconography*.
44 Kaberry, *Aboriginal Women, Sacred and Profane*, pp. 188–189.
45 Kaberry, *Aboriginal Women, Sacred and Profane*, p. x.
46 Kaberry, *Aboriginal Women, Sacred and Profane*, p. 221.
47 C.H. Berndt, 'Digging Sticks and Spears, or, the Two-Sex Model'.
48 Berndt, 'Digging Sticks and Spears, or, the Two-Sex Model', p. 41.
49 Goodale, *Tiwi Wives*, p. xxiii. See also Rudy Rohrlich-Leavitt, Barbara Sykes and Elizabeth Weatherford, 'Aboriginal Woman, Male and Female Anthropological Perspectives' in Rayna Reiter (ed.) *Toward an Anthropology of Women*, Monthly Review Press, New York, 1975, pp. 110–126.
50 Goodale, *Tiwi Wives*, pp. 337–338.
51 Stanner, *White Man Got No Dreaming*, p. 136.
52 White, 'Sexual Conquest and Submission in Aboriginal Myths', p. 136.
53 Bell, *Daughters of the Dreaming.*
54 Annette Hamilton, 'Dual Social Systems: Technology, Labour and Women's Secret Rites in the Eastern Western Desert of Australia', unpublished manuscript, 1978.
55 Annette Hamilton, 'Timeless Transformations, Women, Men and History in the Australian Western Desert', PhD Thesis, University of Sydney, 1979, p. xxi.
56 Hamilton, 'Timeless Transformations', pp. 78–79.
57 Bell, *Daughters of the Dreaming.*
58 Bell, *Daughters of the Dreaming.*
59 See A.P. Elkin, 'The Yaduduruwa', *Oceania* 31 (1961), pp. 166–209; R.M. Berndt, *Kunapipi*; K. Maddock, 'The Jabuduruwa', PhD Thesis, University of Sydney, 1969; John Bern, 'Ideology and Domination' and 'Politics in the Conduct of a Secret Male Ceremony'.
60 Bern, 'Politics in the Conduct of a Secret Male Ceremony', pp. 418–419.

61 See C.H. Berndt, 'Women's Changing Ceremonies in Northern Australia', pp. 30–39, for a discussion of Munga-Munga in the Victorian River Downs area and suggestion that Munga-Munga came from the Roper River area.

62 Diane Bell, 'In the Tracks of the Munga-Munga', submission to the Cox River Land Claim, Darwin, Northern Land Council, 1982 (reprinted in Penny Magee and Morny Joy (eds) *Claiming our Rites: Australian Feminist Essays in Religion*, Allen and Unwin, Sydney, 1994, pp. 213–246).

63 Stanner, 'Some Aspects of Aboriginal Religion', see Chapter 1 above.

64 Stanner, *White Man Got No Dreaming*, p. 118.

65 See Bell and Ditton, *Law: the Old and New*.

66 Transcript of Evidence, Aboriginal Land Rights (NT) Act, 1976, re Kaytej, Warlpiri and Warlmanpa claim, 1981, p. 191. (I have edited out the questions of counsel so that only the answers of the witness remain in the text).

67 *Australian Encyclopaedia*, Vol. 5, The Grolier Society of Australia, Sydney, 1977; see also C.R. Badger, *The Reverend Charles Strong and the Australian Church*, Abacada Press, Melbourne, 1971.

68 The following of my publications explore these issues: 'Indigenous voices and visions: Implications for a global, gendered, environmental agenda', *Pendidikan Tinggi-Higher Education: A journal on the culture and scientificity of knowledge*, Malaysia, 1995, pp. 7–22; 'In the tracks of the Munga-Munga' in Penny Magee and Morny Joy (eds) *Claiming our Rites: Australian feminist essays in religion*, Allen and Unwin, Sydney, 1994, pp. 213–246; 'Representing Aboriginal women: who speaks for whom?' in Oliver Mendelsohn and Uprenda Baxi (eds) *The Rights of Subordinate Peoples*, Oxford University Press, Delhi, 1994, pp. 221–250; *Daughters of the Dreaming*, Allen and Unwin, Sydney (Second Edition), 1993; 'Aboriginal women's religion: A shifting law of the land' in Arvind Sharma (ed.) *Today's Woman in World Religions*, State University of New York Press, Albany, 1993, pp. 39–76; 'Considering gender, are human rights for women too? An Australian case study' in Abdullahi Ahmed An-Na'im (ed.) *Human Rights in Cross-Cultural Perspectives*, University of Pennsylvania Press, Philadelphia, 1992, pp. 339–362; 'Choose your mission wisely: Christian colonials and Aboriginal marital arrangements on the northern frontier' in Deborah Bird Rose and Tony Swain (eds) *Aboriginal Australians and Christianity*, Australian Association for the Study of Religions, Adelaide, 1988, pp. 338–352; Diane Bell, Max Charlesworth, Kenneth Maddock and Howard Morphy (eds) *Religion in Aboriginal Australia*, University of Queensland Press, St Lucia, 1984.

CHAPTER FOUR

# On 'Understanding' Aboriginal Religion

*Tony Swain*

> *'Only Connect . . .'*
> E.M. Forster, *Howard's End*, 1910

When Ronald Berndt delivered the Charles Strong Memorial Lecture for 1979, he touched momentarily upon an issue which I would like to take as my present theme. He said:

> The search for meaning is central to systematic anthropological research; but methodological devices used in that process often remove it from the empirical situation. Consequently, the end product that tells us what particular religious phenomena mean to particular believers or practitioners can differ considerably from an explanation offered in more general terms. The process of interpretation can have its dangers. It can hide or, at best, overshadow what people have to say about their religion. To put this another way, the understanding of Aboriginal religion has been greatly affected by theories about religion.[1]

My objective on this occasion is to discuss the possibility of studying Aboriginal religion in a way which is cognisant of the meaning their beliefs and practices have for Aborigines. The dilemma Berndt identifies will not, however, be solved by simply building a new methodology when the foundations are inadequate. I am going to argue that it is imperative for students of Aboriginal culture to come to grips with a post-positivist epistemology which is capable of dealing adequately with the meaning of religious phenomena.

I do not intend knocking down straw men by making an extensive critique of positivist studies of Aboriginal religion, but as an introduction to my arguments it is appropriate to offer a few historical comments.[2] British anthropology actually emerged from the Aborigines Protection Society – a Christian/humanitarian organisation formed to guard against the abuse of peoples indigenous to British settlements such as Australia. In a series of metamorphoses, the initial aim of garnering knowledge in order 'to secure to [natives] the due observance of justice and the protection of their rights'[3] was transformed into the search for causal scientific laws equivalent to those found in the natural sciences.

Such a model of anthroplogy was accepted for over a century of Aboriginal studies, and it is only during the past few decades that it has been seriously questioned. A teleological interpretation of the work of positivists reveals that they continuously, almost reluctantly, edged closer to confronting Aboriginal religion as it was expressed by Aborigines. The first pre-evolutionary studies of Aboriginal beliefs were undertaken in order to ascertain if they were religious at all, and consequently, whether Aborigines shared in sentiments seen as definitive of humanity. To the credit of most evolutionists, they at least conceded that Aborigines were both human and religious, but they saw Aboriginal religion in terms of the childhood of civilisation, and as dwelling at the opposite pole to themselves on an evolutionary human continuum. Following the lead of Durkheim, functionalists argued that the evolutionary interpretation of Aboriginal religion as being merely a primordial form of higher beliefs was illegitimate. A religious tradition, they said, must be understood in the context of the society in which it is found. As we will see, they did much towards making the study of the way societies cognise and classify their world a central issue in anthropology, but they ultimately insisted that the study of Aboriginal religion was intelligible only to the extent that it could be reduced to sociological laws. To go further would necessitate abandoning positivist ideals.

It has been said that Comte, the father of positivism, saw 'the history of science as a whole [as] one of a progressive movement inwards towards the study of man himself'.[4] I, in contrast, see the history of the scientific study of Aboriginal religion as a whole as one of a progressive movement inwards towards the study of its meaning to Aboriginal man himself. As I would now like to show, this entails the formation of a post-positivist anthropology.

## I

### Positivism

Ironically, the first stirrings of dissatisfaction with positivist explanations of Aboriginal religion originated with a scholar whose thinking is often described as a paradigm of positivism. Although Emile

Durkheim accepted the doctrine that only science could produce truly objective knowledge in the form of causal explanations, he nonetheless parted company with his contemporaries regarding the nature of scientific method itself. In particular, he denied the empiricist claim that logical categories are induced from experience. Specific phenomena are a-conceptual and can never be transformed into general categories. Thus, in his words, 'classical empiricism results in irrationalism'.[5]

Durkheim's theory of the origin of scientific categories was elaborated in a book commonly considered to only investigate the essence of religion. But if we recall that it was originally to be entitled *Elementary Forms of Thought and Religion*,[6] then we might more readily accept it as equally concerned with the origin of science. 'Scientific thought', says Durkheim, 'is only a more perfect form of religious thought'.[7]

This thesis had already been expounded in conjunction with Marcel Mauss in 1903. In their essay on *Primitive Classification*, Durkheim and Mauss broke new ground by studying the manner in which Aborigines categorised their world. Their goal was to investigate 'the most rudimentary classification made by mankind, in order to see with what elements they have been constructed'.[8] These classifications, it is stated may

> be said without inexactitude to be scientific, and to constitute a first philosophy of nature. The Australian does not divide the universe between the totems of his tribe with a view to regulate his conduct or even to justify his practice; it is because, the idea of the totem being cardinal for him, he is under the necessity to place everything else that he knows in relation to it.[9]

Of course, the authors would add that the cognitive categories used by Aborigines are in the final analysis, derived from social categories.[10]

Later on, when Durkheim made his famous pronouncement that the totem was a visible manifestation of the Aborigines' sense of their collective existence, he again stressed that here lay the roots of both religion and science. The identification of a totem with a social group postulates the operation of an invisible force, and it is only with the establishment of such invisible kinships that science can develop. Thus, for instance, to call a man a kangaroo is not a mystical participation as Lévy-Bruhl would have us believe, but an identification analogous to the scientific claim that heat is a 'movement'.[11] Lévy-Bruhl's disappointing notion of a pre-logical mentality was similarly unacceptable to Durkheim who emphasised that Aborigines, in fact, often discriminate where our differentiation fails. Primitive thought does lack certain intellectual refinements so that 'when it connects, it confounds; when it distinguishes, it opposes'.[12] Thus, writes Durkheim

> The explanations of contemporary science are surer of being objective because they are more methodical and because they rest on more carefully controlled observations, but they do not differ in nature from those which satisfy primitive thought.[13]

Although we might not subscribe to Durkheim's suggestion that religion is only science in its infancy, there is nonetheless much to be commended in his willingness to accept the cognitive legitimacy of Aboriginal concepts. However, he seemed unaware that in making such claims he had undermined what was left of his positivist thinking; for if logic springs from society and hence imposes itself upon individuals, then what is the explanatory status of a causal social science? In earlier works, Durkheim rescues science by arguing that it has become objective insofar as the 'element of social affectivity has progressively weakened, leaving more and more room for the reflective thought of individuals'.[14] But to propose that the individual must free himself of social preconceptions is to posit a logic and a rationality which are extra-social. In later statements, he merely claims that science is more methodical, controlled, critical and unbiased than religion ,[15] but fails to show how this has been achieved.[16]

Durkheim's approach to Aboriginal religion 'has dogged anthropological studies on this topic',[17] but few of his followers could maintain the subtlety of his thinking. This was certainly the case with A.R. Radcliffe-Brown who, as Australia's first professor of anthropology, made functionalism (in its various forms) orthodox in this country. In one sense Radcliffe-Brown went further than his predecessor by asking why animal and vegetable species – and furthermore, why particular species – were used in totemic classification. This was Durkheim at the level of specifics. One analysis, for example, showed that the species of Eaglehawk and Crow were chosen in a certain myth because they displayed characteristics analogous to the social oppositions found in Aboriginal kinship. Radcliffe-Brown concluded that Aborigines make their universe meaningful by socialising it. In his words:

> The resemblance and difference of animal species are translated into terms of friendship and conflict, solidarity and opposition. In other

> words the world of animal life is represented in terms of social relations similar to those of human society.[18]

Radcliffe-Brown was certainly near to inquiring into the meaning of Aboriginal religious phenomena. However, in the final analysis, he insisted that these were only intelligible to the extent to which they expressed or reflected the social order. That is, he offered his explanation in terms of a social causality, and his conception of anthropology as *A Natural Science of Society* (1948) was couched in crudely positivistic terms which retrogressed to a notion of science innocent of Durkheim's refinements. Anthropology, Radcliffe-Brown declared, was:

> the purely inductive study of the phenomena of culture, aiming at the discovery of general laws, and adapting to its subject matter the ordinary logical methods of the natural sciences.[19]

**Objectivism**

Obviously, such notions of science served as a sentry barring entry to the arena of meaning. In the last three decades of Aboriginal studies, scholars have become increasingly disenchanted with the restrictions imposed by such scientific ideals. As Susan Heckman has recently argued, this is symptomatic of a crisis reverberating throughout the social sciences.[20] A certain methodological vacuum exists, however, since the ousting of positivism. According to Heckman's analysis, attempts to fill the void can be divided into their objectivist and subjectivist forms. The demarcation between these two might be best illustrated for our purposes by quoting from two letters written by Radcliffe-Brown to his rebellious colleagues. The first is addressed to Claude Lévi-Strauss, and reads:

> I use the term 'social structure' in a sense so different from yours as to make discussion so difficult as to be unlikely to be profitable. While for you, social structure has nothing to do with reality but with models that are built up, I regard the social structure as a reality.[21]

The second letter is to E.E. Evans-Pritchard. It says in part:

> You complained that I have never given an example of a 'law' in social anthropology. It is of course obvious that we do not mean the same thing by the word 'law' and I therefore suspect that I shall never waste my time looking for what you might call a law.[22]

Despite the fact that both Lévi-Strauss and Evans-Pritchard are here united in undermining Radcliffe-Brown's scientific epistemology, they are nonetheless saying very different things. Lévi-Strauss is not denying the objective existence of structures, but they are to him somehow above or outside their empirical manifestations. This is what Heckman calls the 'objectivist critique' of positivism. Evans-Pritchard, on the other hand, is not refuting the existence of empirical structures, but rather questioning the legitimacy of attempting to derive objective laws from them. His 'subjectivist critique' insists that social phenomena must be treated with regard for their unique forms. In his *Nuer Religion*, Evans-Pritchard states this in the following terms:

> in a study of religion, if we wish to seize the essential nature of what we are inquiring into we have to try to examine the matter from the inside also, to see it as Nuer see it, to examine how they differentiate at each level between one spirit and another.[23]

Since both objectivists and subjectivists have claimed to unravel the problems of religious meaning, we must examine them in turn.

Lévi-Strauss has had a profound influence upon recent studies of both Aboriginal kinship and religion. Part of the appeal of his approach to mythology is his claim that he does not impose meaning upon a myth, but rather allows it to 'reveal its nature and to show the type to which it belongs'.[24] This meaning, furthermore, does not reside with the believer's subjective understanding, but rather is incorporated into the objective structure of the myth itself. Consequently, Lévi-Strauss insists – no doubt tongue-in-cheek – that they might feasibly be intepreted by computer.[25]

It is well known that the meaningful structure sought by Lévi-Strauss takes the form of synchronistic binary oppositions. These have a dialectical form. In so-called 'primitive' thought a contradictory aspect of reality is resolved by being transformed into a mythological language. Lévi-Strauss is explicit: 'the purpose of myth is to provide a logical model, capable of overcoming a contradiction'.[26]

Lévi-Strauss is supplied with an instance of an Aboriginal conceptual contradiction by Warner who made the following passing remark in his *A Black Civilization*.

> The snake is the fertilizing principle in nature according to Murngin symbolism: This explains why it is identified with the men's group rather than with the women: otherwise one would suppose that the male principle, being identified with the positive higher social values, would be associated by the Murngin with the dry season – the time of the year of high social value.[27]

Lévi-Strauss sees this as a crucial dilemma for these Aborigines. The men who are said to be socially superior (i.e. more sacred and ritually pure) are identified with the inferior season, while the allegedly profane women are associated with the preferred dry season. Lévi-Strauss claims a resolution has been realised, not, in this case, through being transposed into mythological terms, but rather through the ritual division of men into initiated and uninitiated classes. In this way 'the uninitiated stand in the same relation to the initiated in the society of men as women do to men within the society as a whole'.[28] The men can thus subsume the more desired natural phenomena by periodically incorporating the uninitiated (and hence socially female) males into their ranks.

Lévi-Strauss sees such attempts at mediating problematic contradictions as indicating that 'the savage mind is logical in the same sense and the same fashion as ours', and thus he applauds the 'numerous texts of Durkheim and Mauss [which] show that they understood that so-called primitive thought is a quantified form of thought'.[29] He is similarly appreciative of Radcliffe-Brown's cognitive interpretation of 'totemic' myths. In his polemical *Totemism* he systematically affirms Radcliffe-Brown's claim that '"totemism" as a technical term has . . . outlived its usefulness',[30] by arguing that what is known as 'totemism' 'constitutes not even a mode of classification, but an aspect or moment of it'.[31]

The essential difference between Lévi-Strauss and his functionalist predecessors is that he has abandoned positivism and hence the concomitant insistence upon social causality. What was previously seen as the imprint of society upon religion is now recognised as a simultaneous manifestation in both social structure and religion of a binary predisposition of the human psyche.

Lévi-Strauss so claims to deal adequately with the problem of meaning. Mythology becomes a language – or, more accurately, a meta-language. It is to be understood rather than reductionistically explained. We shall have grasped the significance of Aboriginal religion when we have decoded its message.

Lévi-Strauss and his adherents in Aboriginal studies have certainly shown that it becomes possible to investigate the meaning of religious phenomena once we have abandoned a positivist scientific epistemology. However, the objectivist foundations of structuralism entail the subscription to a neo-Kantian idealism. Durkheim himself was justifiably wary of such *a priorist* conceptions. It is no explanation at all, he said, to suppose that logical categories are 'inherent in the nature of the human intellect'.[32] Many critics of Lévi-Strauss would agree.

The dangers of an *a priorist* theory of knowledge are evident. In Lévi-Strauss' own terms, if a binary logic is common to both 'savage' and 'civilized' thought we must ask, whose thought is represented in our mythological analysis – theirs or ours? The blurring of such boundaries is acknowledged when he says of *The Raw and the Cooked* that 'this book on myths is itself a kind of myth'.[33] Surely this is courting disaster. It is an open cheque which could cover the cost of even the most extravagant mythological interpretation. Lévi-Strauss' approach could feasibly be used to reveal what Aboriginal religious phenomena mean to anthropologists, but it hardly increases our understanding of the meaning they have in Aboriginal society. As Horton and Finnegan write (although I would wish to qualify some of their terms):

> The scholar comes away from Lévi-Strauss saying 'so what?' for the good reason that Lévi-Strauss takes him nowhere near [the] underlying motives and intentions, hence nowhere near the 'meaning' or the 'message'.[34]

II

This brings me to the attempts of the subjectivists to construct a post-positivist anthropology. With two notable exceptions, very little interest has been evinced in trying to understand Aboriginal religion from this reference point. This neglect was identified – so far, fruitlessly – by Kenelm Burridge, over a decade ago. He wrote:

> the reality of religious life as the religious themselves have expressed it, has been almost totally lacking in studies of Aboriginal religion. Much of the necessary data is there to be culled. But as yet, apart from Stanner, there is little sign of the quality of insight and methods of analysis of, say, Evans-Pritchard or R.G. Lienhardt or Turner being applied to the Australian material.[35]

Given the passage from Berndt which I quoted at the beginning of this lecture, it is surprising to find he disagrees with Burridge. Berndt claimed that despite Evans-Pritchard's critique of functionalism, he 'has added little to our understanding of Australian religion'.[36] Surely, however, this is the very point that Burridge is making, and it most certainly is the one I wish to make. The problem is precisely that the type of analysis made by Evans-Pritchard in interpreting African religion is conspicuous by its absence in Aboriginal studies.

I now want to examine the feasibility of developing a phenomenological understanding of Aboriginal religion. After expressing certain reservations with this approach, I shall move on – as Burridge would say – from phenomenology to ontology.[37]

## Phenomenology

Since such perspectives have been neglected in the study of Aboriginal religion, it is probably wise to first refer to some relevant historical antecedents of the 'subjectivist' stance. I shall begin with the hermeneutic tradition and its most noted figure, Wilhelm Dilthey. Dilthey has been called 'more positivistic than the positivists'[38] because he would not allow the facts of the human sciences to be interpreted using laws which had not emerged from these facts. He claimed that the positivists failed to take the totality of social reality into account, and so tended to 'mutilate historical reality in order to adapt it to the ideas of the natural sciences'.[39] The important distinction he and other hermeneuts made was between the process of 'interpretative understanding' (*verstehen*) and the causal explanations of the natural sciences. Dilthey's unsatisfactory (but, as we shall see, strangely resilient) proposal for achieving such understanding was that through empathy, we can re-live or imaginatively reconstruct the experiences of our human subjects. Dilthey's thinking made a great impression upon Edmund Husserl's phenomenology. These two scholars, in turn, profoundly influenced Geradus van der Leeuw's attempt to formulate a philosophical foundation for a phenomenology of religion. Van der Leeuw's explicit concern with epistemological issues is almost unique amongst phenomenologists of religion, but his thoughts, nonetheless, are representative of the kind of assumptions which underlie many of their works.

Van der Leeuw claimed that his phenomenological approach could produce a purely objective understanding of religious manifestations.[40] The process begins with Dilthey's notion of empathic (van der Leeuw's 'intensely sympathetic') 'understanding' by which the religious expressions and experiences being studied are interpolated into our own lives. To truly understand we must bracket (in Husserl's terms) all preconceptions, and consequently come to perceive the 'essence' and the 'meaning' of what is experienced. The historian of religion's task is to reconstruct the significant and meaningful organisation of experience. That is, he comes to understand, but not to causally explain, a meaningful structure. Those structural connections perceived as sharing in a common essential nature are then coordinated into 'ideal types'. In sum, the process is one of making objective forms out of subjective experience.[41]

As has been shown recently, such a phenomenological philosophy is implicit in Mircea Eliade's works.[42] To date, Eliade is the only scholar adopting this strategy in studying Aboriginal religion. Some caution is necessary here, since he has occasionally denied that his position is purely phenomenological. He does not like methodological straitjackets. Nonetheless, van der Leeuw himself acknowledges Eliade's work as parallel to his own,[43] and Eliade has periodically insisted that phenomenology – a word which he uses interchangeably with hermeneutics – is essential if we are to 'understand' what we study.[44] He makes this explicit in his *Australian Religion*. In the opening pages, he focuses on the necessity of considering 'the understanding of the *meaning of a particular culture*, as it is understood and assumed *by its own members*',[45] and with his closing words he reveals how this might be achieved. He says:

> the ultimate goal of the historian of religions is not to point out that there exist a certain number of types or patterns of religious behaviour . . . but rather to understand their meanings . . . Ultimately, the historian of religions cannot renounce hermeneutics.[46]

These are indeed fine sentiments, and if justified they have solved the problem with which we began. But are they justified? Has Eliade really founded his work on an understanding of the meaning that their religious life has for Aborigines? I suggest that he has not.

The first point I would like to emphasise is that Eliade is not a specialist in Aboriginal studies, but an historian of religion, with interests ranging through the spectrum of religious traditions. A strong advocate of comparative methodology, he insists that meaning is only discerned through the use of comparative studies. Particular religious manifestations, such as those found in Australia, are thus but one expression of a universal system of religious symbols and structures. The essence or ideal type of these symbols must consequently be sought only after examining many of their culturally-bound forms. This is the procedure which guided the formulation of Eliade's book on Aboriginal religion. In that book, each of the chapter headings correspond to one of his comparative studies – for example, those on sacred time and space, initiation and shamanism. Some parts are even lifted verbatim from those previous works.[47] Hence we must immediately qualify Eliade's claim that he is elucidating the understanding Aborigines have of their culture, for in practice, he begins with a meaning which is archetypal and trans-cultural. This is not an uncommon approach in the phenomenology of religion.

The success of Eliade's schema is therefore dependent upon the degree of correlation between the essential meaning of general and specific symbolic forms. The problems inherent in the search for universally valid essences or types is illustrated nicely by Maurice Merleau-Ponty's discussion of how Husserl's own thinking would relate to the study of Aboriginal religion. The early Husserl did not deem the existence of objective manifestations necessary for the discovery of essences. He would have thus rejected Durkheim's analysis of Australian totemism as the essence of religion because for him essences were empirically unobtainable. Merleau-Ponty says:

> There are many religious phenomena which are more rich and more varied than Australian totemism. Must we believe that they are mere superstructures based on the sacred as it is experienced by these tribes? This cannot be postulated, and it is precisely the object of Husserl's questions to obtain such a clarification. What is religion, or what is the essence of religion?[48]

Husserl would therefore have claimed that essences must be determined prior to studying particular religious traditions. This may sound absurd, but Husserl argued that by imaginatively varying the facts, he could conjure to consciousness every conceivable experience.

In later years, Husserl rejected this position. This came about through his extraordinary interest in a book outside his usual sphere of reference. It was Lévy-Bruhl's *Primitive Mythology: the Mythic World of the Australian and Papuan Natives* (1935). How, asked Husserl, could someone rooted in a historical tradition ever have imaginatively created the non-historical worlds of these societies? He felt compelled to write to Lévy-Bruhl of how important it was 'to feel our way into a humanity whose life is enclosed in a vital, social tradition, and to understand it in this unified social life'.[49] But, we might ask, is it possible for a phenomenologist to do this without the prior knowledge of essences previously spoken of by Husserl? If the Aboriginal worldview really is alien to us, how might it be grasped and its essential forms be perceived? Such problems of intersubjective understanding are a confessed stumbling block for philosophical phenomenologists.

As Douglas Allen notes, Eliade claims to embrace the latter Husserlian position,[50] but his critics frequently suggest he is lapsing into the former, and that the archetypal forms he identifies reveal more of his own ontology than that of the people he studies.[51] His treatment of Aboriginal 'high-gods' provides a neat instance of this. The significance Eliade bestows upon them is quite disproportionate to their place in Aboriginal religious life. Although by stretching our imaginations and taking an ethnographic leap of faith we might perceive something approximating the idea of an Aboriginal 'high god', we are nonetheless left wondering if perhaps what we are really witnessing is not an *a priori* essentialism conforming to Eliade's thesis that '"true" religion begins only after God has withdrawn from the world'.[52]

The commonly levelled charge that phenomenologists are partisans of essentialism, Platonism and even Jungianism[53] is, I suspect, an inevitable consequence of their fallacious claim that they are creating objective ideal types out of intentional subjective meanings. As we have just noted, Husserl was confounded by the problem of understanding the forms of an alien 'life-world'. Phenomenologists like Eliade are not taking this issue seriously enough when they posit that this difficulty can be overcome through a process of empathy: a simplistic solution that Husserl himself was careful to avoid. When discussing van der Leeuw, I indicated that empathy is the first theoretical link in the phenomenologist of religions' chain that leads to objective essences. Unfortunately, it is also the weakest link. It is easy to be deluded into believing we have gained an empathic understanding of other people's religious life, when in fact we have merely seen ourselves reflected in their culture. Having then failed to achieve an intersubjective intuition, phenomenology cannot claim to be cognisant of subjective meanings.

In the final analysis, therefore, my disagreement with a phenomenology of Aboriginal religion originates with my dissatisfaction with their answer to the cardinal question, how do we understand the meaning of religious phenomena in Aboriginal society? Indeed, all proposals of this nature fail to acknowledge the glaring discrepancy between theory and Aboriginal reality. For if we define understanding (as phenomenologists do) in terms of grasping an intended meaning, then we are doomed from the outset, because, in this sense, Aborigines do not understand their own religion. Stanner put it well when he said:

> The problem of . . . 'meaning' . . . is one to which I have no satisfactory answer. Whatever may be the situation in other societies, in aboriginal Australia it is impossible to ask questions bearing directly on the

> matter . . . The usefulness of both direct and indirect questions falls off sharply. Even old men of intelligence and stamina who survive many inquisitions are apt to shrug, and say: 'it is a thing we do not understand'.[54]

## Ontology

At this point, it might be useful to recapitulate briefly. I began by showing that although scholars such as Durkheim and Radcliffe-Brown brought to our attention the importance of studying the way Aborigines classify their world, they could not, within the positivist paradigm, arrive at an understanding of the meaning of these worldviews. I then maintained that the attempt to overcome this limitation is a focal issue in recent studies in the humanities. So far I have looked at two proposed solutions. Lévi-Strauss' objectivist approach was rejected because it rested upon an *a priori* idealist structure which I suggested is imposed upon rather than grows out of, a specific ethnographic context. If this is so, then his structuralism cannot truly be said to unveil the meaning of Aboriginal beliefs and practices. On the other hand, the phenomenologists have correctly insisted we begin with an 'interpretative understanding' of the meaning religious expressions have within a specific culture, but their definitions of 'understanding' and 'meaning', couched as they are in terms of subjective intentionality, would make our task virtually impossible. Certainly they have never convincingly explained how we are to empathetically comprehend the meaning of another person's religious life.[55]

Is the dilemma posed by Berndt in my opening quote then to be deemed insoluble? I think not. I now suggest that defeat can be avoided if we amalgamate certain aspects of our two post-positivist theories. We must, I believe, begin with the phenomenologists' concern with 'understanding' if we are to ensure that the meaning we discern is one that actually exists in the Aboriginal world. But understanding and meaning cannot be defined in terms of subjective intentions, and here structuralists are correct in insisting that meaning must be sought in the objective forms of religious life.[56]

An inspired statement on how this synthesis might be realised comes from yet another disenchanted positivist.[57] Ludwig Wittgenstein was at pains to redefine meaning in such a way as to avoid reference to subjective mental processes. He said:

> Try not to think of understanding as a 'mental process' at all – for that is the expression which confuses you. But ask yourself: in what sort of case, in what kind of circumstances, do we say, 'now I know how to go on'.[58]

The implications of Wittgenstein's philosophy for social sciences has been argued in an extremely controversial way by Peter Winch. The difference between Winch's so-called 'ordinary language analysis' and phenomenology might most simply be illustrated at the level of the meaning of a word. A phenomenologist 'regards the meaning of the word as an indication of the speaker's subjective experiences – regards the meaning, in short, as what the speaker meant'.[59] But Winch retorts: 'What is it for a word to have a meaning? leads on to the question: What is it for someone to follow a rule?'[60]

Winch is very concerned to salvage the hermeneutic concept of 'understanding' (in particular as it is found in Max Weber's works), and to do so – if I might misuse a phenomenologist's term – he 'brackets' the whole arena of subjective meaning. The role of a social scientist is demarcated as elucidating what might be called the 'rules' of a particular conceptual system, or more simply, its ontology. It is ontology, insists Winch, which governs society:

> A man's social relations with his fellows are permeated with his ideas about reality. Indeed, 'permeated' is hardly a strong enough word: social relations are expressions of ideas about reality.[61]

Winch thus turns positivism on its head while simultaneously side-stepping pure subjectivism.

The anthropological implications of Winch's thesis were elaborated upon in his 'Understanding a Primitive Society' in which Evans-Pritchard's *Nuer Religion* is identified as illustrative of the approach he is proposing. The article owes its origin to a critique by Alasdair Macintyre which claimed that both Evans-Pritchard and Winch had failed to accept that any study of another society's worldview must be evaluative. Macintyre instances a remark by Spencer and Gillen that some Aborigines carry about a stone or stick as though it embodied their soul. He maintains that although we might prescribe rules governing this behaviour, it is also necessary for us to assess the intelligibility of the actions of these Aborigines. He states, 'we cannot rest content with describing the user's criteria for an expression, but we can criticise what he does'[62] and thus:

> We can only understand what it is to use a thoroughly incoherent concept, such as that of a soul in a stick, if we understand what has to be absent from the criteria of practice and of speech for this incoherence not to appear to the user of the concept.[63]

Such beliefs and practices, in other words, are only comprehensible in terms of our own notions of what is coherent, and thus ultimately in terms of 'scientific' rationality.

In replying to what he rightly saw as latter-day Frazerism,[64] Winch re-emphasised that intelligibility is implied in the very concept of language, and that consequently, the onus is upon us to broaden our categories of understanding rather than to lay cultural reality upon a Procrustean bed. He says:

> We are not seeking a state in which things will appear to us just as they do to members of [society] S, and perhaps such a state is unattainable anyway. But we are seeking a way of looking at things which goes beyond our previous way in that it has in some way taken account of and incorporated the other way that members of S have of looking at things. Seriously to study another way of life is necessarily to seek to extend our own – not simply to bring the other way within the already existing boundaries of our own.[65]

The task Winch sets for anthropologists is a *dialectical* one in which we somehow bring our subject's concept of apprehensibility into relation with our own, and hence create a new unit of intelligibility.

How can we begin this dialectical process? Winch suggests we might initially approach an alien society's 'form of life' by acknowledging certain 'limiting notions' which (almost by definition) set boundaries to the human conception of existence. These notions would include those about birth, death and sex. Thus, he conjectures – and it is meant as no more than a conjecture by someone claiming no expertise in Aboriginal ethnography – that might not an Aborigine carrying his soul in an inanimate object be engaged in the totally comprehensible activity of expressing a concern with his life as a whole and its intrinsic connection with death? Since within a person's life this can only be expressed quasi-sacramentally, then 'the form of the concern shows itself in the form of the sacrament'.[66]

At this point Winch is probably overstepping the bounds of his knowledge of Aboriginal life. Yet his reference to Aboriginal sacrament brings us to William Stanner who made the concept focal to his understanding of Murinbata religion. I feel there are many points of agreement between Winch's thesis and Stanner's brilliant monograph *On Aboriginal Religion.* Burridge's identification of Stanner's work with that of Evans-Pritchard (whose contribution is commended in turn by Winch), would suggest that in an indirect way, others have also seen this similarity.

I have already quoted Stanner to the effect that it is impossible directly to intuit the subjective meaning their religion has for Aborigines. Like Winch, Stanner expends a great deal of effort in avoiding causal sociological reductionism on the one hand[67] without lapsing into an unjustifiable subjectivism on the other.[68] With these restrictions operating, the anthropologist, he said,

> is likely to feel for a long time unable to pass beyond the anterooms of meaning, because the rites are made up of an infinitude of symbolisms, most of them obscure, for which the aborigines make no attempt to account and, if asked to, usually cannot.[69]

Stanner nevertheless insists that the meaning which Aboriginal religious thought has is intelligible to us. Although their thinking is greatly governed by the use of simile and metaphor which produce a multitude of symbols,[70] it is also true that Aboriginal myth and ritual are cognitive and communicative. Stanner parallels Winch's thinking when he argues that Aboriginal religious life is philosophical, or more explicitly, ontological. Stanner's methodology, which by and large grew out of his concern to understand what he witnessed in the field, was at heart a technique for getting beyond the 'anterooms of meaning', and thus for grasping the Murinbata's ontology.

Unfortunately, I cannot here do justice to Stanner's sympathetic and yet highly systematic analysis. It can be briefly noted that he begins by suggesting that despite our inability empathetically to seize the meaning of Aboriginal religious experiences, we can nonetheless 'try to relate [them] to things familiar to our own intellectual history',[71] or attempt to find within our tradition a point from which we can extend our categories of understanding. It is difficult to know how significant – or merely coincidental – it is that at this point both Stanner and Winch look towards the concept of sacramentality.

Stanner then goes on to analyse in detail rites and their homomorphic myths, and so to identify a central ontological motif.

> Murinbata religion might well be described as the celebration of a dependent life which is conceived as having taken a wrongful turn at the beginning, a turn such that the good of life is now inseparably connected with suffering.[72]

By the end of his study Stanner has formulated a dozen propositions which summarise the Murinbata ontology.[73] I suspect these would correspond reasonably well with what Winch calls the rules of a specific society's ideas about reality.

## Conclusion: A New Humanitarianism

I am not able here to extend my discussion of Stanner's masterly interpretation of Murinbata religion. However, to facilitate the transition to some concluding remarks, let me quote his anthropological credo which encapsulates the position I am advocating. He says:

> The first duty of anthropology in dealing with aboriginal religion is to try to elicit the kind of reality the facts of study have for the people responsible for them. The data might be described as natural facts of human conviction about the ultimates of life. In other words, they are products of human passion, aspiration and imagination. They are what they are because aboriginal mentality is what it is. In this sense they have their being, as realities studied by anthropology, within what could be called an ontology of life. It is that reality which anthropology must set up for study as best it may . . .
>
> The tradition of anthropology has always gone beyond the study of man simply as Homo sapiens and Homo faber. Beyond, too, the rather inelegant conception of Homo socius . . . the true subject of study is really Homo convictus . . . That is, man to whom it is natural to act socially within a system of life depending on overwhelming convictions about ultimate values.[74]

There is much that is profound in this passage, and I would like to try to delineate the issues surrounding the question: why has Stanner's innovative approach remained a unique Australian contribution?

It is worth noting that Evans-Pritchard's parallel studies of African religions have also received less acknowledgement than they deserve. One recently proffered explanation for this is that it is consequent upon his disinclination to reduce ethnography to an instance of a methodology. He had no desire to cherish a theory to be put 'into a balloon, puffed up with a lot of air, and floated into the academic skies with a large label attached'.[75] Stanner was similarly far too preoccupied with trying to understand Aboriginal religion to be concerned with constructing theoretical programs. There was almost an intuitive cast to his methods. 'My approach', he said, 'has been to try, as far as possible, to let Murinbata religion exhibit itself'.[76]

However, I feel this point should be made more strongly. I am inclined to the position that the absence of methodological blueprints is not merely the result of a preoccupation with ethnographic reality, but rather that there is something inherently contradictory in trying to understand another culture's ontology while remaining fettered to a methodology. This does not undermine my support for the views of

Winch and Stanner. From the outset I have insisted I was dealing with epistemological issues, instead of simply offering yet another methodological prescription. Winch also maintained that he purposely avoided discussing methdology when he tried to build a philosophical foundation for social science.[77] The distinction is fundamental. Radcliffe-Brown, Lévi-Strauss and Stanner all use a methodology which could be labelled 'small-s' structuralist. In particular, the works of the latter two authors have a degree of superficial similarity. With their methods, I have no quarrel – nor any particular interest. But Radcliffe-Brown was an arch-positivist, Lévi-Strauss a latterday idealist, and Stanner was working with ideas which approximated to a qualified 'phenomenology'.[78] I do not imagine that Stanner would wish to be remembered for his idiosyncratic methodology. His true contribution was his attempt to grasp an Aboriginal ontology with whatever methods proved promising.

Part of the reason for the lack of supporters for the goals and ideals of scholars like Evans-Pritchard and Stanner thus stems from a misplaced concern with methodologies rather than with what I believe are more cardinal issues. Their works are overlooked because they do not encourage methodological discipleship. The misguided passion of the humanities for methodology is one that is readily fostered, but rarely queried. One refreshing exception is Cantwell Smith, who rightly reminds us that:

> However 'scientific' the methodological obsession may be, or may appear to be, if it gets in the way of our understanding what we are supposed to be studying . . . then it is out of place in our work.[79]

There is another closely-related reason why I suspect Stanner's work has been relatively uninfluential. Although there are few positivists left in the human sciences, scholars still cling to a belief that to be 'scientific' (whatever that might mean) is to produce generalisations which are valid for all cultures. As I have shown, this is true of Lévi-Strauss' and Eliade's approaches. Stanner, on the other hand, tends towards fideism. He displays a faithfulness to what is unique in Aboriginal religion as it exists for Aborigines. Whether his analysis of Murinbata religion benefits comparative studies is immaterial. In his work, understanding the people being studied invariably takes precedence over any endeavours to formulate transcultural laws, forms, structures or essences. With such priorities I am in entire agreement. I am thus not only suggesting that the study of Aboriginal religion does not need a specifically identifiable method, but more importantly, that we should seriously reconsider just what we hope to achieve by being so-called social 'scientists'. Again, Cantwell Smith puts it succinctly when he says: 'to subordinate one's understanding of man to one's understanding of science is inhumane, inept, irrational and unscientific'.[80]

No doubt many might feel I have gone too far. Yet to my way of thinking I have merely identified the nemesis of positivism. Stanner once suggested that Murinbata ontology rested upon a conviction that life had taken an 'immemorial misdirection'. Perhaps this is equally true of the academic study of Aboriginal religion. At the beginning of the lecture I mentioned that British anthropology was born of a Christian/humanitarian organisation seeking to understand native races in order to lay a foundation for their compassionate concerns. I suggest that anthropology's wrong turning coincides with the eclipse of those ideals and with the subsequent emergence of positivist scientific anthropology. Of course, I am not advocating we return to a nineteenth-century paternalistic philanthropy. But I am saying we must return humanitarianism to the humanities. We must accept that our understanding of Aboriginal religion has to begin with Aborigines, not with science. This, I feel, is what Ted Strehlow was grasping at when he said, almost paradoxically, that it would only be when we abandoned our search for abstract scientific laws and turned instead to acknowledge the place that their spirituality has in our common future with Aborigines, that Australian 'anthropology would blossom into maturity at last as the true Science of Man'.[81]

## NOTES

Unless otherwise stated, the bracketed date is the date of first publication. Other dates indicate the specific edition from which the quote is taken.

1 'Profile of Good and Bad in Australian Aboriginal Religion', Charles Strong Memorial Lecture, 1979, reprinted in Chapter 2 above.
2 See T.J. Swain, *Interpreting Aboriginal Religion: An Historical Account*, Australian Association for the Study of Religions, Bedford Park, SA, 1985.
3 Quoted in G.W. Stocking, 'What's in a Name: the Origin of the Royal Anthropological Institute', *Man* n.s. 8 (1971), p. 369.
4 A. Giddens (ed.) *Positivism and Sociology*, Heinemann, London, 1974, editor's introduction, p. 1.
5 E. Durkheim, *The Elementary Forms of the Religious Life*, Free Press, New York, 1915, p. 27.

6 W.E.H. Stanner, 'Reflections on Durkheim and Aboriginal Religion' in W. Pickering (ed.) *Durkheim on Religion*, Routledge and Kegan Paul, London, 1975, p. 288.
7 Durkheim, *Elementary Forms of Religious Life*, p. 477.
8 E. Durkheim and M. Mauss, *Primitive Classification*, Cohen and West, London, (1903) 1969, p. 9.
9 Durkheim and Mauss, *Primitive Classification*, p. 81f.
10 See D. Bloor, 'Durkheim and Mauss Revisited: Classification and the Sociology of Knowledge', *Studies in History and Philosophy of Science* 13 (1982).
11 Durkheim, *Elementary Forms of Religious Life*, p. 271.
12 Durkheim, *Elementary Forms of Religious Life*, p. 271f.
13 Durkheim, *Elementary Forms of Religious Life*, p. 270.
14 Durkheim and Mauss, *Primitive Classification*, p. 88.
15 For example, Durkheim, *Elementary Forms of Religious Life*, pp. 270, 477 and 479.
16 See P.Q. Hirst, *Durkheim, Bernard and Epistemology*, Routledge and Kegan Paul, 1975, London.
17 R.M. Berndt, *Australian Aboriginal Religion*, E.J. Brill, Leiden, 1974, fasc. 1, p. 1.
18 A.R. Radcliffe-Brown, 'The Comparative Method in Social Anthropology' in *Method in Social Anthropology*, University of Chicago Press, Chicago, (1951) 1958, p. 116.
19 A.R. Radcliffe-Brown, 'The Methods of Ethnology and Social Anthropology', *South African Journal of Science* 20 (1923), p. 138.
20 S. Heckman, *Weber, the Ideal Type, and Contemporary Social Theory*, University of Notre Dame Press, Notre Dame, 1983.
21 Quoted in A. Kuper, *Anthropologists and Anthropology: the British School 1922–1972*, Penguin, Harmondsworth, 1975, p. 70.
22 'Two letters from Radcliffe-Brown to Evans-Pritchard', *Anthropological Society of Oxford Journal* 8 (1977), p. 50.
23 E.E. Evans-Pritchard, *Nuer Religion*, Oxford, London, 1956, p. 121f.
24 C. Lévi-Strauss, *The Raw and the Cooked*, George Allen and Unwin, London, (1964) 1970, p. 4.
25 C. Lévi-Strauss, 'The Structural Study of Myth' in P. Bohannan and M. Glazer, *High Points in Anthropology*, A.A. Knopf, New York, (1958) 1973, p. 426.
26 Lévi-Strauss, 'The Structural Study of Myth', p. 426.
27 W.L. Warner, *A Black Civilization*, Harper and Row, New York, (1932) 1958, p. 377.
28 C. Lévi-Strauss, *The Savage Mind*, University of Chicago Press, Chicago, (1962) 1966, p. 94.
29 Lévi-Strauss, *The Savage Mind*, p. 268.
30 A.R. Radcliffe-Brown, 'The Sociological Theory of Totemism', in *Structure and Function in Primitive Society*, Routledge and Kegan Paul, London, (1929) 1952, p. 117.

31 C. Lévi-Strauss, *Totemism*, Penguin, Harmondsworth, (1962) 1969, p. 218.
32 Durkheim, *Elementary Forms of Religious Life*, p. 27.
33 Lévi-Strauss, *The Raw and the Cooked*, p. 6.
34 R. Horton and R. Finnegan (eds) *Modes of Thought*, Faber and Faber, London, 1973, editors' introduction, p. 56.
35 K. Burridge, *Encountering Aborigines: A Case Study*, Pergamon Press Inc., New York, 1973, p. 199.
36 R.M. Berndt, *Australian Aboriginal Religion*, fasc. 1, p. 1.
37 Burridge, *Encountering Aborigines: A Case Study*, pp. 159–168.
38 C. Antoni, *From History to Sociology*, Merlin Press, London, (1940) 1962, p. 18.
39 Quoted in H. Holborn, 'Wilhelm Dilthey and the Critique of Historical Reason', *The Journal of the History of Ideas* 11 (1950), p. 98.
40 G. van der Leeuw, *Religion in Essence and Manifestation*, 2 vols., Harper and Row, New York, (first edition 1933) 1963, p. 677.
41 See J. Waardenburg, *Reflections on the Study of Religion*, Mouton, The Hague, 1978.
42 D. Allen, *Structure and Creativity in Religion: Hermeneutics in Mircea Eliade's Phenomenology and New Directions*, Mouton, The Hague, 1978, pp. 107–113, and passim.
43 van der Leeuw, *Religion in Essence and Manifestation*, p. 701.
44 See Allen, *Structure and Creativity in Religion*, p. 111.
45 M. Eliade, *Australian Religion: An Introduction*, Cornell University Press, Ithaca, 1973, p. xviii.
46 Eliade, *Australian Religion: An Introduction*, p. 200.
47 For example, M. Eliade, *Rites and Symbols of Initiation*, Harper and Row, New York, (1958) 1965, pp. 99ff., compared with *Australian Religion: An Introduction*, pp. 150ff.
48 M. Merleau-Ponty, 'Phenomenology and the Sciences of Man' in M. Natanson, *Phenomenology and the Social Sciences*, 2 vols., Northwestern University Press, Evanston, (1964) 1973, p. 97.
49 Quoted in Merleau-Ponty, 'Phenomenology and the Sciences of Man', p. 102.
50 Allen, *Structure and Creativity in Religion*, p. 155.
51 Allen, *Structure and Creativity in Religion*, pp. 208–212ff.
52 M. Eliade, *No Souvenirs: Journal 1957-1969*, Routledge and Kegan Paul, London, 1973, p. 74.
53 See A. Hultkrantz, 'The Phenomenology of Religion: aims and methods', *Temenos* 6 (1970), p. 77.
54 W.E.H. Stanner, *On Aboriginal Religion*, Oceania Monograph No. 11, University of Sydney, Sydney, 1963, p. 43.
55 See T. McCarthy, 'On Misunderstanding "Understanding"', *Theory and Decision* 3 (1973).
56 See W. Outhwaite, *Understanding Social Life: the Method Called Verstehen*, George Allen and Unwin, London, 1975, p. 82f.
57 See K.O. Apel, *Analytic Philosophy of Language and the Geiteswissenschaften*, D. Reidel Publishing Co., Dordrecht, (1965) 1967.

58 L. Wittgenstein, *Philosophical Investigations*, Basil Blackwell, Oxford, (1958 translation) 1968, p. 61, sect. 154.
59 A. Schutz, *The Phenomenology of the Social World*, Heinmann Educational Books, London, (1932) 1972, p. 112.
60 P. Winch, *The Idea of a Social Science and its Relation to Philosophy*, Routledge and Kegan Paul, New York, 1958, p. 28.
61 Winch, *The Idea of a Social Science and its Relation to Philosophy*, p. 23.
62 A. MacIntyre, 'Is Understanding Religion Compatible with Believing' in B.R. Wilson (ed.) *Rationality*, Basil Blackwell, Oxford, (1964) 1970, p. 68.
63 MacIntyre, 'Is Understanding Religion Compatible with Believing', p. 69.
64 P. Winch, 'Understanding a Primitive Society' in B.R. Wilson (ed.) *Rationality*, Basil Blackwell, Oxford, (1964) 1970, p. 102.
65 Winch, 'Understanding a Primitive Society', p. 99.
66 Winch, 'Understanding a Primitive Society', p. 110.
67 For example, Stanner, On Aboriginal Religion, p. 16f.
68 Stanner, *On Aboriginal Religion*, pp. 43 and 159.
69 Stanner, *On Aboriginal Religion*, p. 60.
70 Stanner, *On Aboriginal Religion*, p. 14.
71 W.E.H. Stanner, 'The Dreaming' in T.G. Harding and B.J. Wallace (eds.) *Cultures of the Pacific*, Free Press, New York, (1956) 1970, p. 307.
72 Stanner, *On Aboriginal Religion*, p. 39.
73 Stanner, *On Aboriginal Religion*, pp. 151ff.
74 Stanner, *On Aboriginal Religion*, pp. 25 and 27.
75 Horton and Finnegan, *Modes of Thought*, 1973, p. 40.
76 Stanner, *On Aboriginal Religion*, p. 107.
77 Winch, *The Idea of Social Science and its Relation to Philosophy*, p. 136; P. Winch, 'Mr Louch's Idea of a Social Science', *Inquiry* 7 (1964), p. 202f.
78 Stanner's term, 'On the Study of Aboriginal Religion', mimeograph of a paper presented to the Association of Social Anthropologists, Australian Branch, 1961, p. 11.
79 W.C. Smith, 'Methodology and the Study of Religion: Some Misgivings' R.D. Baird (ed.) *Methodological issues in Religious Studies*, New Horizons Press, Chicago, 1975, p. 9.
80 Smith, 'Methodology and the Study of Religion: Some Misgivings', p. 9.
81 T.G.H. Strehlow, *Central Australian Religion: Personal Monototemism in a Polytotemic Community*, Australian Association for the Study of Religions, Bedford Park, SA, (1964) 1978, p. 53.

CHAPTER FIVE

# Aboriginal Spirituality: Land as Holder of Story and Myth in Recent Aboriginal Art

*Rosemary Crumlin*

I come before you as one of you, an outsider, a stranger to her own land. I am a relative newcomer to Aboriginal art, its myths and stories, its secret-sacred rites, its shimmer of colour and its complex rhythms, just as I have been stranger for most of my life to the vast spread of this wonderful land. But I come with an abiding interest in religious art, particularly the religious expression of the twentieth century in the Western world. I have pursued the search for contemporary religious imagery relentlessly in recent years, hoping that the genius of the artist would throw light on my own questions. In this context I was responsible for the exhibition at the National Gallery of Victoria, Images of Religion in Australian Art, and the associated book,[1] and I am at present working towards a project which will bring together 70 great religious images of the century and then, through reflection and conversation, a book which will be interdisciplinary and insightful as the millennium draws to a close. In between, like a surprise filling in a sandwich, has been my encounter with Aboriginal art and so with many Aboriginal people and communities.

It is this journey, the in-between, that I want to share with you. To be with the journey, you must leave the place where you are secure, well respected, academically safe as it were, and step into the realm of story and myth and symbol.

Late in 1989 Frank Brennan approached me with a proposal: 'The World Council of Churches is to be in Canberra next year', he said. 'The voice of Aboriginal people needs to be heard; they have asked to be heard. For them, their art is their voice to the world; it has given them respect and earned them prestige. Would you be interested to mount an exhibition of Aboriginal Christian art to be shown in Canberra at the same time as the meeting?' I thought not. Almost all the Aboriginal Christian art which I had seen to that point was little better than other Christian art in churches – it was emotionally weak and heavily derivative from a corrupted Renaissance figurative tradition. And it bore heavily the persuasion of the missionary, or so it seemed to me.

Having said a firm 'no' for all of these reasons, I was persuaded to rethink the boundaries of Frank's proposal and present to him another. As all Aboriginal art is deeply spiritual, why not mount an exhibition to reflect the diversity of Aboriginal art and include some Aboriginal Christian art if we could find some in which the people (artists) had managed to rethink traditional Christian symbolism into their own culture. (It is only lately that I have come to see the pomposity of such a demand when western Christian art has rarely been able to rethink its own symbols and continues to be wedded to a range of symbols that have lost their power to communicate.) The story of the search for these works is told in the book of the exhibition[2] which also presents all the images of the exhibition.

It is out of this context that I come. My primary focus is on the art itself and in a real sense I move with it as 'outsider', but with a sense of wonder and gratitude and enthusiasm. I remain astonished at its complexity, at its many-layered reality and at its power to communicate something of the depth of life and of what it is to hold responsibility for this land and the spirit that dwells within it. Out of a culture that is wholistic, it is at once map, image, myth, symbol and secret code.

So much for confessions at the beginning of a lecture to memorialise a Scottish Presbyterian minister and scholar who set up the Australian Church in 1885 under the symbol of the five star Southern Cross.

For the rest of this time I would like to share with you some actual works of Aboriginal art from two communities. Each work embodies a story or myth and is located firmly in the landscape that is the country of these people. It is my hope that, as you encounter the symbol that is the whole work (as Susan Langer has said), you will come to experience in the deepest reaches of your being something of the religion, the culture, the politics and the myths and stories of these people. Many Aboriginal people believe that if they but show us *whitefellas* their art, we will understand that they are the centre of the world, that theirs is the garden of paradise and the spirit dwells in them in a remarkable way.

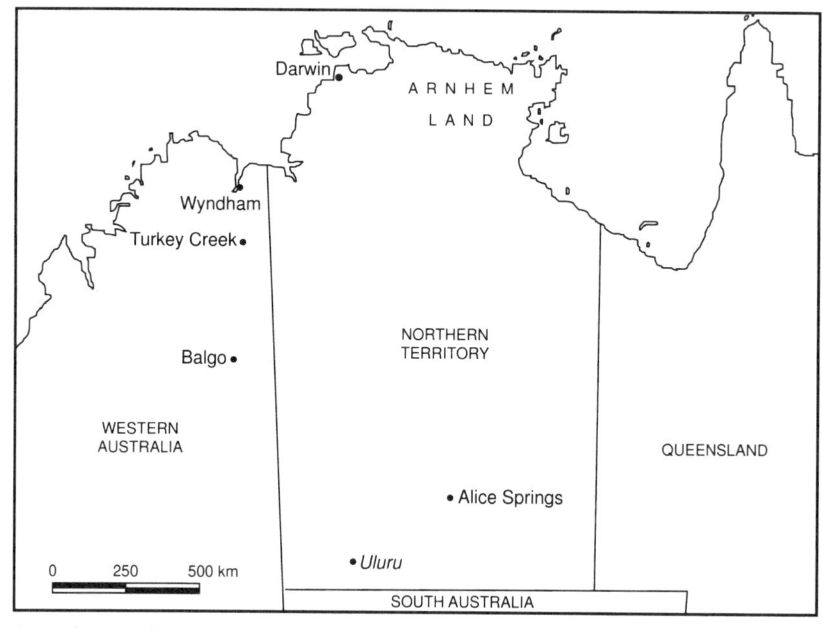


Map showing location of Balgo and Turkey Creek.

I hope you experience this process as odd. It may be that you have come prepared to take notes, to listen attentively and critically. I invite you to do and be other for this time.

I speak with the permission of the creators of these paintings – the traditional owners of Balgo and Turkey Creek. Where possible I shall use their own words about their works. (Plates follow p. 102.)

### *TJIBARI (A WOMEN'S HEALING SONG)* (PLATE 1) BY BAI BAI NAPANGARTI, JEMMA NAPANANGKA, MILLIE NAMPITJINPA, KUNINTJI NAMPITJINPA

The day we flew into Balgo in the tiny five-seater plane the temperature was well over 40 degrees. Red, red earth, some huts and small houses scattered around, the remnants of a football field, a few children and lots of dogs. No adults in sight.

Balgo is at the edge of the Great Sandy Desert in Western Australia. It was set up as a buffer community in the late 1930s by the Pallotine priests for nomadic, traditional peoples of the desert. It was to be a safe place where they could come for food and faith, and as time went on, for education of the children. The Pallotines are long gone, but the community continues to exist – a church, school, health centre, adult education place, an Aboriginal-run store that opens on pension day. The people are mainly Kukatja from the Gibson Desert, Warlpiri from the Tanami desert to the east, Waimatjari from the west and Tjaru from the north. Kukatja is the principal language, but most speak many Aboriginal languages and some, especially the younger men and women, speak English as a second or third language. There is no regular work to be had in Balgo, no industry, no resources. But the community has upwards of 150 practising artists; they get canvas and acrylics from the art co-ordinators[3] and work sitting on the desert floor or outside at night or inside a hut. Often an elder is surrounded by members of the family who listen as the story is told and the main lines drawn in, and who sometimes help fill in the colour; often too they will all dance the painting into life, celebrating together the myth it encodes.

The women who made this painting together did so because they were worried. Television had come to Balgo and the children were obsessed with it, watching the soapies, the ads, 'Sale of the Century' and imitating their favourite characters. In the middle of the desert they were demanding lycra pants, fluorescent bicycle helmets, pop music and consumer foods. Worse still, they were losing interest in the stories of the elders, of the ancestor spirits who dwell in their country, in their developing responsibilities for maintaining the land. 'What shall we do?' the women asked each other. 'What shall we tell our children of who we are, how we came to be here, what it is to be Aboriginal?' (In order to understand the task these women set themselves, you need to try a parallel task. Suppose you had to answer the question, 'What shall we tell our children? How shall we communicate to them what it means to be a member of this family, to live in this place and to grow into responsibility for and with the family, its cousins, uncles, aunts, the way things are done, how these came into being for us, how they must be cherished if this family to keep living?', and so on.)

One group painted this image and danced it into life so that the children and all who came could see and understand the depths of who they were. The painting tells the story of a very long journey made by two young girls in ancestor time who set out to find a great secret. Here is part of what they sang[4] as they worked together and they danced the painting for all to see:

> Two women started leaving Mulirayupungu.
> They tried to make a shade –

the women tried to make a shade,
but it wouldn't stay up.
They got sick of trying to build that shade,
so they started travelling.
They went to another rock,
they stayed there painting their bodies.
These two women were just dancing around.
Next day they started again to another soakwater,
and that's where they did thc same thing.
They painted their body, that's what they did –
the painting and dancing and singing . . .
The next they went to Wilkinkarra –
Wilkinkarra is a big dry lake,
but no trees around.
When you stand in the middle, it's so big,
you might think there's water laying down for years.
But there's no water – it's a salty lake,
so they kept on going.
They went and camped at Killikipunda,
those two women camped.
They carried Yawulyu[5] stuff too,
so they make themselves happy
when they are travelling to find the Living Water,
so they can settle down there to find the New Life.
So those two women kept going.
'We may be getting closer to the Living Water', they said.
And they gave names to the country.
And they went a bit further down.
They were coming near the Living Water.

And so this vast epic voyage, recorded here in writing for the first time, was a search for *living water*. For more than 40,000 years Aboriginal people have called a spring that never dries up living water, and the Balgo women chose this myth to communicate to their children the very depths of who they were. The painting records the journey in layers. The top layer is like an aerial view, a map of the country, and identifiable are the waterholes, the hills, the digging stick they used, the holder for the *yawulyu* materials, and the painted breasts of the two women. The next layer down is that of the story, which is identifiable only to those who know the myth or are willing to listen to it. Underneath these layers is another secret-sacred layer, for parts of this work are 'closed', not to be spoken about, and recognised only by those who have shared the same experience. These are the layers in most ritual Aboriginal painting.[6]

Three other Balgo paintings illustrate the point: *Wanayarra* and *Two Wanayarra* by Susie Bootja Bootja Napangarti, and *Untitled* by Sunfly Tjampitjin.

### *WANAYARRA* (PLATE 2) AND *TWO WANAYARRA* (PLATE 3) BY SUSIE BOOTJA BOOTJA NAPANGARTI

Born around 1932 Susie Bootja Bootja Napangarti is an old woman and a respected elder. Often she paints the myths of her husband's country as well as her own and is sometimes assisted by members of her family as her eyesight is failing. But the paintings are hers, for hers is the authority to tell the stories. In these works she tells of *wanayarra*, the rainbow serpents responsible for creating her husband's country, both the land and the water holes. The eggs, when hatched, spread over the land creating waterholes. *Wanayarra* still live in the caves of the land and are dependent on Susie and her family keeping up a right relationship with the country. She sees this as a sacred command.

### *UNTITLED* (PLATE 4) BY SUNFLY TJAMPITJIN

At 75 years of age, Sunfly Tjampitjin lived much of his life as a nomadic tribesman in Murunpa, north of Yaka Yaka in the Great Sandy Desert. This is his Dreaming country, and this painting depicts a sacred ceremony about initiation. Because it portrays a secret ceremony for men only, the whole of this painting is 'closed' and its meaning cannot be revealed, but its strength and power and masculinity are powerfully communicated.

The flight from Balgo to Turkey Creek takes a couple of hours. From red desert to the majesty of the Bungle Bungles – strings of low hills like rows of the knuckles on your closed fist. As the plane dips low over the Argyle diamond mines the pilot points out that these are the traditional lands of the Warmun people who live in Turkey Creek, and the parts submerged by the flooding for the mines are the women's dreaming sites.

We were going to Turkey Creek because we had heard that the people were 'two-way', that is they were traditional Aborigines but were also Christian; they planned and led their own liturgies and painted Christian myths, but in ways that were faithful to their own heritage. I was dubious; it was a story we had heard many times before of other groups on this journey and had always been disappointed when we came to see the paintings. And we were tired to exhaustion.

Clare Ahern, a Josephite sister, drove us to the L-shaped wooden room beside the little school and as she opened the door the suffocating heat hit us with a blast. We looked around, and I tell you, it was like a miracle and a revelation. The old walls were lined with the most wonderful works – Aboriginal crucifixions, Holy Spirit in the shape of the local owl, a young boy and a young girl accompanied by their guardian ancestor spirits; images of the body marked with the sign of the cross, a dead Christ on a tree platform awaiting resurrection. This, I thought, is what 'holy' means, and I felt I was in a sacred place such as I had never been in before.

I would like to close by looking at a work by each of two elders of the Warmun community. These two men, Hector Sundaloo and George Mung Mung, were the elders and leaders of this group, and it was they who had started the school and went each day to tell stories, paint and teach the children the ritual dances. And it was these two who were the Christian leaders; they composed the music, George played the boomerangs and Hector told the stories. Hector was the *ngapuny* man – the God-man – recognised by the people as their spiritual leader.[7]

## *GOOD FRIDAY* (PLATE 5) AND *PENTECOST* (PLATE 6) BY HECTOR SUNDALOO

Hector completed these works for the Good Friday and Pentecost ceremonies in Turkey Creek. The people danced Good Friday into life as Hector sang the story in Kija, his Aboriginal language:

> Waringarrim perriyan ngurru ngurru
> piny periyan parnanpi jirrayan
> ngurruripe ngapuny ngapuny
> nuwa kural ngiwa jarrak
> nyanini yu kural tungapuny
> yungum purruyu pinpiyaji
> yarri penterrek yinpimji yu
> ngalany ngarri yariny junpam
> ngapuny purruyu kural.

Hector explained:

> This story is blackfellow way given to us by Ngapuny – he tells me the way to do my painting. All the signs are from Ngapuny. The top one is

> the body of Jesus, the bottom is Mary. His mother reminds us to make corroborree for the feeling in Jesus' heart. We must make the drawing of Mary to Ngapuny. Jesus one the cross, and the two robber each side of Him. Mary is standing at the foot of Jesus' cross. That's why we make corroboree for this way. This is Good Friday story.

## *PREGNANT MARY* (PLATES 7 AND 8) BY GEORGE MUNG MUNG

I've spoken about this work many times now, and still feel it a great privilege to mediate the image to a wide group of people. It is, I believe, one of the great religious images of this century and one of the most powerful. It is truly sacred art, born of a deep faith, reverence and understanding of the place of Mary, the Mother of God in Catholic theology. Not that George Mung Mung would have known what Catholic theology was; in fact it was only recently that he was able to write in English. But he was an outstanding artist and a deeply spiritual leader. He died in 1991 while on an initiation ceremony in the Bungles.

The figure is that of a young, unmarried Warmun girl. Her body is painted with the traditional designs reserved for young girls. She is pregnant and carries the child in her womb-shield beneath her heart. The unborn is already a man who dances within her. George said of her:

> This young woman, she's a young woman, this one. The spirit of the little baby comes in a dream to his mother. 'Proper little one', his mother says, 'something has come into me, making me feel strange.' The babe grows and he might be ready at Christmas time. He says, 'Mother, I'm ready now'. And the old woman take her away, and the little one is born, down in the river here.

When George died, Hector said to me of him:

> He was looking forward to a blackfella way and a Kartiya[8] way. He was a two way man. He was a very clever man for the Dreaming.[9]

I do not wish to end our time together with a cold analytic summary of Aboriginal art and its relationship to the land, for I think we have walked quietly with these people who make no separation between religion and life, and whose lives are committed to keeping a right relationship with people and the country. They do not own the land or possess it in our sense of those terms. They are confident and clear about who they are and their art is a remarkably explicit tribute to this. I tip-toe from the room and leave you in the presence of this great art.

## NOTES

1 Rosemary Crumlin, *Images of Religion in Australian Art*, Bay Books, Sydney 1989.
2 Rosemary Crumlin (ed.), *Aboriginal Art and Spirituality*, Collins Dove, Melbourne, 1991, reprinted 1994.
3 The Aboriginal community, under the trade name Warlayirti Artists Aboriginal Corporation, employs a non-Aboriginal art co-ordinator to supply mounted canvases and paints, and to market the finished works.
4 Written down and translated by Patricia Lee, a traditional Aboriginal woman.
5 Women's sacred business – that of 'growing up the land and growing up the children'.
6 Much Aboriginal work is done simply for sale, and does not carry this solemnity which is usually present in the work of traditional elders who have the authority for the story told. I have heard Aboriginal people call the commercial works 'rubbish'.
7 I was later to participate in a baptism ceremony ritualised by George and Hector, where we walked in procession by a river to a spring of living water, stood in reverence as Hector pointed out the trails of the ancestors in a rock we passed and told stories, and watched in silence as a young man was immersed in the spring. And we laughed together, as well as singing and dancing. And I remembered being in Israel.
8 Non-Aboriginal, whitefella.
9 'Dreaming' is the summary term for Aboriginal story and myth, and encodes a way of right living (Law) in relation to the country.

PLATE 1

Bai Bai Napangarti, Jemma Napanangka, Millie Nampitjinpa, Kunintji Nampitjinpa
*Tjibari (A Women's Healing Song)*, 1989
113 x 83 cm, acrylic on canvas

**PLATE 2**

Susie Bootja Bootja Napaltjarri
*Wanayarra*, 1989
120 x 60 cm, acrylic on canvas

PLATE 3

Susie Bootja Bootja Napaltjarri
*Two Wanayarra*, 1989
120 x 60 cm, acrylic on canvas

PLATE 4

Sunfly Tjampitjin
*Untitled,* c.1990
91 x 61 cm, acrylic on canvas

**PLATE 5**

Hector Sundaloo
*Good Friday*, 1992
151 x 186 cm, natural ochres on cotton duck

**PLATE 6**

Hector Sundaloo
*Pentecost,* 1992
97 x 186 cm, natural ochres on cotton duck

PLATE 7

George Mung Mung
*Pregnant Mary,* c. 1983
height 64 cm, wood with natural ochres

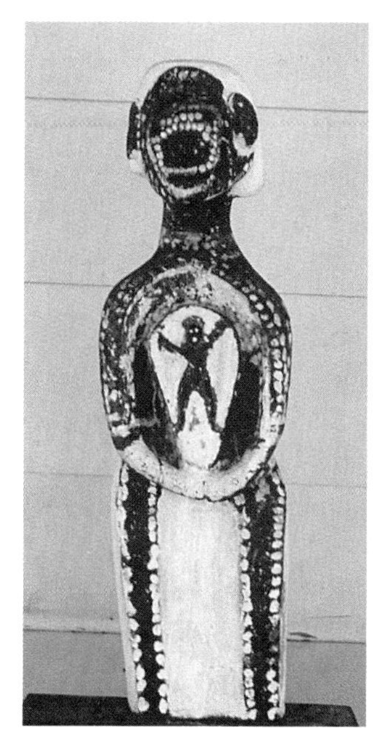

PLATE 8

George Mung Mung
*Pregnant Mary,* (detail)

**CHAPTER SIX**

# Ned Kelly Died For Our Sins

*Deborah Bird Rose*

Images of 'cargo cults' glitter with enticements. They offer representations which invite us, like the mirror on the wall, to discover that we westerners with our fantastic proliferation of goods are indeed the fairest of them all. Images of cargo cults both configure and confine the exotic, addressing us in a language to which we are prepared to listen. Melanesians place a tin can on top of a pole and use it as a telephone to advise the Unites States President to send goods. Here is a message that goods equal power, and that we who can claim to position ourselves as receivers of these messages are masters of both. We can listen, and at the same time we can ignore the moral import of the message. From a position of power, the very form this emulation takes bespeaks an inability to partake equitably in our mastery.

There is, to be sure, much more to cargo cults than my imagery suggests. For a start we might note that cargo cults appear to speak through a code in which control of the object world is equated with control over human worth; succinctly: that wealth equals prestige. This is a code which westerners can comprehend readily. It is a code which Melanesians use with skill, but with an important difference: capitalists accumulate both wealth and power; Melanesians exchange wealth and compete for prestige. In an article focusing on the communicative aspects of exchange, aptly entitled 'Saying it with Shells in Southwest New Britain', Jane Goodale suggests that Melanesians are 'talking about the definition of humanity in these exchanges: that by exchanging so is man defined'.[1] A great deal of evidence from Papua New Guinea suggests that where wealth is an important measure of personal and group esteem, displays of unmatchable and unshared wealth induce those with less to query their own adequacy, to seek the causes of inequality, and to search for means whereby an equitable distribution of wealth and power can be enjoined.

Gary Trompf states that Cargo 'implies a totality of material, organizational and spiritual welfare collectively desired as a replacement for current inadequacy and projected into the imminent future as a coming "salvation"'.[2] Scholars such as Burridge, Lawrence, Worsley, and Trompf have analysed the social, political, moral, and religious dimensions of cargo.[3] Most pertinent to the points I wish to make here is Burridge's discussion of the moral dimensions of cargo.

Part of Burridge's analysis is focused on what he terms the myth-dream: 'a body of notions derived from a variety of sources . . . which finds expression in myths, dreams, popular stories, and anecdotes'.[4] The myth-dream is linked to community – it is shared; and is also linked to aspirations – it encompasses a desired future. In his eloquent analysis, *Mambu*, Burridge contends that the moral dimension of the myth-dream underlying cargo thinking is that of the search for the means to impel Europeans to engage equitably with Melanesians. The dilemma is philosophical: how is it that such inequality came into being? It is also pragmatic: how might those who have more be persuaded to share with those who have less? The dilemma can also become millennial, being predicated on the inducement of a new age, and a new humanity. And finally, it is an intellectual quest: the search for the moral European – one who understands and fulfils the criteria of a moral being.

Just as cargo cults may, but do not necessarily, involve millennial ideals, so too, the search for the moral other is often, but not necessarily, associated with cargo cults. I offer as an example Kenneth Read's (1947) study of the effects of the Pacific war in the Markham Valley.[5] Shortly after the Australians arrived, near the end of the war, Markham Valley People developed a distinction between the British they had known before (called Inggilis) and Australians. One of the men Read worked with explained to him: '. . . But now we see the way the Australians treat us, and now we say that true men have come among us. We know that the English only wanted us to work for them. They did not want to teach us'.[6]

Cargo cults are specific responses to a dilemma posed by colonisation, and they take the form they do in Melanesia, in part, because Melanesians define humanity through competitive manipulation of object-wealth. 'Saying it with shells' is, of course, radically different from saying it with guns and commodities, but the codes converge in the manipulation of goods to impel others to action, and to construct definitions of human worth.

A number of scholars have posed the question: why have Australian Aborigines not developed cargo cults with the same intensity and flamboyance as their Melanesian neighbours?[7] The question seems to imply that Aborigines ought to have responded to European invasion in the same way as Melanesians. Stated so baldly, the immediate response is: why should they? The two contexts are radically different – one an invasion of conquest, dispossession and eradication, the other an invasion of political control and economic manipulation. I think, however, the question can be best understood to indicate scholars' frustration in attempting to understand how Aborigines have responded to invasion.

The deeper concerns underlying this question have been addressed most recently and most articulately by Peter Koepping. In his 1988 paper on 'Nativistic Movements in Aboriginal Australia', Koepping proposes two questions. The first asks whether 'our definition of "real" intellectual opposition [is] so narrow that it fails to encompass the extent of Aboriginal feeling against the invaders'. The second asks whether 'we have few reports because such movements of opposition are well-hidden secrets'.[8] I suggest that the answer to both questions is a qualified 'yes'. There are, of course, types of responses which Aboriginal people define as in some degree secret. 'Balgo business' is an example.[9] The stories I am dealing with in this paper are not secret, but a number of people suggested to me that only since the 1967 Referendum have people felt that it might be worthwhile to share them with Europeans.

Issues of secrecy aside, there is also our failure to attend to what Aborigines have been saying to us, with words and deeds, in art and ritual, for many years. I believe that the greatest impediment to our understanding has been our expectations of what a conquered people could be thought to say to us. Cargo cults make it easy. From a position of mastery it is not difficult to hear from those less wealthy and powerful that they feel inadequate. And as Koepping suggests, we are equally well prepared to hear expressions of resentment, even hatred. Overt resistance, abuse, emulation – we expect these responses, and are mystified by their apparent absence. I will suggest that at least some Aboriginal responses have gone unnoticed because they offer us what, from a position of power, is virtually unthinkable.

But first, I want to make several ethnographic points that will help us to clear our minds of expectations. When we turn our attention to Aboriginal Australia we find that relationships between sentient beings and the object world are pervasively metaphysical,[10] and are less amenable to comparison. A more useful starting point is that of exchange. David Turner has shown with brilliant insight that Aboriginal Australians have sought not to dominate but to accommodate. He defines accommodation between groups of people as 'a part of the one embedded in the other and vice versa without affecting the integrity of either'.[11] He states that this is accomplished through marriage, through trade, and through allocation of rights to produce and to consume resources. I would add, and I am sure Turner would agree, that knowledge, too, is critical to these exchanges. Aboriginal Australians engage in exchanges of human life (usually through reciprocal marriage arrangements) and exchanges of knowledge which is often coded in ritual, and which may also be coded in objects.[12] I suggest that within this system objects can become imbued with meaning which goes far beyond the functions of signs (money) and symbols (gifts). In certain contexts, objects become moulds into which people pour meaning.[13] They become microcosms – vehicles saturated with significance. Manipulation of objects, in ritual and in exchange, allows human actors to position themselves in relationships through which the metaphysical order is made manifest in the human order.

Let us say that where Europeans 'say it' with commodities, using this term in the Marxist sense, Melanesians 'say it' with gifts, using this term as Marcel Mauss would have us understand it.[14] Aborigines, then, 'say it' with human beings, with rituals, with objects, and so on. Through exchange, these persons, events, and things become matrices of shared physical, social and metaphysical being. In contexts of greatest significance, it is fair to say that Aborigines 'say it' with microcosms.

And whereas Europeans conquer with guns and economic manipulation, Melanesians compete with valuables, as well as with weapons. Aborigines, in contrast, accommodate through reciprocal sharing within and through a cosmic order.

From the vantage point of these brief comparisons, we might expect that when Aborigines found that it was not possible to resist invasion, they would seek reciprocal accommodation with Europeans through offers of marriage, knowledge, and access to resources. We might expect them to accommodate European ideas, events, and items within their own cosmology. They might seek to transfigure or transform European objects through ritual. And we might expect them to be baffled and angered at Europeans' failure to respond. What, indeed, have Europeans given back to reciprocate the profound gifts they have been offered?

In many parts of Australia Aborigines have not judged themselves to be inadequate, nor have they found Europeans to be superior. Rather, they have found Europeans to be ignorant, at best, and grossly immoral at worst. I offer as an example stories of Captain Cook which are told from the Kimberley,[15] across the top end,[16] to Queensland.[17] They demonstrate the search to identify, classify, and define the immoral European. As Hobbles Danayari said in one of his narratives about Captain Cook and the immoral law of oppression:

> You, Captain Cook . . . You kill my people. You been look around, see the land now. People been here, really got their own culture. All around Australia . . . We remember for you. I know. Why didn't you look after London and Big England? Why didn't you stop your government, Captain Cook? You're the one been bring him out now, all your government from Big England. You been bring that law.[18]

For most Aborigines, like most Melanesians, evidence of the immoral European is readily available. Many Aboriginal Australians have done us, the invaders, the honour of supposing that we are not all Captain Cook clones – that among us there are moral human beings. The supposition of a moral other is elaborated differently by different people and in different contexts. In parts of Arnhem Land it is told in song, dance, story, and visual arts that there was an earlier Captain Cook. The first and true Captain Cook did not destroy, and in the end he was himself destroyed.[19]

In this paper I concern myself with another example of the moral European – Ned Kelly. The Ned Kelly stories with which I am familiar belong to Aboriginal people in the Victoria River District of the Northern Territory. I heard some of them during my initial two years of anthropological fieldwork (1980–2) in the communities of Yarralin and Lingara. On subsequent research trips I have been told more stories.

Yarralin and Lingara people are the survivors of 100 years of colonisation. They are cattle station people, having worked most of their lives in the pastoral industry. Most of them worked on two stations which were geographically gigantic and owned by powerful companies: Victoria River Downs, and Wave Hill stations. Since the pastoral strikes of 1966–72, Aboriginal people in this area have had access to some control over some of their traditional homelands. Yarralin community is located on a small block of land the title for which is held, in part, by Aboriginal people. Lingara people have obtained a small excision of several square kilometres for themselves and their descendants.

The language identities of Yarralin people are a mix of Ngarinman, Karangpuru, Bilinara, Mudbura and Ngaliwurru. All of the people in Yarralin and Lingara speak English; North Australian Kriol is the most commonly spoken language, and is the mother tongue of the children. Older people are fluent in several traditional Aboriginal languages as well. The stories presented here are told in English; non-standard but quite comprehensible.

I first heard about Ned Kelly from my friend Hobbles Danayari. During the wet season of 1981 we visited a neighbouring community for purposes of young men's initiation. It was raining, and the community we were visiting had no houses – only a few shelters made of corrugated iron and tarpaulins. The shelters were full of people, and I was having difficulty finding a place where I could camp and stay dry. Hobbies perceived my distress and, taking up a large fighting stick, walked up and down the centre of camp, haranguing people: 'This lady came all the way from America to dance for your little boy, and what's wrong you can't give her a good feed and a place to sleep?'

The result of his diatribe was that people came out of their shelters and decided that a good place for me to sleep would be in the abandoned motorcar that they were using as a warehouse for their wet season supplies. They moved out some of the tinned food, and put the rest on the floor, so that I could sleep on the back seat, and told me that if I was hungry I could eat some of the weetbix. Hobbles, being a gentleman, proposed to sleep in the trunk, but they had lost the key, and so he settled into the front seat. For hours he told me stories of the most remarkable kind. One of these was about Ned Kelly: how Ned once visited Wave Hill station long before any whitefellows had come into the Victoria River District. There he taught people how to make tea and cook damper. Although there was only one billy of tea, and one little damper, everybody got fed.

Initially, for me, this story raised very interesting questions about Aboriginal concepts of time, space and events. I cannot deal with these issues fully in one paper, but I will address the crucial questions: What was Ned Kelly doing at Wave Hill? Why Ned Kelly? Why was he there before other Europeans?

I will first examine the question of origins, orienting myself to what is referred to, in Kriol and in English, as Dreaming. In the beginning, Yarralin people say, the earth was covered with salt water. The waters pulled back and the earth was exposed. Out of the earth, out of holes in the ground, emerged all the life we now know. Plants, of course, grew directly from the earth, and all the animals and other beings, including the sun, the moon, the rainbow, and so on, came out of the earth and started walking around. They walked in human shape; flying foxes were human in shape, the moon was a male human being. Men and women walked separately; they carried ceremonies, negotiated laws, created the system by which life now continues to exist. In their travels they demarcated country, speaking different languages, doing things differently in different places, naming places, creating places, and carrying out ceremonies. These original beings, who are now called Dreamings, established the moral principles and laws through which the cosmos can be sustained as a living system.[20] Through their actions, Dreamings demarcated a spatially identified moral universe.

At some point, most Dreamings became mobilised, both in place and in shape. The males and females, for example, who later became flying foxes, are now referred to as Flying Foxes. Their travels are demarcated in real geographical space. They started at the western edge of Ngarinman country, travelled from named place to named place, and finished at the eastern edge of Ngarinman country. All along their track there are Dreaming sites: where they walked, where they stopped to perform certain actions, where they finished. All of these flying fox Dreaming sites are now important places, because the original life which became flying foxes, and the law initiated by flying foxes, are localised there.

Following Yarralin people's usage, we can distinguish Dreaming life from ordinary life. One way of expressing this distinction is temporal: Dreaming precedes ordinary. Ordinary life belongs to the present in which we now live. It is characterised by temporal sequence, and is marked by beginnings and endings. Within what I will call ordinary time there are rhythmic patterns that recur. Seasons are one such rhythm: hot weather, followed by rains, followed by cold weather, followed by hot weather. In addition, these rhythmic patterns are also marked by regular, significant events, which erase the particular, leaving only the pattern. Rain, for example, washes away the marks of the actions of people, plants, and animals from the face of the earth;

human and animal tracks are washed out, plants die. The earth remains. On a different scale, the same is true of individuals. In ordinary time, life is terminated by death. In ordinary time, what I refer to, rather loosely, as information, does not accumulate indiscriminately; not only is visual evidence of action washed out, but the individuals who made the signs are also washed away. It is no accident that one Kriol term for death is 'washed out'.

I have set up some of the characteristics of ordinary in order to contrast them with Dreaming. That which is Dreaming does not die, does not get washed out, but has the potential to exist forever. All of the people with whom I worked emphasised the importance of continuity and endurance; frequently they contrasted the value they place on continuity with the disregard European Australians appear to display toward this value.

Riley Young, for example, one of the leaders of Lingara community, contrasted his validation of his rights to land with a European pastoral lease. In speaking of his 'lease' he was referring to a stone which is a Dreaming site:

> My lease can't wash out. No rain will wash him out him, no anything will take it away. That's mine lease. White man lease, you read him out on the paper, you change him next year, nother lease. That's what they call special lease, you know, whitefellow law. Mine lease you can't wash him out. He stand up there, no matter rain can be hit him, you can't wash him out. He'll be there for years and years, till I die, till another man will take over that lease. Same lease. That lease forever. We call him, that lease, blackfellow law.

Dreaming life is different from ordinary life in that that which exists as Dreaming endures. There is, also, something we might reasonably call a temporal distinction between Dreaming and ordinary. Dreamings were once mobile with respect to form and movement. They are now fixed.

I found that most senior Yarralin and Lingara people traced their genealogies back about three generations – to their grandparents, and there it stopped. Grandparents, for most people, came straight out from Dreaming. This was stated most explicitly by Old Tim Yilngayari: 'Oh, my mother was never born. She came out from Dreaming'. The point at which Dreaming became ordinary, then, is only about 100 years ago. The change from Dreaming to ordinary is ragged in the sense that it always relative to the speaker. The important points are that it precedes us, and that we are not it.

The relationship between Dreaming and ordinary can be conceptualised in two ways. If we were to locate ourselves, hypothetically, in Dreaming, we would see a great sea of endurance, on the edges of which are the sands of ordinary time. Their origins are in Dreaming but their existence is ephemeral. If, by contrast, we locate ourselves in ordinary time and look toward the past, we see a period of about 100 years – a present ordinary time marked by changes which do not endure, by sequence which can be accurately described in temporal terms, and by the obliteration of the ephemeral. Dreaming can be conceptualised as a great wave which follows along behind us, obliterating the debris of our existence and illuminating, as a synchronous set of images, those things which endure.

When we start talking about Dreaming, then, synchrony becomes a salient feature. Dreamings all exist all the time, so to speak. Stanner refers to Dreaming as an 'everywhen' – it's a useful term.[21] One example will suffice to make the point. Tony Swain studied Christianity among Warlpiri people at Yuendumu, and he asked some Warlpiri Christians who came first: Adam, Moses, or Jesus. Their answer: none came first, they all lived on the one day.[22] Some people tentatively suggested that Moses might have travelled through the Tanami desert. Swain argues, quite correctly, I think, that Warlpiri people are attempting to transform Biblical concepts of time into Aboriginal concepts of space.

In sum, both Dreaming and ordinary exist in real, named, local space. Both are grounded in the earth, and both ultimately derive their life from the earth. Ordinary time, which individuals experience as days and nights, dry seasons and wet seasons, youth, middle age, and old age, is a period in which our western concepts of time have a certain explanatory power. Dreaming, in contrast, is marked most powerfully by synchrony, and it, too, is located in real named space.

In ordinary life there is a temporal dimension to the concepts of before and after. They are contingent on the temporal locus 'now'. As Ricoeur says, 'the now is constituted by the very transition and transaction between expectation, memory, and attention.'[23] For Yarralin people, 'now' as a temporal locus is differentiated from past and future along a number of lines, most of which indicate people's attempts to construct continuity between before and after. Thus, for example, we here now, meaning we here in this shared present, are differentiated from early days people by the fact that they preceded us and made the conditions of our existence possible. In relation to them, we are called the 'behind mob' – those who come after. Sequence and succession are the salient features. As Riley Young said with reference to his Dreaming 'lease' – he holds it till he dies and another man takes over. The future is the domain of those who come after us. They are sometimes referred to as the new mob, or new generation, and sometimes simply as those 'behind to we' – those who come after. It is our job to assure that those who come behind us are taught the law and have a place and responsibilities to take over from us.

In Dreaming, the only temporal co-ordinates from which one could define a before or after are major disjunctions. Salt water covered the earth before it pulled back into oceans; Dreamings walked in the shape of humans before they became fixed with respect to place and shape. Within the period demarcated by these disjunctions, synchrony prevails. Adam, Moses, and Jesus were all there together; none was first. However, there is sequence defined by movement through real geographical space. In Yarralin most (not all) Dreamings travelled from the west to the east. Sequentially, before means west, after means east. Before and after are contrasts which are contingent on the spatial locus of the speaker. When, in Yarralin, people spoke of Dreamings which were before, they referred to all those sites west of Yarralin, while the Dreamings which were after were all those sites east of Yarralin. If one spoke from a different place, before and after would be different. The geography remains fixed, as are the tracks. Only the spatial locus of speakers in ordinary time moves around. This Dreaming geography is more complex than I can pursue. The practice of fixing people in country through ties of 'ownership' and the use of songs which, as the country is sung, give a temporal dimension to geographical movement add significantly to the permutations available within the basic time/space co-ordinates. However, elaborations of time, space and mobility do not obscure the basic points under discussion here.

In Dreaming we find that events are organised spatially and morally. In another paper I have developed the argument that in Dreaming moral principles are asserted through what I have called key events.[24] These are Dreaming actions with specific moral content; other events, other persons, other images may be conflated with the key event if they share in the same moral content. Key events are thus open ended in that they attract and accommodate specificity. Events in the present will, if they are determined to be memorable, be packed away into Dreaming by being conflated with Dreaming events. The result is a view of the past in which events are organised by content and by space, but not predominantly by temporal sequence.

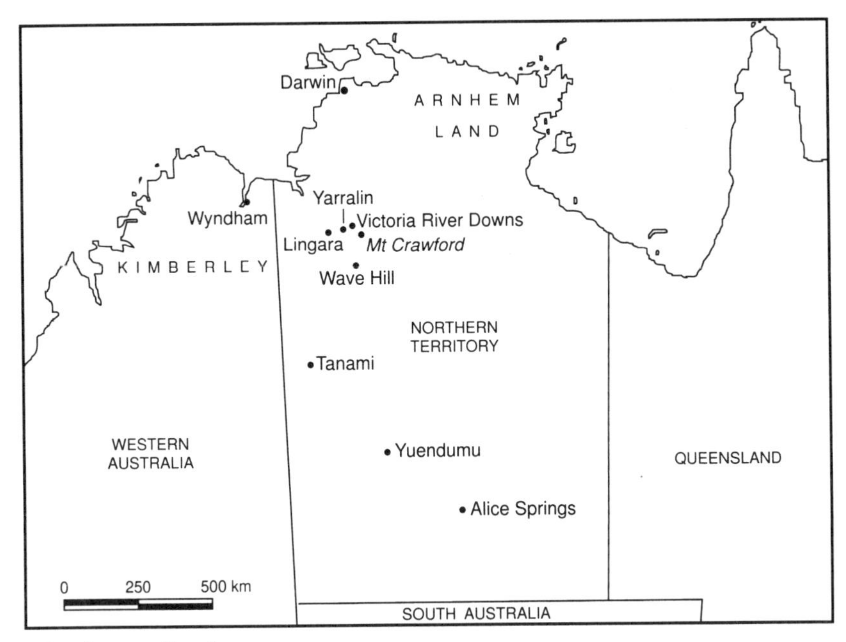

Map showing Yarralin country.

It is now possible to examine another Ned Kelly story. During a research trip in 1983–4 one of the men I worked with regularly offered me a whole set of new terms, one of which was *miki*. His explanation left me puzzled, and in any case I wanted to find out how widespread the knowledge of this term might be. Most of the people I asked found the term quite obscure, but Big Mick Kankinang offered an explanation. I reproduce it here, slightly Anglicised:

> Miki? Early day people might be see him. This world been salt water before, every way, every land. This world been covered up. All the salt water every way. Two men came down from sky. Ned Kelly and Angelo. Come down, get a boat, travel round that sea, salt water. Can't findem any bank. Those fellows travelling. This leaf been fall down. 'Hello! Green leaf here!' Twofellow still – travelling la boat. They hit a high ridge. 'Hello! Pull up here.' Put em anchor. Go down [out of the boat] and stand up. 'What me and you gotta do?' 'We'll have to do something.' They been makem river, and salt water been go right back. That's for Ned Kelly and Angelo. Dry now, every way. Twofellow just walking now. Some bush blackfellow been go longa business [doing ceremony]. They come down. 'Hello! Some blackfellows there!' Blackfellows been talk, 'What's this fellow here?' The blackfellows understand English. Twofellow travelling

> now, longa dry land. Walking. Go longa Wyndham. Wyndham people look those two whitefellows: 'Oh, really different men. Different to we. We'll have to get em policemen.' Four policemen been come. Had a bit of a row longa twofellow. Twofellow get a gun and shoot four policemen la Wyndham. And travel back, go back this way.
>
> Captain Cook been come down to Mendora [beach, in Darwin], gotta boat, from England they been come. Captain Cook come longa this land, longa Sydney Harbour. Good country him been look. Captain Cook shot and broke a leg for one fellow belonging to that country Sydney Harbour. Get a boat and going back again. Bring longa this country now horse and cattle. Captain Cook got a revolver. Photo there all around Daguragu, he's holding a revolver. Where that breed up bullock and horse, that's where the Ned Kelly going back to England, Ned Kelly by himself now, he lose his mate. Ned Kelly got his throat cut. They bury him. Leave him. Sun go down, little bit dark now, he left this world. BOOOOOOOMMMMM! Go longa top. This world shaking. All the white men been shaking. They all been frightened!
>
> This Miki been working for blackfellows, making gutters [to drain off the salt water]. Right la Crawford Knob there, some blackfellows there, that Miki been come out there. He's not here now. He's finished from that salt water time. Him blackfellow, first blackfellow. That Dreaming been come up, and that blackfellow got law now. That Miki been finished altogether.

It is not difficult to appreciate that this story illustrates the points I have been addressing. A number of characters in European mythology are here in this story – God, Noah, and Jesus are all located in the person of Ned Kelly. Ned Kelly is here located in real geographical space; he is at Crawford Knob in Karangpuru country. He goes to a centre of European colonial settlement: Wyndham. And finally he goes to England. He is here in Australia at the very beginning of the world, indeed, he is instrumental in facilitating the division between earth and water that was part of the origins of life. Ned Kelly is Dreaming; and more than that he is allocated a creative position in Dreaming. No matter how many Captain Cooks, police, and settlers came later, it is unmistakably the case that Ned was here first, actively making the Australian continent.

Furthermore, Ned Kelly encountered Aborigines, and his encounters did not result in death, dispossession, or dispersal. In that, he was quite unlike Captain Cook. European people, here located in Wyndham, recognised that Ned Kelly was different – and they condemned him for it. Judging him, and his mate Angelo (sometimes referred to as a group or 'mob' of angels), to be dangerously different, they called out the police. Ned, being Ned, shot the police. In doing so, he aligned himself with the moral position of those who were being dispossessed.

The inclusion of Captain Cook in this story sets up a dynamic tension between those who come to harm people and country, and those whose coming is beneficial. Other stories make it clear that Captain Cook is the originator of an immoral process by which people's land was stolen, their labour appropriated, their lives extinguished, and their knowledge of the truth denied. Hobbles always stated that Captain Cook is dead now; he is dead, and his immoral law ought to have died with him. In contrast, Ned Kelly was opposed to what Captain Cook and his mob were doing to Australia. He went to England – the place of origin of alien animals, alien laws, and intruders. There he was killed, and there, apparently, he rose up to the sky. The stories do not explain why Ned Kelly went to England. I suggest that this sequence is meant to indicate that England is being brought into the same universe of moral principles as Australia. England, or English people, cannot claim that Ned Kelly has nothing to do with them. He died and rose again right there in England. His morality applies to English people as much as it does to Australians.

Big Mick told this story with a great deal of expressive evocation of the emotions involved, and part of the story he told as a subtle joke. He said, in subsequent discussions of the story, that when Ned Kelly rose up to the sky, there was such a great shaking of the earth that all the buildings in Darwin trembled and all the Europeans cowered in fear and wondered what was happening. He found this to be very funny. As I understand the joke, it is based on the Aboriginal perception that Europeans typically fail to recognise the significance of events, because they fail to understand Dreaming. Rather than being frightened, they should have known exactly what was happening, for it is all part of Europeans' own Dreaming.

The humorous effects of this story are awesome: here are two sets of people – Aborigines and Europeans – who find the same story funny, find it funny for different reasons, and in laughing at the story are, in a gentle way, laughing at each other. The fact that we take our cultural constructs to be given in the world causes us to be startled when we see others constructing the world so very differently. Underlying our perceived ridiculousness is our shared humanity, without which it would be impossible even to recognise each other's laughter, much less to make the attempt to understand each other's worlds.

Big Mick's humorous assessment of European Australians is based on the premise that they ought to have known what was happening. But many European Australians might wish to reject the validity of this premise and query, instead, the significance attributed to Ned Kelly. As I understand Kelly in Australian culture, it seems to me that he exists both as an historical actor and as the vehicle for a particular myth-dream.

In his historic persona he is, to some white Australians, a man of monumental, and tragic, proportions. To others he is a quintessential Australian outcast – horse thief, murderer, Irishman and Catholic. Many others respond without feeling the need to be either 'for' or 'against' Ned Kelly. For Professor Molony, of course, Ned Kelly is both man and myth: a well-spring of Australian longing for freedom and for land.[25] I would suggest that Kelly remains the national hero precisely because of the ambivalent and ambiguous responses he generates. Sidney Nolan captures some of this ambiguity, representing Ned in archetypal austerity; man and mask fuse as a spectre haunting the Australian consciousness. As myth-dream Ned Kelly is both invader and outcast; his position encodes the longing to belong and the fear that white Australians will never belong – will always be castaways in the continent of Australia.

In spite of the many ambiguities, Ned Kelly – man, myth-dream, and Aboriginal Dreaming figure – provides a superb bridge between cultures. Part of the basis to this statement rests on a related issue which I have not been able to address: the status of historical facts. It is clear that Yarralin people do not privilege objectivity, nor do they privilege the specific. The question of what 'really' happened is not a question of fact but a question of meaning. If we follow Professor Molony's interpretation of Ned Kelly, and I think we ought to in this context, we would have to agree that, like Jesus, Ned Kelly stood up for the rights of the oppressed; and that he stood against that officialdom which enforced the power of the ruling classes.

We ought also to consider, as Molony does in the final page of his book, that Ned Kelly was passionately in favour of land rights:

> The seasons of a century have come and gone and some men speak again of rights to the land, of resisting those who rape its heritage, and of raising a republic of the free. To many, such ones are visionaries, dreaming like prophets of an Australia still to be born. The legend that is Kelly stands with them. Ned shared their vision, dreamt their dream and, with them, loved the native land.[26]

Yarralin people would agree.

There is more to the story than that which is shared. If Ned Kelly stories offer a bridge of understanding, they also issue a challenge. For white Australians, Ned Kelly the historical actor is dead. Yarralin people have resurrected him twice over – both in the story and by locating him in Dreaming. For them, Ned Kelly is still and always alive. In addition, they have given birth to an indigenous Ned Kelly: he belongs to the continent because he helped make it.

Aboriginal people in the Victoria River District have not found Ned Kelly to be ambiguous. They have analysed his actions and defined him as purely moral. And in indigenising him, they have declared him to be not truly other, but truly us. In fact, Yarralin people take it further. Through Ned Kelly an equitable social order is established as an enduring principle of life. Captain Cook was an invader who had no place here, and as Yarralin people assert, he is dead now. Ned Kelly is indigenous; he is resistance against invasion and injustice. In another story Hobbles Danayari asserted that it was actually Captain Cook who killed Ned Kelly.[27] There is perfect symmetry in the stories, for the immoral Captain Cook is now dead, while Ned Kelly lives.

Yarralin people's stories of Captain Cook and Ned Kelly offer us a mirror in which we can see ourselves. In no way does the image inscribed in these stories tell us that we are the fairest, the most deserving, the most worthy. But it does tell us that we are not without redemption.

Revealing us to ourselves, these stories also offer us a different future. Social justice, they say, is not to be achieved through the destruction of the past, but rather through recognition. We are the successors, the 'behind mob'; and it is up to us to determine to which law we will adhere. These stories tell us that truth is revealed in myth, and that people are capable of changing their society to conform to that truth. There is no 'new age' or 'new humanity' – there is us – and only us – as we are and as we can be. We have only to listen, to learn and to act.

This, I believe, is why we have had such difficulty understanding Aboriginal people's responses to invasion. Unlike cargo cults which flatter our sense of mastery and, on the surface, suggest that it is others who want to change, Ned Kelly stories suggest that it is we who are in dire need of radical change. The last thing one would expect, or be prepared to hear, from a position of power, is that the dispossessed claim to have indeed understood. That they have accepted. And that they are offering us redemption.

## NOTES

1 J. Goodale, 'Saying it with shells in Southwest New Britain', unpublished manuscript, 1978, p. 2.

2 G.W. Trompf (ed.) *Cargo Cults and Millenarian Movements: Transoceanic Comparisons of New Religious Movements*, Mouton de Gruyter, Berlin and New York, 1990, editor's introduction, p. 17.

3 K. Burridge, *Mambu. A study of Melanesian cargo movements and their social and ideological background*, Harper Torchbooks, New York, 1960; P. Lawrence, *Road belong cargo*, Manchester University Press, Manchester, 1964; P. Worsley, *The Trumpet Shall Sound: a study of 'cargo' cults in Melanesia*, Schocken Books, New York, 1968; Trompf (ed.) *Cargo Cults and Millennarian Movements*.

4 Burridge, *Mambu*, p. 27.

5 K. Read, 'Effects of the Pacific War in the Markham Valley, New Guinea', *Oceania* 18 (1947), pp. 95–116.

6 Read, 'Effects of the Pacific War in the Markham Valley, New Guinea', p. 109.

7 H. Petri and G. Petri-Odermann, 'A Nativistic and Millenarian Movement in North West Australia' in T. Swain and D. Rose (eds) *Aboriginal Australians and Christian Missions*, Australian Association for the Study of Religion, Bedford Park, SA, 1988, pp. 391–396; F. Rose, *The Wind of Change in Central Australia*, Akademie Verlag, Berlin, 1965.

8 P. Koepping, 'Nativistic movements in Aboriginal Australia; Creative adjustment, protest or regeneration of tradition' in T. Swain and D. Rose (eds) *Aboriginal Australians and Christian Missions*, Australian Association for the Study of Religion, Bedford Park, SA, 1988, p. 398.

9 See B. Glowczewski, 'Le "juluru", culte du "cargo"', *L'Homme* 23 (1983), pp. 7–35.

10 See N. Munn, 'The transformation of subjects into objects in Walbiri and Pitjantjatjara myth', in R. Berndt (ed.) *Australian Aboriginal Anthropology*, Australian Institute of Aboriginal Studies, Nedlands, WA, 1970, pp. 141–163.

11 D. Turner, 'Transcending War: Reflections on Australian Aboriginal Culture,' *Anthropology Today*, Spring 1987, p. 14.

12 See E. Kolig, 'The mobility of Aboriginal religion' in M. Charlesworth, H. Morphy, D. Bell and K. Maddock (eds) *Religion in Aboriginal Australia: An Anthology*, University of Queensland Press, St Lucia, 1984, pp. 391–416.

13 See W. O'Flaherty, 'Ethical and Nonethical Implications of the Separation of Heaven and Earth in Indian Mythology' in R. Lovin and F. Reynolds (eds) *Cosmogony and Ethical Order*, University of Chicago Press, Chicago, 1985, pp. 179–80.

14 M. Mauss, *The Gift: Forms and functions of exchange in archaic societies*, W.W. Norton and Co. Inc., New York, 1967.

15 E. Kolig, 'Captain Cook in the Western Kimberleys,' in R. and C. Berndt (eds) *Aborigines of the West: Their Past and their Present*, University of Western Australia Press, Perth, 1980, pp. 274–82.

16 D. Rose, 'The Saga of Captain Cook; morality in European and Aboriginal law', *Australian Aboriginal Studies* 2 (1984), pp. 24–39; C. Mackinolty and P. Waingurranga, 'Too Many Captain Cooks' in T. Swain and D. Rose (eds) *Aboriginal Australians and Christian Missions*, pp. 355–360.
17 M. Kennedy, *Born a half-caste*, Australian Institute of Aboriginal Studies, Canberra, 1985.
18 Quoted in Rose, 'The Saga of Captain Cook; morality in European and Aboriginal law', p. 34.
19 Mackinolty and Waingurranga, 'Too Many Captain Cooks'.
20 For more details, see D. Rose, 'Consciousness and Responsibility in an Australian Aboriginal Religion,' in W. Edwards (ed.) *Traditional Aboriginal Society. A Reader*, Macmillan Company, Melbourne, 1987, pp. 257–269.
21 W.E.H. Stanner, *White Man Got No Dreaming: Essays 1938–1973*, Australian National University Press, Canberra, 1979, p. 24.
22 T. Swain, 'The Ghost of Space: Reflections on Warlpiri Christian Iconography and Ritual' in Swain and Rose (eds) *Aboriginal Australians and Christian Missions*, pp. 452–469.
23 P. Ricoeur, 'The History of Religions and the Phenomenology of Consciousness' in J. Kitagawa (ed.) *The History of Religions: Retrospect and Prospect*, Macmillan, New York, 1985, p. 16.
24 D. Rose, 'Jesus and the Dingo' in Swain and Rose (eds) *Aboriginal Australians and Christian Missions*, pp. 361–375.
25 J. Molony, *I am Ned Kelly*, Penguin Books, Ringwood, 1980, p. xiv.
26 Molony, *I am Ned Kelly*, p. 257.
27 H. Middleton, *But now we want the land back*, New Age Publishers Pty Ltd, Sydney, 1977, p. 121.

CHAPTER SEVEN

# Riders in the Chariot: Aboriginal Conversion to Christianity in Remote Australia

*Peter Willis*

## INTRODUCTION

This lecture attempts to interpret the significance of Aboriginal conversion to Christianity in remote Australia by analysing the context and processes surrounding the conversion, baptism and subsequent Christian life of a Miriwung group living on the outskirts of Kununurra in the late 1960s. The interpretation is based on an exchange theory approach to human interaction in which the meaning of the processes is extracted by looking at the various human exchanges contained in them.

It is suggested that from this perspective the missionary strategy in these remote settlements can be described as attempted patronage – the strategic bestowal of goods and services to encourage the Aboriginal target group to reciprocate by becoming affiliated with them as their clients. The Aborigines for their part, it is suggested, employed a patterned strategy called 'riding' or 'kinship riding' when relating to non-violent whites possessing useful resources (to which category most missionaries belonged).

My general thesis is that for Aboriginal people the religious outcomes of their encounter with Christian missionaries in remote Australia can best be understood as an amalgam of two orientations possessed by Aboriginal leaders while employing their general 'riding' strategy. The first is an orientation towards securing the patronage of the missionaries by attempting to meet their expectations without losing their own integrity and autonomy. The second is an orientation towards exploiting their incorporation into the missionary society by forming what can be called religious alliances with members of the missionary community to further their interests.

The suggestion of this paper is that where traditional life and kinship and territory remained – as they did on remote Christian missions – Aboriginal religion continued for its adherents, including those who became Christians, to be the foundation of their spiritual being. Aboriginal converts, while often carrying out the prescriptions and practices of the missionaries, did not replace their religion with Christianity. They rather located it within categories of their own religious world and married the demands and enrichments of both, according to their own philosophy and religious system and according to the demands of the sociopolitical environment, which are expressed particularly by their own needs and the needs of their various missionary and non-missionary interacting partners.

My approach in this lecture is to examine in detail a case study in which I was involved – the proselytising, baptism and subsequent religious life of the Miriwung in Kununurra. I want then to look at Aboriginal religion and what meaning 'conversion to Christianity' could be presumed to have in such a context; to provide a brief outline of the theory underlying the hypothesis proposed; and to apply it with some additional corroboration to the case study in question. This approach is exploratory and hopefully will form the foundation for further research in this area.

## THE CONVERSION OF THE MIRIWUNG

I will begin at the opposite end of the continent, at Kununurra in north-western Australia.

On 1 November 1969 on a sunny Sunday morning, the convent school at Kununurra was converted into a temporary church to accommodate several hundred people whose routine Sunday Mass was to include the baptism of 60 Aborigines, most of the remainder of the Miriwung Aboriginal people who had recently migrated to Kununurra from cattle stations in the region.

### The Miriwung at Kununurra

Kununurra is near the northern coast of Western Australia, close to the Northern Territory. The region was occupied by pastoralists in the late nineteenth century. The Duracks, well-to-do Roman Catholics, were prominent among these settlers, and the diaries and journals of the family patriarch were to provide the foundation for Mary Durack's book *Kings in Grass Castles*.[1] This book and her subsequent writing speak often about 'the natives' and how they collaborated with the settlers in the setting up and maintaining of the cattle industry. It was their descendants who nearly a century later crowded into the school to be baptised and confirmed.

For a short time I had visited these people when they lived out of town on cattle stations as the new parish priest of Kununurra, in the course of my missionary activities. For several years before me other priests permanently stationed in the eastern Kimberleys since the 1950s had actively evangelised them. The priests had been given hospitality by the pastoralists and were permitted to 'visit the camp' and to 'evangelise the natives'. Where the pastoralists were active Catholics, a 'station Mass' was celebrated, attended by virtually the entire station population.

With the downturn of the cattle industry in the late 1960s and early 1970s and the introduction of award wages for Aboriginal stockmen, an increasing number of Miriwung and their relatives who could not get work on the stations came to live with their relatives in Kununurra. This was a new and less protected environment for the Miriwung and they availed themselves, particularly in the early times of their settlement, of the protection and support offered by the Catholic priest and nuns – some of the very few people they had known during their life on the cattle stations. The Catholic nuns looked after the children and supported the parents with clothing, food and transport.

More than 100 Miriwung came to live in Kununurra. They spoke their own language, sang their own songs and had an active ceremonial life to which I and the sisters were frequently invited. At the same time, they attended Mass and prayers and participated enthusiastically as so-called 'catechumens' or 'Christians-to-be' in all aspects of Catholic life. They had been promised baptism *when they were ready* and *when they knew more* about the Catholic faith. For the time being they participated in the Mass and other ceremonies but were not permitted to receive Holy Communion.

## Baptism and Christian life

When they came to Kununurra a number of the Miriwung leaders, both men and women, began to ask if 'their mob' could be baptised. They were considerably influenced in this by the example and proselytism of two Aboriginal elders of their group who had been baptised while confined in a Catholic leprosarium and who were the only ones able to take Holy Communion during Mass.

When they asked to be baptised in 1969 there was some urgency, since a senior nun whom they all knew was about to go to a new post and they felt that once she was gone they would have to 'start again with the new sister' and they might never get baptised.

It was my task as their parish priest to decide if they were ready for baptism. From their fervent and regular participation in Catholic religious practices and their apparent agreement in principle with Catholic morality, there was every indication that they were.

As far as basic beliefs were concerned the Christian focus on the one transcendent God roused no quarrel with the Miriwung catechumens, whose ancestral spirits were closer to home. They seemed quite impressed with the Christian teaching and happy to accord it acceptance.

The clearest challenge for Christian missionaries tended to be in reconciling Aboriginal polygyny with Christian monogamy and certain other practices, particularly the use of violence in regulating social behaviour. There were however no polygynous marriages among the Miriwung at Kununurra, nor was violence condoned as an acceptable form of social regulation. It is to be recalled that these people were the children of the children of people raised under the cattle station regime which intruded upon and controlled the activities of Aboriginal workers and 'encouraged' them to adopt monogamy and to become docile and obedient workers.

There was among some the usual crop of disordered behaviour – fighting, drunkenness, etc., together with occasional non-participation in essential church services – the Sunday Mass, prayers and sacraments, but these practices were disavowed in principle.

It has remained a difficult task to identify the depth of a person's commitment to Christianity. There were, however, a number of convergent factors supplementing a person's personal statement and request for baptism. 'Conversion' understood in this way had some verifiable dimensions. A lengthy period of sober living with one partner, regular attendance at church services and participation in church social activities could be said to create a presumption of inner conversion. Certainly in other parts of Australia this would satisfy a great many ministers of religion, if accompanied by affirmation of personal faith and desire for admittance to membership, as was the case with the Miriwung.

Although according to the criteria outlined above the people seemed ready for baptism there was still the question of their ceremonial life. Catholic missionaries were obliged to advise Aboriginal applicants for baptism whether the continuance of their ceremonial would be appropriate once they became Catholics.

Missionaries in earlier days tended to describe all Aboriginal ceremonial as pagan and therefore to be eschewed by people seeking baptism. In later times they permitted certain ceremonial but forbad practices involving so-called 'mutilation' to be carried out in areas under their jurisdiction. The rulings in the early days were not restricted to Aboriginal catechumens directly, but concerned all the Aboriginal people living on or visiting mission settlements under their jurisdiction. The question in those early days of missionary control was whether any performance of Aboriginal ceremonial (even by Aboriginal people not interested in Christianity who were living on a mission) should be permitted, since it was held by some that even to permit 'pagan' practices was somehow to condone them.

In later years a working ruling was established to assist priests preparing traditionally-oriented Aboriginal people for baptism: Aboriginal *religious* ceremonies were incompatible with Catholicism and could not be practised by Aboriginal people seeking baptism. Non-religious *cultural* ceremonies – sometimes called 'play-about corroborees' in Aboriginal English – could be allowed. In practice this was difficult to ascertain, since the distinction between religious and cultural entities did not seem to be seen in Miriwung thought as a contradiction. It seemed rather a continuum of two realities that overlaid one another. In any case ceremonies seemed sometimes to be performed with a number of levels of meaning at the same time. It was thinkable that different levels of meaning could also have different levels of sacredness. The question inevitably became something that the missionaries were obliged to rule on with what knowledge of Aboriginal ceremonial they could muster.

After exhaustive inquiry I finally ruled that the ceremonies which the Miriwung catechumens invited me to must be compatible with Christianity, since the Aborigines, whom I and the nuns had exhaustively instructed, thought they were. The elders mentioned above, who had been baptised while at the Derby leprosarium and who were most active evangelising Christians, participated actively in them. (In most cases they were among the group in charge of the ceremonies.) They spoke of them as compatible with – even enriching – their Christian life.

Thus the older members of the newly baptised converts remained deeply engaged in the full range of their own ceremonial and ritual and on at least two occasions took on additional Aboriginal ceremonial from other places.

If the Catholic church had given evidence of its ritual and social beneficence, the Aboriginal people were enthusiastically reciprocal, particularly in terms of ritual. Church officials and laity were often invited to Aboriginal ceremonies. Those that showed an interest were invited to more and more.

I was invited to the most solemn and secret ceremonies among the Miriwung, Katjarawang and Ngarinman in the eastern Kimberleys, covering most of the men's ceremonial repertoire. It was during one of these ceremonies that I began to think of and apply the interpretation of Aboriginal acceptance of Christianity outlined in these pages.

I had attended special rites of passage by which initiated men were introduced to a new law. After the ceremony I drove back to Kununurra with one of the ritual leaders, an old friend and informant who had led all the people for me to baptise. I asked him if any 'white-fellows' ever 'went through the Law' (the local Aboriginal English way of describing the initiation sequence for newcomers into their group). He said that one or two young stockmen wanting to live with Aboriginal girls had been put through the Law. I asked about myself – did people like me go through the Law? He looked at me and said: 'You already, you our Father'. Whatever else was being conveyed, it was obvious that the Miriwung had located me and my Christian ritual role within their scheme of things.

My informant was a committed Christian, with piety and fervour to match. When his brother fell ill he took a taxi to the hospital where he recited Catholic prayers with great fervour and conviction, to the edification of some and the bewilderment of other hospital staff. The same man held to his own traditions and was worried that the 'young fellas' were not following the Law. It was evident that for him somehow Christianity and his other religious accomplishments complemented each other.

In later years there was a change in the relationship between the Catholics and the Miriwung. Other Christian proselytisers arrived and attracted a following, although usually from Aborigines not already closely affiliated with the Catholics. The regularity and fervour of Aboriginal participation in Catholic activities diminished during this time. This occurred at the same time as the Miriwung's dependence on my services and those of the Catholic nuns was reduced by the provision of alternative welfare and transport services – social security and government-granted vehicles. The Miriwung attenuated their participation in Church activities as they gained access to alternative resources and protectors – the welfare department and paradoxically the police. The welfare department, once it was established, provided an alternative supply of money orders and food during times of scarcity. The police gave nearly all the male leaders of Aboriginal households some affiliation with their power and immunity by making them honorary 'trackers'. There was also a competing church, the United Aboriginal Mission, and a group linked informally to it (called 'the Shedley Mob' by the Miriwung, after the leading family of that group), who attempted to recruit people on the native reserve along similar lines as those attempted by the Catholics.

The exclusive nature of the early exchanges between the closed Miriwung/Catholic church circle was increasingly breached and no longer constituted the exclusive arena from which help might come in difficulties.

I want now to look briefly at Aboriginal culture and religion and what conversion to Christianity might mean within such a tradition.

## ABORIGINAL RELIGION AND 'CONVERSION'

### Aboriginal religion and lifestyle

Aboriginal people had a lifestyle and religion directly linked to nature and to the land. They occupied as owners (or as users linked to owners by birth or conception), various territories, according to links with so-called totemic ancestral creative beings who were associated with specific places and flora and fauna. Ownership rights over land brought ritual responsibilities to carry out ceremonial by which the ancestral creative power could be continued in order to nurture the land and increase its fruit.[2]

Aboriginal people had what was called a hunting and gathering economy (now, in view of more developed notions of Aboriginal management, sometimes referred to as husbanding, or perhaps better, nurturing and harvesting). They travelled through their territory (or 'range') hunting animals and gathering vegetables and seeds in a careful and skilful way, using fire and other technology to ensure the appropriate conditions for the increase of food species. They did not establish permanent residence at one point on their lands, but moved from place to place following seasonal food sources, usually along so-called 'Dreaming tracks' mapped out not in written form but enshrined in ceremonial songs of their totemic ancestors – creative spiritual beings linked to animals, plants and places in the natural world – from whom they, the existing humans, derived their descent.

As communal occupiers of traditional territory, Aboriginal groups maintained their economic and social order by making the relationships with their totemic ancestors and their law the foundation upon which human relationships were ordered. Aboriginal social order was a family-based one. Kinship terms comprehended everyone in a personal social universe, and with relationships came rights and duties. Much social interaction was governed by strict kinship-based protocol. Actions and exchanges appropriate to various kinship relationships were not a matter of option but of obligation.

Three important levels of existence – the land, kinship and the family – were somehow telescoped into a dynamic and conservative notion translated as 'the Dreaming'. The requirements of this ancient and new dispensation were expressed through 'the Law' which encompassed all, which all had to obey, and from which human authority was ultimately derived.[3]

Ritual knowledge and status provided a foundation for an individual's authority in Aboriginal society. Generally speaking a domestic group or band would be ruled by the consensus of that group's older men who possessed ritual knowledge, and land ownership would be carried out with the informal collaboration of older women, who possessed their own ritual knowledge and land ownership.

There was often tension in Aboriginal society between the older men and women who possessed ritual knowledge and status, and the younger aspirants under their authority. There was also often tension between men and women who grouped separately and whose interests did not always coincide.[4]

A major area of contention was that of marriage, or more particularly the rights to arrange marriages and to allocate partners. The father of marriageable children and his relations could have divergent interests from the mother and her relatives since each belonged to different groups.

The need to arrange marriage partners from other groups was a major force, and required some harmony between groups which may have been opposed and feuding. The exchange of marriage partners between hostile groups had a peace-making function, since affinal relationships brought children who claimed affiliation with both groups. The processes by which this was arranged could, however, generate discontent as different groups promoted their interests.

The daily routine of Aboriginal domestic life with its hunting, gathering and domestic toolmaking, childcare and ritual, was interpersed with larger communal gatherings in which large rituals were carried out – initiation of boys, mortuary and inquest rituals. There were also other so-called 'travelling' ceremonies, which were passed from group to group and which required collaboration from members of a number of groups.[5]

Older men and women collaborated to manage these in complementary ways under the chairmanship, as it were, of older men. These men were accorded status according to the amount of ceremonial they participated in or controlled, and many were interested in gaining access to or control of new ceremonies. In 1975 and 1976 in the eastern Kimberleys I saw groups compete to have ceremonies over which they had ownership rights accepted by others in the group as the ones to be used in initiation and other functions. In such cases the fortune of ceremonies under the sponsorship of a group was an index of the group's status.

Religion was the idiom in which social and territorial relationships were expressed. Robert Tonkinson's book *The Mardudjara* (1976)[6] explains this beautifully for a desert group in Western Australia. Religious ceremonies were also a major way in which social relations were expressed, alliances forged and the like. Thus I witnessed a secret ceremony in 1970, in which a group of newcomers to the eastern Kimberleys were 'put through' a ritual in order to make them members of the group of ritual owners, thus allies and adherents accepting and deferring to the rule of the owners of the local ceremonial and secret places.

Religious experience authenticated the integrated patterns of Aboriginal social and economic life and linked the individual experience with the formal experiences of the group, expressed and promulgated in their ceremonial.

For its adherents, Aboriginal religion was not followed in order to control material reality by spiritual means (the so-called 'magical' function of religion), but to assist them to come to terms with and accept the everlasting realities of life as a corporate related group. Individuals had their own religious experiences within this dispensation. Deborah Rose writes:

> where mysticism in the religions of the great traditions leads people out of this world and toward a transcendent experience of unity beyond,

> Aboriginal religion leads people into this world and towards an immanent experience in the here and now.[7]

W.E.H. Stanner in his Charles Strong Lecture in 1976 (see Chapter 1 above) was to point out that Aboriginal religion was a means by which people oriented themselves to the Dreaming. Aboriginal religion generated in its adherents 'the mood of assent' (in Stanner's phrase) to a wholistic spiritual and physical dispensation laid down in the Dreaming which continues to affect human lives. Different ceremonials generated their own mood within specific contexts: the entry of new members through invitation, the passing of the old in mortuary rituals, the rebirth of the people in special ceremonies of fertility and life renewal.[8]

This brief introduction to Aboriginal religion has indicated that although there was provision for some change within the processes of Aboriginal ceremonial, the macro-system was immutably tied up with their identity, their family and their land. There is thus a presumption that people possessing such an integrated religious culture would be unable to change its main components without a major upheaval in their identity and general direction.

As we turn to consider the meaning of Aboriginal conversion to Christianity, it is important to be aware of the essential contextual dimensions of this act. Aboriginal conversion to Christianity occurred as a result of a particular kind of encounter between two groups with particular orientations. Christianity, as encountered, was the religion of a particular kind of white people who, while possessing desirable goods and claiming certain kinds of superiority, did not exhibit the hostility and violence of other whites – in fact seemed able often to inhibit such acts – and sought to establish an interactive relationship with Aborigines. We also know that Aborigines, equipped with their lifestyle heritage and essentially religious worldview, were often interested in establishing relationships with whites.

Aboriginal conversion to Christianity was the result of a long-term encounter between these two groups. There is a presumption that people will use mechanisms appropriate to their own culture to manage what amounts to an encounter between strangers. These mechanisms must be understood in order to understand some dimensions of the outcome. Before attempting to interpret such outcomes it is necessary to look at the implications of what we Christians were hoping to achieve: conversion to Christianity.

**Conversion to Christianity**

Traditionally there are two major dimensions in the process of Christian conversion: the act of faith and the act of commitment to and acceptance by a church. In Christian theology the act of faith is essentially a personal act in which an individual undergoes an internal spiritual change in the manner of Saint Augustine, who described his conversion (which to him involved an enormous personal death and re-birth) in his *Confessions*. It can also be a familial act involving a whole household somehow subsumed under the authority of the head, as described in the *Acts* of the Apostles: 'and he believed and his whole household with him' (*Acts* 16:33). Although the former case is more common to missionary experience, the latter has some acceptance, particularly where traditional authority and group structure is strong.

A person seeking to become a Christian is required to make a declaration of faith and commitment before a church official. This declaration must then be ratified by the official on behalf of the church and arrangements made for baptism of the new convert. The question then would be how to interpret the announcement of conversion and request for baptism from traditionally-oriented Aboriginal people. What terms would be suitable for their incorporation into the church?

Historically there have been a number of ways in which Aboriginal people have accepted Christianity and been admitted to fellowship in a Christian church. Some conversions appear to take the form of total rejection of traditional ways. For example in 1923 Pastor Stolz reported that:

> The Hermannsburg congregation was a Christian one, for the people had broken with their heathenism, handed over their witchcraft and corroboree utensils and declared their sacred places free.[9]

A similar occurrence took place a decade ago at Bulla camp near Timber Creek in the Northern Territory, when a whole community of Ngarrinman people joined the Apostolic Church based at Kununurra. One of the Aboriginal leaders and the usual spokesperson said to me that he had 'put away all that old business and followed Jesus'. Bulla camp had been a major centre of traditional Aboriginal ceremonial almost until that time.

In other cases, as with the Miriwung in Kununurra, the acceptance of Christianity was somehow achieved without the repudiation of all traditional ways. The meaning of the various forms of Aboriginal conversion to Christianity as an announced and accepted state has part of its explanation in the mission context in which it took place which forms the next part of this lecture.

**The context of conversion**

As we have pointed out above, the meeting between Christian missionaries and Aborigines was never purely one between people interested only in religious matters. The encounter was coloured by other factors: political interests, economic need etc., which means that in looking for the meaning behind Aboriginal religious conversion one needs to look at conversion enacted between people with the cultural repertoires described above encountering each other in specific contexts in which specific issues were in contention.

The sociopolitical context of the encounters between Aborigines and white missionaries is essentially a colonial context. The white settlers and their administration were extending control over the land and its original inhabitants. The missionaries, although possessed of a radically different approach, were effectively part of this program. Endowed with consumer goods and sponsored to a greater or lesser extent by the Australian government, they set out to establish settlements in country known to be occupied by Aboriginal people. Local Aboriginal people were then invited to participate in the activities of the settlement.

Once established, the missionaries then set about persuading the Aborigines of the values of Christianity by word and example and ceremonial. The kind of Christianity offered to the Aborigines was that practised by whites in Australia, modified to suit the dependent affiliate status to which the Aborigines were relegated under the mission regime.

As we mentioned above, the Aborigines for their part were often interested in establishing exchange relations with the highly endowed newcomers but there is no evidence that they wished to surrender their identity and autonomy.[10] Stanner, reflecting on the massive migrations of Aboriginal people towards centres of white settlement, has suggested that Aboriginal people were extremely interested in – amost addicted to – participating in the activities and sharing the goods surrounding the white man's settlements. He viewed what appeared to be irresponsible migration out of one's country with alarm, since Aboriginal culture needed to be grounded in the customs and dreaming of their own country. He could see great value in the missionary bringing enough civilisation to satisfy the needs of Aboriginal people, who would otherwise want to migrate to white urban centres.

Aborigines in addition often cultivated the patronage of whites to form the foundation for exchanges in which they could obtain certain goods and services – food, clothing and transport, and some relief from white harassment. This occurred particularly in places where there were few whites, and where Aborigines were required either as proselytes on missions or more commonly as cheap labour – in tin mines in North Queensland,[11] and the pastoral industry in Central Australia and Northern Australia, particularly the smaller holdings.[12] The next section looks at some theoretical principles, which are informed by comparison with work done with Inuit people in Newfoundland.

## MODELS OF EXCHANGE

### Patrons and Patronage

Robert Paine of Memorial University in Newfoundland discusses a set of relationships between Christian missionaries and the Eskimos or Inuit in western Canada which are similar to those between missionaries and Aborigines in Australia.[13] His ideas provide the basis for the following theoretical considerations.

Patronage is a type of permanent and reciprocal exchange relationship between two parties. It is established when people in need accept unrequested gifts which they hold as valuable and which are usually otherwise unobtainable. By accepting the status of 'one who receives gifts', the recipient then feels obliged to return gifts 'acceptable to the giver' in order to maintain reciprocity. In such exchanges both parties benefit. The bestower or 'patron' gains people (adherents) and the receiver or 'client' gains goods, protection, and sponsorship. There are also costs – the patron has to bestow or at least be seen to be prepared to bestow gifts and the client has to accept a degree of permanent dependence and inferiority.

One of the classic forms of patronage has been when a patron acts as a broker by controlling the mediation of goods to his client. The broker, in order to maintain his or her position as provider of goods and services, needs to secure the exclusive mediation of goods so he or she can bestow access to goods and services otherwise unobtainable. Missionaries were often the only go-between or link and as such wielded considerable power of access, particularly when mediating government goods and services. The brokerage on these exchanges – the handling charges, as it were – was bestowed as an act of patronage.

Patron/client relationships are established in two phases. The first phase is that of gift distribution. The aspiring patron attempts to distribute goods, preferably those in his exclusive possession, over as wide a range as possible. Paine notes:

> Ideally the patron offers items and services that are new to the culture and to which he alone has access, thereby actually creating the need for them.[14]

The patron tries to create a 'general dependence on his goods and services'. Having established this general dependence, he is then able to nominate what values are acceptable to him as counter-offerings. I think it is also true that the return offering does not 'settle the score' but maintains reciprocity while at the same time symbolising the client's acceptance of his dependent position.

Ultimately what distinguishes the patron from his client is that 'only values of the patron's choosing' are circulated in their relationship. Further, the client has to demonstrate to his patrons and others his acceptance of the values which the patron has chosen for circulation between them.

The second phase is the permanent state of indebtedness on the part of the client and the continued power of the patron:

> [T]he client may be made liable at any time for any number of different prestations [offerings], all of which the patron alone has determined as appropriate to their relationship.[15]

The client is thus directed by the patron on the choice and timing of return goods and services. The relationship is thus different from other exchange relations, either those based on 'general reciprocity' as occurs between friends, or that based on kinship where reciprocity is predicated on a set of giving and receiving relationships where the power to nominate the values in circulation is not restricted to one partner. This is because the patron is not placed in debt by reciprocal return offerings from the client and because the patron has the say in what goods and services are suitable returns to his beneficence. In the other more equal exchange relations mentioned above each is indebted to the other at different times. This is not the case in patronage. Patronage is about structured inequality, paternalism on the one hand and 'obedience' and 'gratitude' on the other.

Patronage can dig deep. In many cases it can be the foundation of attempts to annex the client's attitudes and values. Paine says:

> The patron chooses for the client those values in relation to which the patron protects the client; moreover the patron expects the client himself to embrace these values.[16]

Clients have to bear the cost of this real or potential dependence:

> The costs to the client can be very little; some of the clients' own values may be supported by the patron and the clients may succeed in sustaining a deception over their embracement of the patron's values.[17]

It seems to me that this is due to a feature qualifying the reciprocity in a patron/client relationship. Reciprocity in such relationships is partly real and partly notional: expressions of obedience and gratitude may suffice to serve the relationship. Real offerings, gifts and services may rarely be required.

The patron/client relationship can then continue with fewer real offerings involved, but without being formally terminated. Indeed, to be known as patron or client, as protector or protégé, may itself be of value. It may enhance prestige, it may protect from harassment.

**Responding to patronage: riding**

I have suggested elsewhere that many Aboriginal would-be clients developed a strategic style of reciprocation to the bestowals of their white would-be patrons.[18] 'Patronal' bestowals (in response to which one is expected to become a 'grateful' client) were re-interpreted as quasi-kinship based 'normal' behaviour. White gift givers could then be treated like any other visitors to the camp, as if they were kin relations from whom bestowals were not wonderful acts of generosity expecting thanks and generating dependence, but appropriate behaviour to be expected of kinfolk lucky enough to gain access to resources. Gratitude was inappropriate. The bestowers had just done the job appropriate to their status. The missionaries, by defining themselves by kinship terms – father, sister, etc. – were inviting such re-codification.

I suggest that in addition to re-defining the relationships between themselves and whites many Aborigines, in order to pursue their own agendas, had also developed a special kind of strategic participation in white enterprises which I have called 'riding' or kinship riding. As we have seen, many Aborigines wanted to link up with whites in order to gain access particularly to food, transport and protection from other whites. We have also seen that in most cases whites were only interested in forming unequal relationships with Aborigines where they, the whites, were in charge. Within such oppressive regimes, which Aborigines felt in almost all contexts, riding became one of the only ways to work towards one's own objectives, particularly if they involved using white resources. Since in many parts of Australia white control of resources spilled over from the things they brought and developed into areas which once Aborigines would have had free access to, this was not uncommon.

By means of selective co-operation and participation in enterprises sponsored by patrons known to be friendly, 'riding' was an attempt to achieve one's own objectives under cover of their patron's initiative, sponsorship and protection.[19]

In the context of oppressive colonial regimes, 'riding' should be seen as an act of corporate leadership by which Aboriginal leaders attempted to negotiate the survival and interests of their group. Leaders had been able to negotiate some status for their authority by 'managing the camp for the boss' – i.e. looking after the Aboriginal group living on the station. In this way Aboriginal groups had the authority of their leaders endorsed by their white bosses. They had also been able to negotiate some modified autonomy under the regime of the cattle station by using times (particularly the three months summer lay-off season when they were not needed for work) to pursue their own agendas, supported to a limited extent by station resources – food and transport. The continuance of the authority of traditional leaders maintained through this form of 'riding' was a key to the survival of the traditional cultural identity of small Aboriginal groups on cattle stations and other locations in remote regions of Australia. This was particularly useful during the time of modernisation, when their children started returning from strongly assimilationist mission schools with little interest in or respect for traditional authority or culture.

## INTERPRETING ABORIGINAL CONVERSION

### Introduction

In the interpretation followed here I am suggesting that the form that Aboriginal conversion took was not one of the client responding to the patron's wishes. I am suggesting that it was essentially a culturally appropriate response to a set of political, social and religious initiatives which missionaries had adopted, and that it coincided with early

Aboriginal attempts to create culturally appropriate symmetrical and equal alliances with approachable whites, using strategies of exchange and encounter from within their own repertoire. Both partners wanted to be related. This interpretation suggests that each had different expectations of what that relationship should be.

Aboriginal conversion to Christianity in this context can then be defined as a specific reciprocal act by which an Aboriginal group or individual displayed formally and solemnly their affection for and approval of the commitment and support of the missionaries, without becoming their clients and accepting their attempted patronage in any strict sense. This was effected furthermore by what amounted to a kind of 'going through' their rituals of acceptance and recruitment as they might with the owners of rituals to which they had been beholden in traditional contexts. In this way, from an Aboriginal perspective, an alliance between the whites and themselves became ritually expressed and sealed.

The difference is of course that they refused to internalise the role of subordinate clients, to become grateful and obedient and to seek to become like their masters. They offered a lot in return but as quasi kin and allies, not as servants.

Such interpretations make sense of the often enthusiastic Aboriginal adoption of Christian behaviour – frequent and fervent attendance at and participation in church services, home prayers and the like – while at the same time refusing to become obedient servants and continuing the ceremonies and observances of Aboriginal religion, beliefs and practices.

This disjunction may not have been spelled out to the missionaries. The Aboriginal people's untroubled continuance of their ceremonial may not have been disclosed to the missionaries in detail, not necessarily because it might upset them, but because in the nature of Aboriginal Law these things are not talked about before non-initiates.

As we have seen, there was provision within Aboriginal traditional culture for religious change on three counts. The first by Dreaming, when a ritual leader creates or dreams a new ceremonial. The second is by religious exchange, when new rituals are taken into the group's repertoire. The third is an adjunct to social and political exchange, when new ceremonies are the ritual part of new relationships and alliances.

In the interpretation I am following here I am suggesting that Aboriginal leaders used this third traditional competence when meeting and negotiating with the missionaries – among whites the group most able to be dealt with and managed. Political and social exchanges among Aborigines were linked to alliances giving shared access to country, to relationships (marriage partners) and to ritual. The meaning of individual exchanges was to be found in the aspiration of the participants and their negotiating style, together with the circumstances in which they found themselves.

These principles of Aboriginal/white exchange can now be applied to interpret the original case study. The circumstances of the conversion of the Miriwung and the undoubted establishment of a reciprocal alliance between the Catholics and the Miriwung in Kununurra can now be revisited.

**Interpreting the Miriwung conversion**

The Aboriginal people were migrants from cattle stations in the area living as tenants in Kununurra in two-room huts on a small area of land called the Native Reserve. They had moved reluctantly out of their country and out of a stable regime which, although authoritarian, was predictable, safe and relatively well resourced. They had minimal resources, no vehicles or cash reserves. Those that had paid employment were far outweighed by children and dependent relatives. They were ill-clad and sickly, and often hungry. The Miriwung, in coming to Kununurra, were thus in a dislocated and vulnerable position.

The Reserve and the Catholic convent school were the focal points for an important set of exchanges between the Miriwung and the missionaries – myself and the two Catholic nuns. The sisters and I recruited children for their school. These children and their parents and relatives were often given food and clothing, taken to hospital or to the shops in the convent car. On Sundays the sisters took the parish car and the convent car to the Reserve to drive people the two kilometres to the church. It was thus a set of exchanges between an endowed recruiting group and a group of indigent marginal recipients.

The nuns and I, who knew and looked after these people, were successful in recruiting them and they called themselves 'the Catholic mob'. They used the Catholic church's name and affiliation when dealing with police, welfare and service providers. The whites often came to us about 'your Aboriginal flock' and we accepted the affiliation. The Miriwung also, as we have seen, often asked to be baptised.

In Kununurra the Miriwung participated in Catholic church life as a group and sought baptism in the same way. Following my interpretation, when these people sought baptism as an ordered Aboriginal group, conversion was a kind of federation-style affiliation to the Catholic group. When the old men attempted to bring all their people as a group into the Church, they were bringing a group whose internal identity and structure remained. In this way their authority too was recognised and re-enforced in the Church.

Such a group derived its identity from Aboriginal religious culture. I would suggest then that in retrospect it was as a religiously formed and maintained entity that this group sought to strengthen links with the Catholic Church, their benefactors and protectors, by being baptised and confirmed.

Understood in this way, the act of baptism could be concluded to have had important effects on the linked parties. The Catholic Church had ratified an existing affiliation. It now had 60 new members to care about and of course to be pleased about. The Aborigines had a formal public testimonial to the acceptance of their conversion by the Catholics and to the protection afforded members by the Church which had currency in Aboriginal and non-Aboriginal circles.

This interpretation provides an explanation for the enthusiastic participation of the Miriwung in Catholic religious ceremonial on the one hand, and their repeated invitations to us the missionaries to attend their ceremonial on the other.

I am suggesting then that an exchange approach can be useful in understanding Aboriginal conversion within a missionary context, since it has a strong interactional dimension. As such it needs to be analysed by looking at the different interests and approaches of the participants involved in its component interactions.

I suggest that the Catholic Church, within the process of its evangelisation, engaged in strategic bestowals of goods and services in order to make the people grateful, dependent and reciprocal. What the church wanted in return was for them to affiliate with the church and thus ratify their recipient status and to adopt Catholic religious practices. This could be described as attempting to establish patronage relationships over the Aboriginal group by inviting them to become clients and affiliates. Once constituted as clients, Catholic Christian behaviour could be required as the appropriate acts of reciprocation to their Christian patrons.

It appears that the Aborigines had their own agenda in response to this. They were happy to take on another ritual system to enrich their ritual repertoire, and they were happy to accept affiliation with the church. They were also prepared to 'go along' with the church's claims to patronage and to cultivate their beneficence. The leaders were also interested in cultivating endorsement for their authority in this new non-station environment. Earlier in this lecture I have called this strategy 'riding'. The clients 'ride' on the patrons' beneficence but without commitment – a kind of sociopolitical hitch-hiking.

It seems then that the hypothesis of 'patrons and riders' could be used to make sense of exchanges between the Catholic missionaries and their Miriwung converts.

## CONCLUSION

In concluding this interpretation I want to summarise the two main points of my argument. The first is that religious changes on remote missions which occurred as a result of the missionaries' activity were linked in sociopolitical exchanges between decision-makers from Aboriginal and Catholic Christian groups. These exchanges took place within the context of attempted patronage by the missionaries and selective acceptance by the Aborigines, and derive at least a dimension of their meaning from the influence of these exchanges. The second is that religious change for Aborigines needs to be understood in terms of Aboriginal culture and religious style. Aboriginal religious style allows for the exchange of ceremonial.

It is culturally appropriate for Aboriginal leaders to seek to increase their access to, participation in and ownership of ceremonial. But since Aboriginal culture does not separate fundamental religious beliefs from Aboriginality, it is difficult to imagine how a traditionally oriented Aboriginal person could change his or her worldview and still retain Aboriginal identity with its overlaid perspectives of self and relations, territory and dreaming.

When this appears to have occurred, and Aboriginal people still retain their identity, it must be presumed to be occurring somehow *together with* rather than *instead of* being in competition.

A consequence of this interpretation is the suggestion that at least some forms of Aboriginal Christianity can be understood as kinds of additional ceremonial sets incorporated into Aboriginal religion. In this case their current ceremonial repertoire now includes Catholic Christian practices and accords some status to those Aborigines affiliated with it.

Aboriginal religion would thus have incorporated another way for people to generate 'the mood of acceptance' referred to in the beginning of this lecture, in which they come to identify and accept their changing role in a disposition which Martin Wilson has felicitously called 'new, old and timeless'.[20]

Such an interpretation provides an explanation for the interest some Aboriginal ritual owners in other places in remote Australia have in being involved in Christian ceremonial. Thus on Elcho Island the owners of certain sacred *rangga* or sacred ceremonial boards, who, in 1959, departed radically from traditional practice by erecting these emblems usually kept secret in view of everyone near the church,[21] were engaging in Aboriginal religious acts within a Christian context. Another example is the incorporation of ceremonial paintings in the Uniting Church at Yirrkala done at about the same time,[22] the Christian Pulapa at Yuendumu, and the religious songs – *Djaanba* – used in the Catholic ceremony at Kununurra.

Perhaps while the missionaries were thinking they had incorporated the Aborigines into their church, the Aborigines had incorporated the church into their world, without the missionaries knowing. There is a blessed irony if the humanists among the rapacious colonisers are manipulated to provide a base and nest for the dispossessed Aborigines, so that our demise becomes their rebirth. Not as we wanted but as they did, so that the missionaries, like John the Baptist in a different context, may decrease so that the Aborigines may increase.

Missionaries have come under fire for destroying Aboriginal culture. This interpretation suggests that Aboriginal culture was not destroyed but rather its infrastructure was extended, and that the missionaries, by their concern to deal with the Aborigines and to promote their welfare as people and as groups, were able to be used by the Aborigines in their terrible struggle against colonial and genocidal forces to provide an essential bridge from then till now.

## NOTES

1 Mary Durack, *Kings in Grass Castles*, Constable, London, 1959.
2 N. Peterson, *Tribes and Boundaries in Australia*, Australian Institute for Aboriginal Studies, Canberra, 1976.
3 W.E.H. Stanner, 'The Dreaming' in W.A. Lessa and E.Z. Vogt (eds) *Reader in Comparative Religion: an Anthropological Approach*, Row, Peterson, Evanston, Illinois, 1965.
4 L. Hiatt, *Kinship and Conflict: A Study of an Aboriginal Community in Northern Arnhem Land*, Australian National University Press, Canberra, 1965.

5 R.M. Berndt, *Australian Aboriginal Religion*, Four fascicles (in one volume), Institute of Religious Iconography, State University of Groningen, Brill, Leiden, 1974.
6 R. Tonkinson, *The Mardudjara, Living the Dream in Australia's Desert*, Holt, Rinehart and Winston, New York, 1976.
7 D.B. Rose, 'Consciousness and Responsibility in an Australian Aboriginal Religion', *Nelen Yubu* 23 (1985), p. 12.
8 Stanner, 'The Dreaming'.
9 Quoted in E. Leske, *Hermannsburg: A Vision and A Mission*, Lutheran Publishing House, Adelaide, 1977.
10 W.E.H. Stanner, 'The Murinbata – 1935–1953', Paper presented at ANZAAS conference, 1954.
11 C. Anderson, 'Aborigines and Tin Mining in North Queensland: a Case Study in the Anthropology of Contact', *Mankind* 13 (1983), pp. 473–498.
12 J.R. Collmann, 'Social Order and the Exchange of Liquor: a Theory of Drinking among Australian Aborigines', *Journal of Anthropological Research* 35 (1978), pp. 208–224.
13 R. Paine, *Patrons and Brokers in the East Arctic*, Memorial University Press, Newfoundland, 1976.
14 Paine, *Patrons and Brokers in the East Arctic*, p. 14.
15 Paine, *Patrons and Brokers in the East Arctic*, p. 16.
16 Paine, *Patrons and Brokers in the East Arctic*, p. 19.
17 Paine, *Patrons and Brokers in the East Arctic*, p. 13.
18 P.A. Willis, 'Patrons and Riders', MA Thesis, Australian National University, 1980.
19 Willis, 'Patrons and Riders', p. 101.
20 M. Wilson, *New, Old and Timeless*, Chevalier Press, Victoria, 1974.
21 R.M. Berndt, *An Adjustment Movement in Arnhem Land*, Cahiers de L'Homme, Mouton, Paris and The Hague, 1962.
22 H. Morphy and R. Layton, 'Choosing Among Alternatives: Cultural Transformations and Social Change in Aboriginal Australia and French Jura', *Oceania* 13 (1981).

CHAPTER EIGHT

# Land Rights – The Religious Factor

*Father Frank Brennan SJ*

As life changes for Aborigines, so too does their relationship to land and to each other. Changes in these relationships effect changes to the religious life of myth and ritual, which also inform those relationships. The state, which has authorised Aboriginal dispossession and cultural invasion, has a duty in justice to provide protection of Aboriginal interests in land and aspirations for community self-determination, so that Aborigines may more readily determine the changes offered by new technology and lifestyles. Land rights legislation is essential, providing a protective regime of space and time, acknowledging Aboriginal spiritual responsibility for as well as economic opportunity from their country. Though the religious factor is invoked for the recognition of land rights and the right to restrain outside interests from interfering with the land (even in the public interest), Aboriginal landowners are also seeking political and economic bargaining power to maintain their legitimate self-interest. Attempts to authenticate Aboriginal spiritual relationships with land are usually made by those who are not Aboriginal attempting to weigh up Aboriginal claims over against the claims of others whose value system and worldview more readily accords with that of the state's decision-makers. We are yet to let Aborigines make decisions for themselves and for the rest of us regarding the best use of their country. Though there is greater willingness now to extend recognition to Aboriginal law regarding land and life, that law is still under threat from outsiders as well as its inheritors who, for a variety of reasons, are 'running away from ceremony'. The more we can allow Aborigines to speak for their country, the more they will be able to maintain and reveal the life-sustaining capacity of the land which, being the only constant in a sea of change, is sacred.

## RITUAL AND LIFE

In 1886, the Austrian Jesuits arrived at Daly River in Australia's Northern Territory to establish a mission amongst Aborigines. They had spent four years amongst Aborigines at Palmerston, on the outskirts of modern-day Darwin. Despairing of the depredations being visited upon these people by European and Chinese settlement, they went further afield to work amongst Aborigines guaranteed freedom from colonial and economic expansion. The mission at Daly River lasted until 1899. 1892 was 'perhaps the darkest year in the Mission's seventeen years',[1] influenza and the pending great Depression taking their toll on the people and the mission. On one of his begging tours in 1892, Father Donald MacKillop wrote:

> Australia, as such, does not recognize the right of the blackman to live. She marches onward, truly, but not perhaps the fair maiden we paint her. The blackfellow sees blood on that noble forehead, callous cruelty in her heart; her heel is of iron and his helpless countrymen beneath her feet. But we are strong and the blacks are weak; we have rifles, they but spears; we love British fairplay, and having got hold of this continent we must have every square foot. Little Tasmania is our model, and, I fear, will be, until the great papers of Australia will chronicle, 'with regret', the death of the last blackfellow. There is a feeling abroad, too, which might be worded thus – It is in God's providence that the native races here, as elsewhere, must disappear before the British people. This, of course, I do not admit. The laws of nature, not God's providence, require that in given circumstances an inferior race will disappear before a superior, but so do they require that death will follow starvation, or be the consequence of poisoning.[2]

Forty years later, W.E.H. Stanner arrived at Daly River and spent six months 'making a sociological survey of the remaining tribes of the Daly and Victoria Rivers'.[3] He noted, 'The rites at puberty are now for all river tribes the most important of their remaining ritual. In the midst of generalised ritual decay they stand nearly unaltered.'[4] He found that initiation fell naturally into four periods: (i) an indeterminate period of isolation; (ii) a period of two to three days during which circumcision occurred; (iii) a period of about a week while the boy awaited the healing of his wound and underwent ritual washing and (iv) an indeterminate period during which he re-entered the normal life of his group, assuming his new status and resuming 'in the old or now modified forms the associations which have been ruptured by the impact of the puberty rites'.[5] Stanner observed:

> Initiation is more than the dramatisation of an individual life crisis. It is far more than mere circumcision. The rites at puberty, no matter how dramatic their emphasis, only punctuate by formal organised ceremonial a social process that runs far deeper and wider . . . In time, in significance for individual and group, initiation is no affair of the moment. For perhaps fifteen years it is a rod which disciplines the very routine of daily life.[6]

He noted that puberty in women was marked by less elaborate ritual, but ritual none the less. There was no equivalent extensive ritual at birth or marriage. Stanner observed that for the Mulluk Mulluk people at Daly River the religious background of life had almost disappeared. 'Most of their own beliefs have been forgotten, and they retain only a few scraps of the Christian theology taught them forty years ago.'[7] He noted that other tribes which had not suffered the same cultural shock retained their beliefs to a much greater extent. He distinguished between river tribes which had endured great contact and bush tribes which seemed to be very little altered.[8]

Stanner returned to the north-west coastal strip of the Northern Territory in 1934–5. He then accompanied Father Richard Docherty MSC on the journey from Darwin to establish a mission settlement at Port Keats among the Murinbata people. When he came to write his papers on Aboriginal religion from 1959 to 1963, he relied on what he had learned from people in the area from Port Keats to Daly River. He described the Karwadi ceremony as an initiation and an integral part of the process of socialisation of persons. He insisted that the ceremony was not only an initiation, because Aborigines had said that the intent of Karwadi was 'to make the young men understand'.[9] Stanner described the ceremony as 'a liturgical transaction, within a totemic idiom of symbolism, between men and a spiritual being on whom they perceived themselves to be dependent'.

Where Stanner found evidence of the lineaments of sacrifice, other anthropologists have insisted that the evidence supports only a complex rite of passage. Where Stanner found evidence of a high culture born of a religious disposition given to an embracing of the transcendent beyond self and the social order, others have found evidence only of a religious belief system supporting and being maintained by the social order. Rejecting Durkheim's 'primacy of society over religion', which held that religion is the most primitive of all social phenomena, out of which comes 'by successive transformations, all the other manifestations of collective activity, law, morality, art, science, [and] political forms',[10] Stanner faithfully reported Aboriginal 'operations and transactions about things of value' which were handed on through myth and rite even though there be no articulated understanding or rationale of the living heritage – a transmission of some very perceptive truths about human experience and the human condition grounded in a landscape embraced as a 'humanised realm saturated with significations'.[11] Though the tradition was grounded in the past, it was not static; he found flux to be the norm for Aboriginal life before and after colonial contact. Pragmatism and adaptability can result from and are not necessarily antipathetic to a religious dispensation which allows the individual and the community to accept the inevitable and to survive the tragic.

The Karwadi ceremony commenced each day with the mime of the blowfly. The initiated men, crouched in a circular excavation in the ground, started the mime with a low murmurous hum while moving backwards and forwards until their heads touched. The youths then came into the centre of the circle, knelt, and imitated actions of their elders. According to Stanner:

> The esoteric symbolism is not explained to the initiates, for no one seems able to interpret it. All that is known, or is now discoverable, is that the proceedings must start every day with . . . the mime of the blowfly, which goes to rotting flesh.[12]

In this shallow, circular hole, the Mother, the key actor in the Karwadi rite, manifested herself. The hole was conceptualised either as a 'nest' or a 'wallow'. Stanner interprets:

> The first is a fairly clear symbol of family and sociality. The second is in some sense its reverse. The buffalo in this region, usually a solitary wanderer, makes or seeks a wallow against the heat of the day or to free itself from irritating pests and parasites. The symbol thus denotes what seem like positive and negative statements of the same truth about life: at the centre of things social, refuge and rottenness are found together. In other words, there is an intuition of an integral moral flaw in human association.[13]

More than most other Australians, contemporary Aborigines speak of the romantic notion of community while being faction-ridden with the undertakings and routines of community living. The wallow and the nest are readily posited for any sit-down place where people congregate for business for any length of time.

In 1978 Stanner returned to Peppiminarti (between Daly River and Port Keats) for the Karwadi ceremony, which was attended by local people and invitees from Kununurra at least 1,000 kilometres away. On this occasion Stanner was puzzled throughout the ceremony by the behaviour of the Peppiminarti people. They impressed him as:

> possibly not (or no longer) knowing what is good form on such high occasions, or possibly having become too self-conscious to express deep emotion in a characteristic Aboriginal way. A good illustration is the marked reluctance they showed later to draw blood from their own veins to assist their *yunguana*. The Kununurra visitors on the other hand showed no such reluctance. The Peppiminarti elders were shocked in an old-maidish way by such savagery.[14]

Whereas four decades before, each day of the ceremony would commence with the mime of the blowfly which goes to rotting flesh,[15] the first mime of the Kununurra mob at the 1978 ceremony was 'a simulation of an aeroplane, with two engines, approaching or taking off from an airstrip'.[16] Stanner was of the view that at least for the Kununurra people, 'the proximate purpose of the ceremony was to increase the political authority of the elders over the young men becoming *yunguana*'. Though in the more traditional ceremonies there is always a lot of horseplay, it was a new experience for Stanner to observe an elder punching up an initiant saying, 'This is what will happen to you if you don't watch out'. Stanner was persuaded that as far as the Kununurra people were concerned,

> the whole point of the Karwadi ceremony as they helped to stage it on this occasion was to raise a new position in the hierarchy of cult values, not 'understanding' or a 'sense of mystery' or the other loftier things I attributed to the Daly River and Port Keats people, but the secular values of the 'religious law' represented by the cult leaders in a drink-sodden and crime-ridden Aboriginal community.[17]

In the 1930s Stanner had a reputation of being 'a lawyer' who 'stood up for black fellows'. However he concluded that the reason he was asked to attend the 1978 ceremony 'was not simply an expression of the affection and trust in which I am held, but rather a ploy to strengthen the ability of the cult leaders to stand well in the eyes of the visitors and in the eyes of the younger Peppiminarti people'. He had come to return various sacred items for the ritual which had come into his possession 40 years before.

On my periodic visits to Daly River, I meet a community of mixed tribal origins in a state of constant flux, besieged by outside demands and highly factionalised when it comes to questions of land. The Nauiyu Nambiyu community has a local council structure which by election empowers certain individuals to make decisions and to negotiate with outside groups including government and land councils regarding community living arrangements. The council also deals directly with the Northern Territory police and Aboriginal police aides in maintaining some semblance of law and order. When the going gets very tough, the ultimate sanction for matters under their control is not the administration of council-supervised punishment, but rather a trip across river to Peppiminarti where they can be straightened out in no uncertain terms by local leaders. However, there are many aspects of life in the Daly River area which are beyond the control of the people: aspects of the good and the bad. Whether it be a pending birth or an emergency evacuation, a visit by big time outsiders or the commencement of proceedings for a serious criminal offence, the principal actors fly in and out on the aeroplane. Refuge and rottenness, life and death, joy-filled awe and foreboding are sensed in the drone of the propeller which heralds the other world. The aeroplane dance is to community living and individual behaviour what the blowfly dance was two or three generations ago. The ritual has kept pace with social change. As in the past, it enacts more than the social order; though used to buttress the social order, it is now more dependent on personal, charismatic power than on the old law which guaranteed respect for and the authority of elders.

## LAND RIGHTS

In 1492, Europeans and the American Indians discovered each other. To each, there opened a New World. For centuries, Christopher Columbus was described as the discoverer, and the Indians as the discovered. Throughout the world, indigenous peoples were then dispossessed of their lands without consent and without adequate compensation. Their societies were destroyed and slavery was common. In 1537, Paul III in the bull *Sublimis Deus* condemned those who held that 'the inhabitants of the West Indies and the southern continents should be treated like irrational animals and used exclusively for our profit and service'. He declared that the

> Indians as well as any other peoples which Christianity will come to know in the future, must not be deprived of their freedom and their

> possessions even if they are not Christians and that, on the contrary, they must be left to enjoy their freedom and possessions.

In colonial times, the European powers carved the globe into spheres of influence. Having asserted sovereignty by act of state, the coloniser would assert control over the local population and resources. Native systems of land title would continue but only until they were extinguished by will of the sovereign. Especially where the native population lived a communal lifestyle, hunting and gathering, without a political system operating beyond the territory occupied by the local language group, the colonisers would take over the land as if it were *terra nullius*. The assertion of sovereignty often resulted in the expropriation of native lands without consent nor fair compensation.

After the Second World War, the United Nations committed itself to a decolonisation process. Native peoples with an identifiable population and land base were entitled to self-determination. Local populations could make a free choice whether or not to be integrated into the adjacent society administered by the colonising power. When separated by blue water or by identifiable boundaries, such populations could decide to separate and seek their own development.

In this post-colonial era, indigenous people have become more political in their struggle. Their rights are an international issue. Their claims to land rights, sovereignty and self-determination are being heard, but are restricted by prevalent notions of private property, national sovereignty and assimilation. In many countries, a just and proper settlement is still to be reached. Land rights is an issue in countries where an indigenous population is in the minority and the law of the new settlers has in the past paid insufficient regard for the traditional owners' right to land. It is also an issue where indigenous people are the majority but where communal notions of native land title are giving way to individual notions which are more compatible with the demands of foreign investors.

In international law, self-determination has applied chiefly to people emerging from the colonisation process being guaranteed a choice of future. It is not allowed to just any group. There must be an inquiry whether there is enough homogeneity or unity or common desire to hold the state together; whether it has economic resources and political capacity. Though there is still no definition of 'peoples' in international law, the right of self-determination, carrying with it the entitlement to partition of territory, is exercisable only by a territorial community, the members of which are conscious of themselves as members of such a community.

The international community of nations will not agree to interference in their domestic affairs to the extent that outside agencies would be able to adjudicate the claim of indigenous peoples to separate themselves from the nation state, especially when the nation has long been recognised as a member of the world community of nations with boundaries intact. It would be even less likely if the indigenous population is scattered throughout the land, made up of diverse groups without a long established nationwide political structure, having intermarried with descendants of the settlers over centuries. Land rights for these groups can provide the economic and spiritual base for them to make a realistic choice between their traditional lifestyle and that of other nationals.

In his world travels, Pope John Paul II has spoken often about indigenous land rights and the need to negotiate agreements with indigenous people. To Australian Aborigines he said:

> Let it not be said that the fair and equitable recognition of Aboriginal rights to land is discrimination. To call for the acknowledgement of the land rights of people who have never surrendered those rights is not discrimination. Certainly, what has been done cannot be undone. But what can now be done to remedy the deeds of yesterday must not be put off till tomorrow.
>
> The establishment of a new society for Aboriginal people cannot go forward without just and mutually recognised agreements with regard to these human problems, even though their causes lie in the past.[18]

The Pontifical Commission for Justice and Peace has spoken of aboriginal peoples as being marginalised with respect to their country's development and the need to guarantee the rights of first occupants to land, and to a social and political organisation which allows them to preserve their cultural identity, while remaining open to others.[19] One risk to be avoided is their 'being forced to assimilate without any concern for their right to maintain their own identity'. The rate of their integration into the surrounding society must be their decision.

In seeking an appropriate social and political organisation for indigenous people, we have to move beyond the primitive notion that assimilation is a precondition for justice for all. Equality does not equal uniformity. Equality of treatment requires recognition of differences which indigenous minorities themselves want to maintain in order to develop according to their own specific characteristics, while still having regard for others and for the common good of society and the world community. An assured land base is essential. Any decision to be integrated into the surrounding culture must result from a guaranteed free choice based on the right of minority group members to live together according to their specific cultural and religious characteristics. This requires the provision of realistic alternatives, backed by the equitable provision of government services to indigenous people, whichever choice they make.

Indigenous people are not simply self-identifying groups in the community who are in need of welfare assistance. As descendants of the first occupants and as the primary custodians of indigenous culture and heritage, they have a right to continue the management of their community affairs on their lands as autonomously as possible, provided they do not act contrary to the common good nor interfere with the rights of others, and provided all community members are afforded a realistic choice between their community life and the lifestyle available to other nationals. Though the provision of such choice may require extra resources from government, the cost is justified and necessary, given the history of dispossession of land and kin which was the precondition of the birth of modern nation states which include indigenous peoples within their borders. The evils of assimilation and discrimination will be overcome only by indigenous people determining their future, even if it be inevitably as a part of a nation state in which they are numerically a minority.

Recognising indigenous land rights, a post-colonial legal system is able to reverse some of the wrongs from previous generations and to wrap a protective husk around the relationship of the indigenous people with their land (often spiritual as well as economic), affording them the protections and opportunity needed to determine their own future and to manage their own affairs, no longer foreigners nor second class citizens in their own land. Land rights laws usually preclude tribal elders alienating the land or relinquishing control. The land is to be maintained for future generations. The land is held in trust for the benefit of all tribe members. Special provisions govern access to the land by miners and other developers because such commercial activity can disrupt the spiritual life and traditional lifestyle of the people. The risk of such disruption should be permitted only with the consent of the people.

## AUSTRALIAN LAND RIGHTS LEGISLATION

In 1972 the Aboriginal Land Rights Commission was established and chaired by Justice A.E. Woodward. The government having decided to recognise land rights of Aborigines in the Northern Territory, Woodward was asked to design a process. He set out his assumptions of the aims underlying the recognition of land rights, including 'the doing of simple justice', the promotion of social harmony and stability, the provision of land as a first essential to people who are economically depressed and who have no real opportunity of achieving a normal Australian standard of living, the maintenance and improvement of Australia's standing amongst the world's community of nations, and 'the preservation, where possible, of the spiritual link with his own land which gives each Aboriginal his sense of identity and which lies at the heart of his spiritual beliefs'.[20]

Under the legislation which resulted, Aborigines claiming to have a traditional claim to land which is unalienated crown land outside town or city boundaries can apply to a commissioner who may then recommend to the minister that a land grant be made. A traditional land claim can be made only by traditional Aboriginal owners who constitute

> a local descent group of Aboriginals who have common spiritual affiliations to a site on the land, being affiliations that place the group under a primary spiritual responsibility for that site and for the land, and are entitled by Aboriginal tradition to forage as of right over that land.[21]

There has been much anthropological ink spilt over this definition. The legislative history is clear. Justice Woodward provided drafting instructions for proposed legislation which included a definition of traditional Aboriginal owners almost identical to that which resulted in the legislation.[22] He based his draft substantially on the Northern Land Council's final submission which included a specially commissioned paper by R.M. Berndt on the 'Relationship of Aborigines to their land, with reference also to sacred and/or traditional sites'. Berndt submitted that the personal and spiritual linkage of Aborigines with land is expressed through membership of what can be called a local descent group.[23] The local descent group would be defined most typically in relation to patrilineal descent:

> A local descent group is associated with a stretch of country within which special sites are located. Possession of that country is validated

> through mytho-ritual statements. The sites within it contain the deathless and eternal spiritual manifestations of the mythic characters: just as the members of such a unit are living manifestations of those land-based (spiritually speaking) mystic beings.[24]

Australia's most experienced land commissioner, Justice John Toohey, conducted a review of the Land Rights Act in 1983. At that stage there had been fifteen land claim reports published, each of which had discussed the elements of the definition of Aboriginal owners. The concept had not been confined to an exogamous descent group which is patrilineal and whose members exercise a primary spiritual responsibility for a clan estate. A local descent group could be matrilineal or even ambilineal, including managers as well as owners of land. Though there was a good case for broadening the definition, Toohey concluded that it had been interpreted in a way that allowed sufficient flexibility while retaining 'the advantage of identifying with some precision those who answer the description'.[25] He recommended that the existing definition of traditional Aboriginal owners remain.[26]

The Daly River (Mulluk Mulluk) Land Claim is revealing. In response to the Mulluk Mulluk claim to traditional ownership there was a claim by other Aborigines to Kamu country. In his report of field work in 1932 Stanner reported the presence of members of eleven tribal groups. Seven other tribal groups, including the Kamu, were formerly in contact with the settlement but, according to Stanner, were either extinct or the few survivors had drifted into the sidings or stations such as Pine Creek, Katherine, and Adelaide River. At the land claim hearing 50 years later, Father John Leary MSC, who had re-established the mission at Daly River in 1955, said, 'I have never heard an Aborigine talk about that group. I have some faint recollection of Bill Stanner talking about the group, but was absolutely puzzled as to where they fitted in. I got the impression that they had died out many, many years before.'[27] At the time of the land claim, there was only one elderly member surviving, Mrs Pan Quee, and she had indicated a willingness to pass on her traditional rights to the active claimants of the Mulluk Mulluk-Madngele group. In evidence she lamented:

> Kamu country all been finished up. Nobody alive here, nothing. No old men, old men, my old man, nothing – me . . . Let him have it. Mulluk Mulluk, this country. My country all been finished. I might give him this mob, Mulluk Mulluk. But for hunting I can come up here and camp here and go back here like that, you see. I bring all the children and we camp

> here and we go back again. I give him Mulluk Mulluk this country now because old men, old men, been die. I can't have it – no good health.[28]

Toohey observed, 'Although it may once have been Kamu country, it has for many years been thought of as Kamu and Mulluk Mulluk. Once the Kamu had died out or were thought to have died out, the situation was more one of surviving co-owners. In my view it does insufficient justice to the evidence to describe the Mulluk Mulluk as simply looking after Kamu sites.'[29] In the end, Toohey was satisfied that the Mulluk Mulluk claimants had common spiritual affiliations to the relevant sites placing them under a primary spiritual responsibility for those sites and that land.

Kamu descendants, mostly resident in Darwin, in recent years have agitated their claim with the Northern Land Council for some entitlement to land in the Daly River area. The local community has been happy to share country by the river bank with these Kamu descendants, but they have shown no willingness to share country on which the community is built. It is not a question of spiritual relationship with land, rather a question of power – power of the local community to determine its own living arrangements as a community over against the power of persons wishing to be absentee landlords or wishing to displace present occupants so as to reconstitute on their ancestors' country, when the last surviving traditional owner had indicated the transfer of the land under tradition to another Aboriginal group. Given the history of dispersal, dispossession, and establishment of missions and stations, many links with country have been severed and not just in favour of migrants and their descendants; often other Aboriginal groups have taken over country with encouragement from church, government and pastoralists.

In 1983–4 Mr Paul Seaman conducted the Aboriginal Land Inquiry in Western Australia. The Woodward report served as a useful starting point for him. Seaman observed:

> The great majority of people of Aboriginal descent in Western Australia can make the case that they or their forebears were forcibly dispossessed of traditional lands. Many would be unable to obtain any land under a process which demanded proof of Aboriginal tradition.[30]

He found 'a range of interests from traditional relationships based on spiritual, residential, economic and historical factors to contemporary relationships based on association with settlements, pastoral stations and urban areas'.[31] He could see no value in Western Australian conditions in basing the right to claim land upon a definition of traditional owner similar to that contained in the Northern Territory legislation.[32]

Though Woodward had originally recommended that land be available for claim on the basis of need, the Commonwealth Government rejected all bases of claim from the legislation other than that based on traditional ownership of unalienated crown land. This narrow insistence has resulted in the advocates and commissioners in the land claims process being confronted with the reality that Aborigines succeed either as traditional owners or else are deprived altogether of land grants. Not surprisingly, there has been an extension of land claims under the heading of traditional ownership beyond the bounds of what was expected by the original drafters of the legislation.

In his 1974 report Woodward had said:

> I think it is undesirable from the point of view of the Aborigines themselves that large areas of country, having little value to them should be handed over to their ownership. This would inevitably lead to the result that the total area of Aboriginal ownership would be calculated and could be made to seem that the Aborigines had more than their fair share of land.

He reiterated this warning in 1985 at the Australian Legal Convention and suggested that

> Aboriginal Councils and their advisers give careful thought to the extent of future claims – and even consider the advisability of foregoing or surrendering some land already claimed or granted. I realise that this creates problems for the particular Aboriginals most closely associated with the land in question but, if persuaded that their access to their land will almost certainly remain unrestricted, they may be willing to forego their claims for the best interests of Aboriginals generally.[33]

This advice of course has not been heeded. It completely overlooked the fact that the relevant consideration nowadays is more often that of Aboriginal control over outside access to such land, particularly access by miners which can and ought result in financial betterment and improved social conditions for the Aboriginal land holders. The guarantee of access for the performance of spiritual obligations is not the only concern of Aboriginal land holders. In some instances, it may no longer be the primary concern.

When Queensland came to legislate for land rights, though there had been no public inquiry, the government decided to follow the

Woodward and Seaman recommendations to the extent that land could be claimed on the basis of traditional affiliation, historical association, or economic or cultural viability. The Queensland Aboriginal Land Act 1991 provides that a claim on the ground of traditional affiliation 'is established if the Land Tribunal is satisfied that the members of the group have a common connection with the land based on spiritual and other associations with, rights in relation to, and responsibilities for, the land under Aboriginal traditions'.[34] Aboriginal tradition is defined as 'the body of traditions, observances, customs, and beliefs generally or of a particular group of Aboriginal people, and includes any such traditions, observances, customs and beliefs relating to particular persons, areas, objects or relationships'.[35] But if there be no traditional owners of the land, it can still be claimed by those claiming an historical affiliation, or if there be no historical occupiers, others can make a claim on the basis of need. A priority of bases for claims is likely to reduce dependence on the criterion of traditional ownership, allowing Aborigines a greater parity in power relations with outsiders, without always having to invoke spiritual responsibility for the land in question.

## THE RELIGIOUS FACTOR

Under Durkheim's influence, many commentators saw Aboriginal societies as the epitome of primitive religion paralleling primitive social organisation. Religion was seen to be a social instrument for the preservation of law and order. It is still an opinion popularly espoused that traditional Aboriginal religions, particularly in remote desert areas with small populations, shared much in common with monotheistic religions in that they provided a regime for law and order in societies which had to ensure a strict code of morality for survival of the community. The complexity of myth and ritual and the diversity of religious practice belie any simple reduction. Understandably such reduction has greater appeal for commentators who admit to no religious dimension in their own lives. Admittedly such reduction may be too readily dismissed by those of us who profess a religious dimension in our own lives and protest its being posited as a consequence of our social conditioning.

In contemporary Aboriginal Australia, the religious factor is just one level of relationship, just one justification for, just one perspective on the Aboriginal relationship with land. It is an abiding factor; it is also a changing factor. It can be an independent factor; it can also be an inter-dependent factor. It is a threatened factor – threatened not only by non-Aboriginal non-practitioners of the religious belief system but also threatened by Aboriginal owners who choose or are cajoled, persuaded or simply slip into another way of looking at the world and therefore another way of looking at their land.

Aborigines constantly see their reality in terms of their relationship with creator beings of the Dreaming, with the land and with each other. There is no ready differentiation between the law, religion and culture. The law is seen to be life-giving as well as death-dealing. Life is not a morality play but it can be a tragi-comedy to be lived to the full. There is always time for myth and ritual to be enacted and repeated. Change is neither sought nor a matter for surprise. No change is so great that it need be a challenge to Aboriginal faith. Aboriginal religion is never some idealised system lived in splendid isolation by people yearning for the lives of their ancestors a century ago, having no interest in the attractions of technology and ideas developed in cultural contexts far removed from their own. Contemporary Aborigines are above all else contemporary people open to the world and wanting to assert their own identity. There are many Aborigines in many communities through Australia who are crying out; I have heard them saying:

> We know we have problems. We know they are our problems. We know many of these problems would not have occurred but for the clash of cultures and the enforced dispossession of our ancestors and the continued disadvantage and poverty we suffer. We know that we have to find the answers and work at implementing them. We know we need help. We want help – but help which respects our dignity and accords us our due autonomy as indigenous people. We know our law cannot provide the answers of this new rapidly changing world which attracts, shapes, and sometimes twists our children and our young people. To solve these problems we do not want to become just like the colonisers and migrants to our land. We want to solve these problems our way so we can continue to live our way – though that not be like our ancestors did. Those days are gone. And not like other Australians live. We want our way to be strong so our young people will be proud to choose it whatever happens.

Whether it be the proposed flood mitigation dam at Alice Springs or the proposed mine at Coronation Hill, the religious factor in the Aboriginal relationship to land is invoked by Aborigines and their supporters to buttress their claims when the nation state continues to deny to the Aboriginal owners the power to make the decisions about their land, which are really decisions about their lives. Instead, the decisions are made by non-Aboriginal non-practitioners of the religion trying to offset the incommensurable spiritual factor against the so-called national interest or community interest. If freedom of religion were taken seriously in these cases, Aborigines holding the beliefs would also be holding the power to determine the outcome. Having to articulate one's questioned religious heritage to non-believers whose economic or national interests are presumed sacrosanct simply because they are espoused by the decision-makers demands articulation of the ineffable and independent valuation of the transcendent reality. Inevitably, Bula is parodied as a pot of gold at the end of a rainbow and Urewe Aterle is seen as a wellspring for Commonwealth interference in domestic Northern Territory affairs.

Decisions about land use become politicised because the government will not trust Aborigines as the decision-makers, determining their own religious future by weighing incommensurable values and making their own determination when there is a conflict of aims between them and other Australians who want to use the land for their own interests. Economic and social realities impinge on decision-makers whoever they may be and whatever their beliefs. Aboriginal traditional owners are more likely to make the right or preferable determination simply because it is their decision. Wherever there has been conflict in the past, the decision of the state has been that it is for an instrument of the state (whose personnel are not the Aboriginal landowners), to make a determination as to the balancing of rights and interests, they having translated the Aboriginal religious affiliation to land in a way comprehensible to themselves and the Australian community and having gauged the religious interest over against other incommensurable matters all of which impact upon the common good. When the state determines the weighting to be given to the religious factor in the Aboriginal relationship to land, there will always be grounds for objecting that the decision-maker has wrongly weighted that factor against criteria which are not more objective, but simply more comprehensible and appealing to the decision-maker.

Though the Commonwealth's declaration preventing the proposed Junction Waterhole Dam outside Alice Springs for the next twenty years was hailed as a major breakthrough in the protection of Aboriginal rights, the detriment to others which had to be offset was only the

> infrequent damage to the carpets and other property of white people who have chosen to build on flood-prone land, not to elevate their houses or commercial buildings to the small extent necessary to place them above flood level or otherwise floodproof them, or to buy buildings that are known to be subject to occasional flooding at prices that presumably reflected that fact.[36]

Even for economic rationalists having no concern for Aboriginal sensibilities about sacred sites, the dam was a questionable proposition being 'an unusually expensive option for flood mitigation'. During its life, the dam would have returned only '33 cents for every dollar invested by preventing property and infrastructure damage and business disruption'.[37]

At Coronation Hill, the question was, 'To mine or not to mine?' This recurring question confronts all who have a commitment to sustainable development in Australia. The Hawke Government referred the question to the newly created Resource Assessment Commission (RAC). It provided the government with seven options across the spectrum from 'no' to 'negotiated process for mining applications' to 'open mining'. After a heated five hour meeting, the Cabinet under the leadership of Mr Hawke decided that mining and exploration would not be permitted at Coronation Hill or elsewhere in the Kakadu Conservation Zone and that the whole of the zone would become part of Kakadu National Park.

The RAC adopted what it called an inter-disciplinary approach to arrive at conclusions relevant to decisions that seek 'to optimise the net benefits to the community from the nation's resources'. The criteria used in the evaluation included efficiency of resource use, environmental considerations, sustainability, and equity. In the end, environmental considerations were not determinative as the evidence suggested that 'a single mine, properly managed and monitored, would have a small and geographically limited direct impact on the known biological resources of the conservation zone'. The decision was to turn on so called equity considerations, the one of greatest relevance being the wellbeing and views of the Jawoyn, the local Aboriginal community.

Unable to answer the question, the RAC simply stated the dilemma facing the Australian Government: 'Should it set aside the environmental risks that cannot be eliminated and the strong views held by the Aboriginal people responsible for the conservation zone in favour of securing increases in national income of the order that seems likely from the Coronation project and possibly from other mineral resources in the zone?' The RAC conducted what it called a contingent valuation survey of the Kakadu Conservation Zone. In these days of economic rationalism, such a survey is an attempt to measure values which are incommensurable. Two thousand and thirty four Australians were asked how much they would be willing to pay to prevent possible environmental damage from mining in the conservation zone. The survey rendered precise but farcical results, showing that Australians were willing to pay $123.80 per person per year for ten years to avoid the effects of a major impact scenario. If mining were not to have a major impact, Australians were still prepared to expend $52.80 per person per year for ten years to avoid the effects of minor impact. The researchers claimed that these results supported 'the intuitively plausible proposition that Australians are prepared to pay more to avoid more serious and more likely environmental effects'. No cabinet minister could conceivably have been assisted by the results of this survey.

Governments often claim a mandate for a particular program. Or failing to articulate a mandate, they point to the economic benefits which will inevitably flow to the community at large. In our political system, which does not at present give legal recognition to the Jawoyn claims to the hill, it was for Federal Cabinet to decide, with a discretion unfettered by either the Aboriginal or Commonwealth legal systems. How the ministers reached their decision and on what basis was murky business during a leadership challenge.

Mr Hawke decided that his cabinet should implement the wishes of the majority of the elders of the Jawoyn people as they were expressed to and determined by the RAC. When asked by Justice Stewart, who chairs the RAC, those old men said they did not want mining because mining could disturb Bula whom they believe to inhabit the hill. The Jawoyn beliefs about Bula and the hill are religious beliefs. These beliefs are not shared by any other people than the Jawoyn.

There are barbaric economic rationalists who regard any religious beliefs, no matter how many or how few who profess them, as quaint, non-rational human quirks with no economic rationale. They dismiss out of hand the religious beliefs of the Jawoyn. It is these people who set the pace in the secularist public domain which encourages headlines such as 'Chief Minister Blasts "Stone Age" Mining Ban'. For them, a 50 per cent-plus-one vote and an improved balance of payments settle the matter, whether it be Coronation Hill or a cathedral.

Fortunately, barbaric economic rationalists do not have the last word. There are Australians of goodwill who respect the religious beliefs and emotional commitments of others, even when there is no economic advantage, and even economic disadvantage, to themselves or the general community. They see that the national interest is about more than the balance of payments. The common good is more than economic development. Many of these people willingly concede the need to respect and take account of Jawoyn religious beliefs. But, they ask, what are the limits? And when should the Jawoyn themselves be allowed to decide?

The miners went for broke on Coronation Hill. They and their foreign investment colleagues decided to turn it into the litmus test for Australian economic development driven by foreign investment. Upping the stakes, they decided that a government ban on mining so as to court the green vote or even to protect Jawoyn religious sensibilities was beyond the pale. Setting the limits was at first too difficult for government. That is why they handed it to the RAC. When the RAC handed it back to government, it found that, but for Aboriginal beliefs about Bula, there was no reason why mining should not proceed. In its own fact-finding the RAC was satisfied that the majority of Jawoyn elders held strong religious beliefs about Coronation Hill, and whatever their previous contradictory testimony to government inquiries, they were now opposed to mining.

Even some wishing to accord due respect to Aboriginal beliefs challenged in good faith the process and findings of the RAC. But in the end Cabinet decided not to go behind the RAC findings. It was no longer a question whether the Jawoyn believed in Bula's power and whether or not they wanted mining. Presuming they did so believe and that they did not want mining, it became a starker, simpler question: who should win out – the Jawoyn or the mining company which had invested $14 million?

There was dispute about the benefit the mine would bring to the Australian economy. The RAC said at the end of the day we would only be $82 million better off. The miners claimed we would gain export revenues of $500 million. The simple question this time was answered in favour of the Aborigines opposed to mining. Not only their interests were served by the decision. Inevitably, the decision-makers in that cabinet room also had regard for their own interests. But Aboriginal viewpoints and opinions were a crucial factor in the calculus. For as long as Aborigines are not allowed to make decisions themselves about the exploitation of their land, the decision-makers need to give due weight to their views. There must be better processes than the RAC and a second-guessing, emotional cabinet room wracked by a leadership crisis.

Everyone, including the miners, knows their interests could be better served by a legal process which clarifies rights and interests before $14 million is invested and back door deals are done in Canberra. The miners' in-house theologian Mr Hugh Morgan saw the Coronation Hill decision as evidence of the prime minister's neo-paganism. The Coronation Hill decision has deprived prospective investors of the certainty which they need in order to invest with any sustained regularity. The recent decision-making process shows that there is no principled procedure for determining the hierarchy of values between conflicting claims, especially between developers and Aboriginal and environmental interest groups. Attempts to quantify in dollars and cents the citizenry's commitment to environmental values and the recognition of the religious factor in Aboriginal land rights are bound to fail. The more complex political and moral arguments are not reducible simply to economic considerations. Neither is the result to be effected by a choice between principle and pragmatism. Rather where there is a conflict of principles in their practical application to the case at hand, there is a need for a process determining the hierarchy of those principles and the limits of application of each. There is a need for an effective decision-making process which guarantees participation by those most affected by the decision and its outcome. Cabinet should be left to resolve questions only of the highest policy in the national interest. In hard cases, the right answer will be yielded only by the choice of the right decision-maker and an adherence to the right process which guarantees proper access by all parties to the decision-making process.

Opinion polls or, as they are now known in their more nuanced variety, contingent valuation surveys, can only be a useful starting point for determining the will of the majority. Any outcome which is contrary to the will of the majority obviously requires justification. Justification by clear enunciation and application of principles or through arbitration and determination by an acknowledged authority may be possible. The hardest disputes are difficult to resolve precisely because there is no clear enunciation of principles possible or because there is no singular application of the principles to the contingent situation. Also, there is no authority who enjoys the respect of all disputants (this may even include the Federal Cabinet). There is no established process for involving disputants, guaranteeing them natural justice, locking them into compliance with the umpire's decision, and making them own the decision or at least the process.

The final decision may or may not reflect a community consensus. Rather the decision must be a consistent part of the mosaic of national decision-making which renders sufficient certainty and commitment to shared values (including Aboriginal spiritual values) such that all parties are assured certainty in the instant case, and the community is provided with a predictable and fair range of outcomes for future disputes. This cannot be achieved by equating economics and ethics. Neither can surveys or opinion polls be quoted as the right answer.

Commenting on the Coronation Hill decision, Mr. Morgan said, 'it will become impossible for any government to protect the economic well-being, or even the security, of the country if threats arise from doctrines or groups claiming immunity through notions of sacredness or sanctity'. Economic wellbeing is important, even for the Jawoyn. But it is not always trumps. Some other things are non-negotiable or superior in the community's hierarchy of values. In a civilised democracy we ought take into account and provide protection under the rule of law for the religious sensibilities and world views of others, especially the indigenous people of the continent. That account does not have a cash value. Its limits are set by moral argument about the rights and entitlements of citizens and the common good of the society. Preferably, the compromise between religious sensibilities and economic betterment should be effected by those who profess the religious beliefs, especially when they have a claim in justice to a share in the economic benefits. The greatest problems arise when those with the religious affiliation with the land have no recognised entitlement to share in its economic riches. There is then no incentive nor moral imperative for them to adapt their religious practices and perspectives to the gains available to all parties, which should include themselves.

Whatever the economic cost, there must be some times when we would not permit mining in any circumstances. There are many other times when our economic interest can readily be accommodated with the rights and interests of all. Then even Aboriginal landowners welcome mining and the focus moves to an equitable distribution of the benefits. 'To mine or not to mine?' is no longer a straight economic, political lobbying and public relations question. It has a moral and religious dimension. No one community sector holds the key to the right answer, least of all those whose short-term economic interests will be best served. We need to listen to those who have traditional authority to speak for their country. At times, there is good reason for them to have the last word, whether or not we with a different cultural and religious perspective agree.

Terms such as 'sustainable development' point to a search for principles and a hierarchy of those principles and a process for applying those principles to a contingent situation. The commissioning of the RAC or the appointment of eminent persons to make inquiries is an attempt to solve disputes with recognised and legitimate authority using a fair, transparent process, but with insufficient regard for cultural and religious differences. Ian Keen, one of the anthropologists who advised the RAC has said:

> Given that the legitimacy of the state is accepted, in a pluralist democracy there are no grounds for complaint about someone putting forward a case for setting limits on Aboriginal sacred site claims, any more than it is illegitimate to propose constraints on mining in particular cases. I question the fairness of some of the suggested criteria of sanctity. Is it reasonable to demand, for example, that a majority opinion be sought among people who recognise religious authority on the basis of age, gender and local affiliation? Is it just to insist on a record of ancient and wholly unchanging belief from a people who so evidently adapt old principles to changing conditions?[38]

## TERRA NULLIUS NO MORE

With the advent of airstrips, Toyotas, faxes, telephones, videos and television, there is no Aboriginal community in this country which is spared the pervasive influence of foreign culture and religious values. If I were to ask my Irish forebears who were singing in Gaelic about the theme of their songs, they would probably reply, 'They are about life'. Similarly requests made of Aboriginal people to explain their songs or paintings result in the response, 'It's My Country'. They speak for their country.

'This is my country' is one of the proudest contemporary Aboriginal declarations you will ever hear. Aboriginal artists are even painting their country for sale and display in foreign lands. Art has become the bridge of communication and commerce out of which has grown non-Aboriginal appreciation of the land and Aboriginal access to cosmopolitan goods and services. It is a new way of talking the history and acknowledging the present – a way that does not threaten the descendants of the European colonisers and that need not undermine the integrity of the Aboriginal landowners who have been dispossessed. It is a way of sharing the land through understanding and respect. The painting both tells the story and evokes it; it is the text and the visual aid; it is the map, the code and the very terrain under which lies buried a world of meaning that expresses values transcending all cultures while being embodied completely in this culture, fully accessible only to the initiated.

The new quest for self-expression across cultural barriers has a pathetic 200-year history. The self-interested failure of colonists to recognise Aboriginal land rights was part of a cohesive policy aimed at reducing Aboriginal resistance to European progress, development and economic expansion. On the fringes of the new society built on their lands, Aborigines were marginalised from its benefits. The present generation of Aborigines is the first to know formal equality under the law, the first to enjoy the benefit of affirmative action programs – in housing, health, education and employment – aimed at overcoming past disadvantage and providing equality of opportunity. Their grandparents were supposed to die out; their parents were to be assimilated or at least integrated. They are now supposed to manage their own affairs and to become self-sufficient if not self-determining. They are recognised by the others in the land as people in their own right.

In situations of potential conflict, they have to translate the sacred to others outside the world of religious meaning in profane, or at least mundane, terms so that the violent law of a foreign culture might wrap a protective husk around the life-giving and death-dealing relationship they have with clan, Dreaming and land. That relationship is law in its fullest sense, described by Mr Justice Blackburn in the 1971 Gove Land Rights case as:

> a subtle and elaborate system highly adapted to the country in which people lived their lives, which provided a stable order of society and was remarkably free from the vagaries of personal whim or influence . . . a government of laws and not of men.[39]

'The lands of this continent were not *terra nullius* or "practically unoccupied" in 1788'.[40] So spoke the High Court of Australia in the case of *Eddie Mabo and others v The State of Queensland* on 3 June 1992, the day the Australian legal system came of age. Though the British Crown asserted sovereignty over those deemed to be barbarians in 1788, it would now be barbaric, as it was then, to presume sovereignty automatically wiped the slate clean of native land title. Though a court established by the sovereign has no power to canvass the validity of the assertion of sovereignty over new territory, it has the duty to ensure equal protection of the law for those holding property within the territory. When Eddie Mabo commenced his litigation in 1982 many Australians still saw land rights as a special welfare measure. The defendant state's premier, Sir Joh Bjelke-Petersen, saw it as part of a long-range communist plan to alienate Aboriginal lands from the Australian nation so that a fragmented north could be used for subversive activities by other countries'.[41] Land rights is now legally classifiable as the restitution, recognition and compensation of property rights.

The fiction of *terra nullius* allowed the European community of nations to expand their colonial horizons with minimal concern for indigenous peoples. In the eighteenth century the common law took its lead from international law. In Mabo, three judges, acknowledging their law-making role, said, 'It is imperative in today's world that the common law should neither be nor be seen to be frozen in an age of racial discrimination'.[42]

Governor Phillip may have asserted British sovereignty over the eastern part of the Australian continent on 26 January 1788, but he did not thereby automatically increase unencumbered crown landholdings by another half continent. Native title to the lands continued until the new sovereign dealt with the lands in a manner inconsistent with the continuation of native title. Even after 204 years of unmitigated pastoral, colonial and mining expansion, there are still large areas of vacant crown land especially in Western Australia. It is now traditional Aboriginal law which determines the Aboriginal titleholders of such land. Like international law, the traditional law or custom is not frozen as at the moment of establishment of a colony. There are four developing sources of law which now impinge on determination of land ownership: international law, Aboriginal traditional law, common law as declared by the High Court, and statutory law as legislated by Australian parliaments within their constitutional limits.

*Terra nullius* was clear and simple; it was also unjust and discriminatory. The law of the land is now more complex and more just. The nation state as sovereign retains the power to extinguish the property rights of citizens. The federal government cannot extinguish title without just compensation which is guaranteed under the constitution. State parliaments can extinguish title without compensation, but they cannot do so in a racially discriminatory way. Racial discrimination is outlawed by the Commonwealth Racial Discrimination Act which implements the International Convention on the Elimination of all Forms of Discrimination. Aboriginal 'traditional owners' of vacant crown land, national parks and some other public lands are now entitled to the same protection of their property rights as other landholders.

Though the High Court has ruled by four to three that there is no guaranteed right to compensation for extinguishment of native title by a state government, public servants and politicians will have to recognise native title as they would any other title to land. Wiping out native title without compensation will pass muster only if other title could be so extinguished in the same circumstances. Aborigines now have a property interest in stock routes and vacant crown lands, even if these lands be subject to authorities to prospect or exploration licences. Increasingly developers, pastoralists and miners will have to deal with Aborigines on an equal footing. Govermments will have to treat with them to effect the workable compromises for land use according to Aboriginal law and the common law. The High Court has removed the legal basis for the continued dispossession of Aborigines retaining traditional affiliations with their lands. The court has not undone the injustices of the past. It has set the foundations for just land dealings in the future. By recognising the existence of Aboriginal law and land rights, the court has provided a jurisprudential basis for the calls by Aborigines for self-determination on their lands.

The court has ruled that native title to particular land, its incidents and the persons entitled to land are ascertained 'according to the laws and customs of the indigenous people who, by those laws and customs, have a connection with the land'.[43] It is immaterial that the laws and customs have undergone change 'provided the general nature of the connection between the indigenous people and the land remains'. According to three of the judges, native title can be extinguished if the clan or group, by ceasing to acknowledge its laws and to observe its customs, loses its connection with the land. Two other judges, having observed that traditional law or custom is not frozen, said, 'Provided any changes do not diminish or extinguish the relationship between a particular tribe or other group and particular land, subsequent developments or variations do not extinguish the title in relation to that land'.[44] They were of the view 'that, at least where the relevant tribe or group continues to occupy or use the land', the members would not lose their rights through 'the abandonment of traditional customs and ways'. Another judge said, 'So long as occupation by a traditional society is established now and at the time of annexation, traditional rights exist. An indigenous society cannot, as it were, surrender its rights by modifying its way of life.'[45]

In 1993, the Commonwealth Parliament passed the Native Title Act which provided what Prime Minister Keating described as 'ungrudging and unambiguous recognition and protection of native title'.[46]

In the future, we have to expect further showdowns in the contest between the two laws. During the Noonkanbah dispute, Mr Ginger Nganawilla portrayed the conflict starkly:

> If we are to allow Amax [the mining company] to return to Noonkanbah they must show us Law, not paper law. Paper is nothing. Paper can be washed away. Our Law, Aboriginal law, will last forever. If Amax has this Law then they must show us.[47]

Ironically the enduring Aboriginal law is being recognised by foreign legal systems at a time when it is coming under greater threat from its own practitioners.

## CULTURE FADING AWAY

The primary custodians of the only culture unique to this land have a rich heritage and an abundant resource which gives value to the political struggle, the physical labour and spiritual trauma of living in two worlds. The genius of Aboriginal religion is summed up by Professor Stanner in his description of Murinbata religion:

> It affirms reality as a necessary connection between life and suffering. It sees the relation as continuously incarnate and yet as needing reaffirmation. It celebrates the relation by a rite containing all the beauty of song, mime, dance and art of which human beings are capable.[48]

Aboriginal law, though now recognised for the first time as part of the law of the land even in the eyes of the colonisers, has to survive under challenge from its own practitioners who sense both new horizons and shifting foundations in their lives. If it is to maintain its appeal to contemporary practitioners, the Aboriginal religious worldview has to embrace, or at least encounter and accommodate the worldviews of others. Aboriginal cultures are changing, being lost and retrieved at a rate never before experienced. Aboriginal people themselves know best that their system of law is under threat.

The breakdown of the law, the abandonment of myth and ritual, and violence in these communities are exacerbated by readily available alcohol, widespread unemployment and concentrations of population which draw together groups from various clans and language groups for administrative convenience and economies of scale. Communities of such size, variety and outside contact never existed previously, except for periodic ceremonial, trading and meeting purposes. As permanent societies, they are new creations in the post-contact era resulting from the push and pull of outside service delivery. Such 'communities' as they are erroneously described do not and never have had a simple or uniformly acknowledged law, religion or culture which could provide the basis for a customary dispute resolution structure or process.

In 1981 I was junior counsel for Alwyn Peter who was charged with the murder of his woman, Deidre Gilbert, on the Weipa Reserve in Cape York. Like many defence counsel, I was proud of our win in reducing the charge to manslaughter and obtaining a sentence which guaranteed Alwyn almost immediate parole. An anthropologist put it to me: 'In a reserve situation like Weipa, there is no customary law sanction to protect Deidre and women like her. All you will succeed in doing is removing the limited sanction applicable by the whitefella law. There will be nothing left to protect the black women.' Her words came back to haunt me as I read Marcia Langton's report *Too Much Sorry Business* to the Royal Commission into Aboriginal Deaths in Custody:

> It is clear . . . that the appalling level of domestic violence against Aboriginal women is not being addressed by Aboriginal Law. Many women are hesitant to speak about it, but the daily parade of women with bandaged heads and broken arms, especially in towns and larger communities where there is access to alcohol, is plain for all to see.[49]

The Australian legal system is perceived by these women to be too lenient, too late and ineffective. As Langton put it:

> In many instances, justice is not seen to be done by Aboriginal people, because punishment imposed by a . . . court is often too lenient. [S]tatistics on lengths of sentences for most serious crimes bear out precisely the Aboriginal view that sentences imposed by . . . courts for homicide, rape and other serious crimes are too lenient .[50]

She heard much evidence that elders in communities thought the legal system too humane and lacking in deterrence:

> Many elders, because of the stringency of their traditional Law and because of their experiences of police in the early days . . . feel that 'humanitarian' European laws provide no deterrent to Aboriginal

> offending. Indeed Aboriginal Law seems to have worked to prevent breaches by the threat, if not the actuality in most instances, of severe corporal punishment and even death.[51]

Aboriginal law embraces all we might variously describe as law, religion, philosophy, art and culture. Discrete groups of individuals were able to ascertain with practical precision their relationships, rights and duties with each other, their land and their possessions. It was binding law which was life-giving and death-dealing. As Langton puts it:

> What our people mean when they talk about their Law, is a cosmology, a worldview which is a religious, philosophic, poetic and normative explanation of how the natural, human and supernatural domains work. Aboriginal Law ties each individual to kin, to 'country' – particular estates of land – and to Dreamings. One is born with the responsibilities and obligations which these inheritances carry. There are many onerous duties, and they are not considered to be optional. One is seen to be lazy and neglectful if these duties are ignored and the respect, authority and advantages, such as arrangements for good marriages, opportunities for one's children, are not awarded. As many of our people observe, Aboriginal Law is hard work.[52]

In many areas culture is fading away, law is breaking down, languages are being lost, the ceremonies are dying out. Langton reports one testimony:

> Culture fading away slowly. So many people think they're white these days. Especially young people. Yeah, culture broken down. Yo, they running away from ceremony, cause of nganaji (grog). Young children, school age, they got to learn their culture. But middle age boy and girl they want to run away to the parks, they come back really drunk. Fussing about you know in the ceremony, they fighting, and talking wrong time, too fussy.
>
> When they sober, like we today, we never be break up culture. When that happening, drinking business, they break and kick the culture. When people are making ceremony you know, then they come in and disturbing our ceremony and culture.[53]

Like Langton in the Northern Territory, Commissioner Patrick Dodson in Western Australia 'found that much of the content of discussions related directly to problems arising from alcohol use and how to solve them'.[54] Having said that 'alcohol can be seen as the absolute or, indeed, the only cause of violent behaviour', Dodson concedes that alcohol can 'be seen to exacerbate violent behaviour among Aboriginal people'.[55] He found that in some areas violence was endemic among those who make extensive use of alcohol in circumstances which 'can undermine respect for Aboriginal Law, and social relationships and practices that seek to maintain Aboriginal societies'.

He concluded:

> [V]iolence has increased among Aboriginal society, both in the amount of violence inflicted, and in how, and to whom, that violence is inflicted. What appears to be true, is that, whereas in previous times, members of Aboriginal society often used what may be described as violence or physical force to enforce certain aspects of law and order, today physical force has, in many areas, where excess alcohol use occurs, become almost uncontrollable and mindlessly violent. This is especially so not only with regard to the violence directed towards women and children but also among men themselves.[56]

The evidence quoted by Langton and Dodson and their considered reflections put to rest some of the more romantic notions about contemporary Aboriginal life and the ideal interpretations of Aboriginal law. Aborigines are living under two laws. But one law is losing its sanction, its appeal, its practitioners and its teachers. It is becoming optional. Some desire its continuation and transmission. Others, especially when drunk, can opt out when it suits them or lose it when living in a social situation where that law no longer makes whole sense of the individual's new world filled by Toyotas, videos, satellites, faxes, firearms, computers, cash, grog, school and fast food – all of which have their advantages and disadvantages.

Outstations are set up as sanctuaries for the preservation of the traditional way. But there is a limit to which outstations can be used as reform schools in the old law for young radicals playing up in their communities or in town. Young men facing initiation or some corporal punishment or young women facing a traditional betrothal to a much older man increasingly want to opt out of the traditional law and opt in to the system of individual choices and liberties they see on screen (such as 'Dallas' or 'LA Law') or in the streets of Alice Springs or Katherine. The whitefella legal system in these instances prizes individual rights and individual freedom of choice over collective rights of the group and the requirements for handing on a tough, wholistic law which is hard work. Aboriginal law no longer controls every aspect of their lives. Free to choose, the young may abandon culture even if only for short-term gain or liberty. Affected by alcohol and confronted by change, the elders may lose their confidence and abandon their duties to the law.

Once elders are denied the power to impose their law on the young without their consent, having already been denied the power to impose their law's ultimate sanction even with the consent of all parties, Aboriginal law inevitably becomes an optional way of living for the new generations, who may want to move freely between two worlds.

Customary law is of little use in disciplining the young for grog-related property and motor vehicle offences. Today, law and culture remain strong only while they hold appeal or can be imposed without human rights violations on the young who see and want to roam far beyond the boundaries of their traditional country. Culture is breaking down because, as the old say, the young are running away from ceremony.

The old law which was all-embracing is shattered by outside contact. It no longer typifies the ineluctable human condition enacted as a celebration of the fearful approach to mystery. However some of the law may be salvageable and amendable if reshaped by those who have a memory and a vision of the law, having the skill and authority to impart it to the young, who have geographic and cultural choices previously unimagined. Aboriginal communities might then keep afloat and mobile in the sea of all cultures, remaining true to themselves and their ancestors. Imposed solutions will generate further alienation and despair. Government with and at the request of local communities might keep in check needless violence and even remedy the causes embedded in a shattering colonial history.

## CONSTANCY AND CHANGE

Future generations of Aborigines will want to live in the best of all possible worlds – Aboriginal but open to all the world has to offer, not being swamped by it, being able to stay afloat, able to make sense of it, able to embrace the mystery of it, even able to shape it, and able to hand on to their children, the successors in title, the uniqueness of their culture and the universal possibilities of life in the modern world.

Stanner's last paper was an anthropological report written for the defence team in Alwyn Peter's case. After the case, I was privileged to receive the last letter he ever wrote:

> I am fascinated by the question: how do general ideas about human conduct change so quickly? I can recall about fifty years ago appearing as a witness for the defence in an Aboriginal murder case in Darwin before Wells J. He was notably unimpressed by my arguments but nevertheless

> reluctantly took them into account in mitigation, while looking round the court as if expecting trouble. Or do I mean remarkably quickly?

He died within the week while traditional owners were gathering at Daly River for the hearing of the Mulluk Mulluk land claim. The old men told the young anthropologists how they had, 50 years before, 'been carried on Stanner's shoulders while he hunted and talked with elders long since gone'. Stanner saw and had a reverence and respect for Aboriginal religious practitioners who embraced the mystery beyond themselves and their own. He had seen them embrace the land they walked on, performing the ritual and telling the myth. Their country and their countrymen had embodied all they needed to confront the ultimate mystery of reflective creaturehood. In his last visit to the north, he saw religion subjugated to a tool for social order in a drink-sodden and crime-ridden Aboriginal community. Now, as then, we all inhabit the nest and the wallow. As always, 'at the centre of things social, refuge and rottenness are found together'. Ideas and conduct are forever changing and forever the same.

A few years after Alwyn Peter's case, I was visiting his people on their country at Mapoon in Cape York. One of the key witnesses, Jean Jimmy, had just become a great great grandmother. Congratulating her, I admired the large mango tree under which she sat, presuming it to have been planted by the missionaries a century before. Still rolling her own cigarette, she replied, 'No, I planted this tree. I am very blessed to sit under the shade of the tree that I planted and to see it bearing fruit.' She, too, has passed away. Recently, I was walking along the beach at sunset and encountered one of her daughters fishing. She told me how good it was that the people now had title to their land because they were able to bring Jean home and bury her in her country and with her spirits.

Shortly after, I was in a Toyota with traditional owners of land nearby. Without warning, they cried out to their ancestor spirits. They told me, 'They're still here'. A couple of minutes later we were back on the main dirt road and I was told, 'Highway One'. Both worlds co-exist for those embracing the mystery of being Aboriginal when so much has changed while so much of what ultimately matters remains as it was in the Dreaming. If only we could be more willing to allow Aborigines to make the decisions about country, we could accord dignity to the human person's religious sensibilities and we could witness true self-determination by which Aborigines decide whether to mine, to build a dam, or to maintain the status quo for a while longer while they reflect on what is best for them and for us. Why does it remain so unthinkable that they should make some decisions for us when those decisions relate to their country? Any religion has to come to terms with power, wealth and conflicting demands of interest groups. Even in the midst of agonising worldly decisions, we Australians still have the opportunity to count ourselves blessed in this land. Economic imperatives, like the laws of nature, may cloud our vision. Like MacKillop a century ago, we need to discern the justice of Aboriginal claims to land, allowing them to speak for country, thereby according religious freedom to those whose ancestors settled and humanised this land tens of thousands of years before Abraham set out for Canaan. We might then discover the full life-sustaining capacity of the land which is sacred.[57]

## AFTERWORD (1998)

In 1996, the High Court of Australia ruled in the Wik case that Aboriginal native title rights could still survive on lands granted under pastoral lease to other persons.[58] Over 40 per cent of the Australian land mass is covered by pastoral lease and the majority of new mining activity occurs on such land. The nation is still debating the appropriate balance of rights between Aborigines and pastoralists and between Aborigines and miners. Native title holders anxious to maintain their spiritual relationship with the land are also seeking to maintain a statutory right to negotiate with other stakeholders, thereby enhancing their economic base and political standing. Other Australians not convinced of the religious factor in land rights often view the debate as one simply about money and power, rather than one defining of identity and enhancing of culture and religion.

## NOTES

1 G. O'Kelly, 'The Jesuit Mission Stations in the Northern Territory', BA (Hons) Thesis, Monash University, 1967, p. 51.
2 D. MacKillop, *Sydney Herald*, 23 December 1892.
3 W.E.H. Stanner, 'The Daly River Tribes: a report of fieldwork in Northern Australia', *Oceania* 3 (1932–3), p. 377.
4 W.E.H. Stanner, 'The Daly River Tribes: a report of fieldwork in Northern Australia', *Oceania* 4 (1933–4), p. 1.
5 Stanner, 'The Daly River Tribes', (1933–4), p. 12.

6 Stanner, 'The Daly River Tribes', (1933–4), p. 13.
7 Stanner, 'The Daly River Tribes', (1933–4), p. 21.
8 Stanner, 'The Daly River Tribes', (1933–4).
9 W.E.H. Stanner, 'On Aboriginal Religion, I. The lineaments of sacrifice', *Oceania* 30 (1959), p. 109.
10 W.E.H. Stanner, 'Reflections on Durkheim and Aboriginal Religion', in M. Freedman (ed.), *Social Organisation*, Frank Cass & Co, London, 1967, p. 221.
11 W.E.H. Stanner, 'Religion, Totemism and Symbolism' in R.M. and C.H. Berndt (eds), *Aboriginal Man in Australia*, Angus and Robertson, Sydney, 1965, p. 227.
12 W.E.H. Stanner, *On Aboriginal Religion*, Oceania Monograph 36, University of Sydney, Sydney, 1989, p. 17.
13 Stanner, *On Aboriginal Religion*, p. 44.
14 W.E.H. Stanner, 'Big Sunday at Peppiminarti', unpublished manuscript, 12 February 1979, p. 6.
15 Stanner, 'On Aboriginal Religion, I. The lineaments of sacrifice', p. 113.
16 Stanner, 'Big Sunday at Peppiminarti', p. 10.
17 Stanner, 'Big Sunday at Peppiminarti', p. 11.
18 *The Pope in Australia*, St Paul's Publications, Homebush, NSW, 1986, p. 170.
19 *The Church and Racism: Towards a More Fraternal Society*, St Paul's Publications, Homebush, NSW, 1989, p. 19.
20 A.E. Woodward, *Aboriginal Land Rights Commission 2nd Report*, April 1974, p. 2.
21 See sections 50(1)(a) and 3, *Aboriginal Land Rights (Northern Territory) Act*, 1976.
22 'Traditional Aboriginal "owners" means in respect of an area of land, a local descent group of Aborigines who have common spiritual affiliations to a site or sites within that area of land, which affiliations place the group under a primary spiritual responsibility for that site or sites and for that land, and who are entitled by Aboriginal tradition to forage over that land.' Woodward, *Aboriginal Land Rights Commission 2nd Report*, April 1974, p. 162.
23 Aboriginal Land Rights Commission, Submission by the Northern Land Council, January 1974, p. 20.
24 Aboriginal Land Rights Commission, Submission by the Northern Land Council, January 1974, p. 21.
25 J. Toohey, *Seven Years On*, Australian Government Publishing Service (AGPS), Canberra, 1984, p. 38.
26 Toohey, *Seven Years On*, p. 39.
27 J. Toohey, *Daly River (Mulluk Mulluk) Land Claim*, AGPS, Canberra, 1982, p. 25.
28 Cited in Toohey, *Daly River (Mulluk Mulluk) Land Claim*, p. 27.
29 Toohey, *Daly River (Mulluk Mulluk) Land Claim*, p. 38.
30 P. Seaman, *The Aboriginal Land Inquiry*, Vol. 1, September 1984, para. 3.8, p. 24.

31 Seaman, *The Aboriginal Land Inquiry*, Vol. 1, para. 3.23, p. 30.
32 Seaman, *The Aboriginal Land Inquiry*, Vol. 1, para. 7.14, p. 115.
33 A.E. Woodward, *Australian Law Journal* 59 (1985), p. 420.
34 *Aboriginal Land Act*, 1991 (Qld), Section 4.09(1).
35 *Aboriginal Land Act*, 1991 (Qld), Section 2.03.
36 J.H. Wootten, *Significant Aboriginal Sites in Area of Proposed Junction Waterhole Dam, Alice Springs: Report to the Minister for Aboriginal Affairs*, 1992, p. 136.
37 Wootten, *Significant Aboriginal Sites in Area of Proposed Junction Waterhole Dam*, Alice Springs, p. 134.
38 I. Keen, 'Undermining Credibility', *Anthropology Today* 8 (1992), p. 8.
39 *Federal Law Reports* 17 (1970), p. 267.
40 *Eddie Mabo and others v The State of Queensland*, Deane and Gaudron JJ, *Australian Law Journal Reports (ALJR)* 656 (1992), p. 451.
41 *Queensland Parliamentary Debates* 287 (1982), p. 5172.
42 Brennan J (Mason CJ and McHugh J concurring), *ALJR* 66 (1992), p. 422.
43 Brennan J (Mason CJ and McHugh J concurring), *ALJR* 66 (1992), p. 422.
44 Deane and Gaudron JJ, *ALJR* 66 (1992), p. 452.
45 Toohey J, *ALJR* 66 (1992), p. 488.
46 *Commonwealth Parliamentary Debates*, House of Representatives, (1993), p. 2878, 16 November 1993.
47 Cited in S. Hawke and M. Gallagher, *Noonkanbah*, Fremantle Arts Centre Press, Fremantle, 1989, p. 193.
48 Stanner, *On Aboriginal Religion*, p. 56.
49 Royal Commission into Aboriginal Deaths in Custody, *National Report*, Vol. 5, AGPS, Canberra, 1991, p. 373
50 Royal Commission into Aboriginal Deaths in Custody, *National Report*, Vol. 5, p. 351.
51 Royal Commission into Aboriginal Deaths in Custody, *National Report*, Vol. 5, p. 355.
52 Royal Commission into Aboriginal Deaths in Custody, *National Report*, Vol. 5, p. 361.
53 Royal Commission into Aboriginal Deaths in Custody, *National Report*, Vol. 5, p. 311–2.
54 Royal Commission into Aboriginal Deaths in Custody, *Regional Report of Inquiry into Underlying Issues in Western Australia*, Vol. 2, AGPS, Canberra, 1991, p. 731.
55 Royal Commission into Aboriginal Deaths in Custody, *Regional Report of Inquiry into Underlying Issues in Western Australia*, Vol. 2, p. 761.
56 Royal Commission into Aboriginal Deaths in Custody, *Regional Report of Inquiry into Underlying Issues in Western Australia*, Vol. 2, p. 763.
57 A.M. Howard, 'The Land As Sacred', M.Theol. Thesis, Melbourne College of Divinity, 1990, p. 168.
58 *Australian Law Report* 141 (1996), p. 129.

CHAPTER NINE

# Malo's Law in Court: The Religious Background to the Mabo Case

*Nonie Sharp*

Throughout the Torres Strait Islands the people identify a vast constellation they call Tagai, after a mythical sea hero who set out on a journey with a twelve-man crew. The sky image is of Tagai standing in a canoe with his crew, Usiam (the Pleiades) and Seg (Orion); his left hand is the Southern Cross. 'Usiam time', when the Pleiades comes up, is a sign to the gardeners and the seafarers of the Murray Islands to prepare their garden plots and for their voyages north-westwards.

Tagai's left hand points to the endless repetition of sowings and harvestings among the cultivators of the Murray Islands. Tagai and other culture heroes of the Meriam people had given expression to a religious sensibility and forms of awareness from ancient times. For the Christians of the Murray Islands today the old beliefs give a foundation on which to build. In the words of Bernard O'Dowd in the poem 'Australia', these were 'the auguries that dare to plant the Cross upon your forehead sky'. The Southern Cross is the symbol of the Charles Strong Memorial Trust, for whom I offer this lecture.

## INTRODUCTION

When Edward Koiki Mabo was leaving his home on Mer Island in the Torres Strait in search of the knowledge European Australian culture had to offer, Sam Passi, one of the custodians of the Meriam cultural tradition, said to him: 'Whatever you do, Koiki, wherever you go, always remember [to] bring back that idea [you learn] to Murray Island'. Some twenty years later Koiki Mabo (as Meriam people and his friends called him) brought back such an idea for all Murray Island: he became the first plaintiff in the landmark case which was to bear his name. That was on 20 May 1982, the day the writ was issued on behalf of five Meriam plaintiffs.[1] This is how I like to think about Edward Koiki Mabo's contribution to the Murray Islanders' case. I shall argue that Passi's advice to Koiki Mabo is also symbolic of the religious grounding of the case.

Sadly, Koiki Mabo did not live to celebrate the Islanders' victory on 3 June 1992 when six of the seven judges of the High Court ruled that the Murray Islanders 'are entitled as against the whole world to possession, occupation, use and enjoyment of the island of Mer', except for lands leased to the Australian Board of Missions of the Anglican Church.[2]

On that day the Meriam people's claim to native title was recognised. The Murray Islanders, Justices Deane and Gaudron stated, undoubtedly possess 'a local native system under which established familial or individual rights of occupation and use were of a kind which far exceed the minimum requirements necessary to found a presumptive common law native title'.[3] The Meriam people also became the carriers of the rejection of the fiction of *terra nullius* in Australia as a whole. The Meriam people differ in 'culturally significant ways from the Aboriginal peoples of Australia', Justice Toohey noted, but for the purposes of determining indigenous interests in land throughout Australia as a whole, '[t]he relevant principles are the same'.[4]

In Meriam terms, in instructing the young Mabo, the older man was drawing upon the central principle of Meriam culture – that of giving and returning – expressed in one of the laws of the sacred order of the Meriam culture heroes, Malo-Bomai: that law of Malo (the public name of the two gods) which says, Malo plants everywhere, Malo *wali aritarit*. That particular law has a literal meaning: to the Meriam who are cultivators of the soil, it is an instruction to plant. But the instruction has a religious as well as an economic aspect. In saying the god Malo plants everywhere, that law is invoking a religious sanction with Malo as the exemplar through whom the act of planting is legitimated. It has also a material side: if you do not sow you will not eat; you and your family will not survive. As an instruction to the Murray Islanders of the three tiny volcanic islands which together comprise less than three square miles, who in pre-colonial times numbered some 700 persons, the advice was life-giving in a very practical sense.[5]

The instruction 'Malo sows everywhere' also has a metaphorical meaning, a layer of meaning which is very like the Biblical words, 'As ye sow, so also shall ye reap'. As Koiki Mabo set out on his journey seeking the knowledge of European-Australian society that had been largely denied him at the little 'native school' at Mer, the instruction was saying, give what you have to offer of Meriam culture, sow it down south in Kole or white man's soil and bring back the fruits to the Murray Islands. Sowing and harvesting has moved into another realm, the realm of knowledge, without losing its earthly meaning as cultivating and providing. Those who are familiar with Aboriginal or Melanesian religions will have no difficulty with the switch from the level of procuring a livelihood to another plane. Aboriginal religious thought, W.E.H. Stanner wrote long ago, is expressed in metaphor and simile.[6] But the metaphorical level intrinsic to Meriam thought was not accessible to significant members of the court (the defence counsel), and only minimally to the justice who heard evidence from witnesses over 67 days in the Supreme Court of Queensland and determined issues of fact for the High Court.[7]

Beneath this metaphorical language there exists a religiously grounded mode of being; a being which I shall argue is one in which 'living as a human being is in itself a religious act', in Mircea Eliade's words about Aboriginal people.[8] In the inquiry into issues of fact in the Murray Islanders' case (where fact refers to deeds, sayings or events determined by evidence), the religious character of Meriam life and the spiritual side of their relationship to their land was not perceived by the judge, Justice Moynihan. In acknowledging a major debt to Justice Blackburn in the case of *Milirrpum versus Nabalco*, the case brought by Yolngu clans and heard in the Supreme Court of the Northern Territory in 1970, Justice Moynihan emphasised what he saw as the 'very different relationships with and attitudes to land' among the Meriam.[9] In contrast to Yolngu Aboriginal people, the Meriam people's relationship and attitudes to their lands and adjoining sea property

> was and is not a religious or spiritual relationship of the kind which emerged, for example, in *Milirrpum v Nabalco*.[10]

To say this is to rob the Meriam of the fundamental truth about their culture and the way they see themselves. To deny their spiritual or religious relationship and attitudes to land is to divest them of their 'natural inheritance', of that 'body of patent truth about the universe', to use Professor Stanner's words in the inaugural Charles Strong lecture about Aboriginal people's unquestioned certainty that all living people are linked 'patrilineally with ancestral beings by inherent and imperishable bonds'.[11] *No* Meriam people would question such a proposition as applied to themselves.

In exploring the religious background to the Murray Islanders' land case, or *Mabo* as it is called in legal shorthand, I shall attempt to show how the Meriam came to be divested of their spiritual relationship with their land by Justice Moynihan. In examining the reasons for cutting off the Meriam from their religious inheritance I seek to instate (or reinstate) the full Meriam person and the *raison d'être* of Meriam culture; to locate Meriam ontology within a wholistic being which is at one and the same time spiritual and material, religious and economic.

This lecture on the religious background to the Mabo case consists of five stages. They are:

1 Malo's Law as it appeared in court from the perspectives of Meriam and European Australian witnesses;

2 the role of the Meriam culture heroes or gods Malo-Bomai in the identity of the Meriam (as diversities-in-unity);

3 the conversion of the Meriam to Christianity in relation to underlying cultural principles;

4 an exploration of the misunderstanding and misperceptions of Meriam religiosity and their reasons;

5 a reinstatement of Meriam being in its full stature.

In a concluding discussion I seek to show the utmost importance of an understanding of the wellsprings of Malo's Law for the cultural ensemble of the Meriam people – the restoration of the full stature of the Meriam people – for projects concerned with inter-cultural relations and reconstruction. I argue that that 'other' category of law termed native or traditional title,[12] has as much or as little meaning and quality as the community which 'possesses' it makes possible.

## MALO'S LAW IN COURT

In their statement of claim five Meriam plaintiffs claimed land, foreshore and reef flats at the three islands of Mer, Dauar and Waier at the northern end of the Great Barrier Reef. They were named Murray's Islands by Captain Edwards of the vessel *Pandora* a few days before the ship was wrecked on the reef on 28 August 1791. The claims were brought 'on their own and on behalf of the members of their family groups': those of Mabo, Passi and Rice.[13] Although the size of the family group or lineage varied as between the plaintiffs,[14] the basic principles of land ownership are the same: the eldest male is landholder (*lu kem le*) for land inherited patrilineally *on behalf* of a lineage or family; the younger brothers and unmarried sisters are joint owners or *ged kem le* in Meriam language. Allotments of residential land claimed lie within villages formed within the geographical setting of eight clan territories on the rim of the islands along the sandbeaches, which are themselves part of clan territories; plots of garden and plantation land, owned by either women or men, are found in the interior of the islands; they may be as small as 900 square feet. Together they form a patchwork of numerous allotments which, along with rock formations, cover the entire islands: there is no unowned land, or any concept of 'vacant' land. As slash-and-burn horticulturalists, the Meriam fallow their garden plots. All these allotments have boundaries, the oldest of which are mounds of earth formed out of rotted vegetable matter, shell and bone (*daip*). Imaginary lines also join boundary markers (*nener*) which are natural topographical features, stones or shells, or sometimes today, concrete markers.

Each plaintiff spoke about his own land, and when pressed, about land of his close relative or adjoining neighbour, and nothing more. The plaintiffs and many of the Meriam witnesses said explicitly, in our law we don't speak for someone else: 'My place only there [on Komet clan land]'.[15] They were not claiming land collectively on behalf of the whole island; but each person spoke about his land knowing that the principles he was expressing were repeated across the island. The plaintiffs and the 24 Meriam witnesses called by the plaintiffs explained to the court the details of their land, how they came to know about it and its boundaries, how it was passed down to them. The connection between each claimant (speaking only for his own property) and the whole community was explained to the court by plaintiff James Rice: 'I can picture the whole of Murray Island speaking about the same thing as I do here'.[16]

Those principles were identified by the plaintiffs and many witnesses as Malo's Law or *Malo ra Gelar* in Meriam language. Its watchword is 'Hands off!' as plaintiff James Rice said. *Malo tag mauki mauki, Teter mauki mauki* are two tenets of Malo's Law which became everyday words in court. Again and again Meriam witnesses explained these rules against trespass – keeping quietly to one's own path, to one's own land – as a set of principles they felt bound to follow. 'Who told you Malo's Law?' Reverend Dave Passi was asked by counsel. 'I was brought up with it. It is the general knowledge in Murray Island', he replied.[17] As another witness implied, that practice is deeply cultural, what one might call the common sense of the Meriam: 'Well, it is sort of built in us', another witness explained.[18]

That 'common sense' was made explicit by the plaintiffs in court. In their written statements or 'proofs of evidence' requested by the court, they listed the various laws which made up Malo's Law. Most of them began with *Malo tag mauki mauki*, but the number of laws they listed varied – James Rice listed 24 laws, Sam Passi listed seven. All of them included the law against trespass, keeping to one's secret ways, planting everywhere, letting unneeded fruit drop on the ground. Most of them gave the law, 'Stars follow their own path . . .', a law about land tenure and succession, as well as a law against trespass.

Malo's Law is part of Meriam oral tradition; it is a law told to children in its social context as a *lived* law: it is woven into the fabric of everyday life – built into people, as the witness I have mentioned put it. On 23 January 1962 a leading cultural and political Meriam figure, Marou Mimi, wrote down thirteen laws of Malo in Meriam language and in English in his diary,[19] and in 1970 Margaret Lawrie published Malo's Law in a collection of myths and legends of the Torres Strait Islands.[20]

Much of the time of the court was taken up with questions concerning the way in which what witnesses were calling Malo's Laws (of respecting other people's property) were today merely the manifestation of the teachings of the Old and New Testaments to which the Meriam people had been exposed since 1872; or the 'common sense' associated with rules against trespass in English law. The main defendant, the State of Queensland, had contended that the activities of missionaries, pearlers and governments had totally and irrevocably altered the way of life of the Meriam people.[21] The defendant had called several Meriam witnesses: one of them claimed that he had first heard Malo's Law in the late 1930s when Marou Mimi placed a taboo on a garden (a Meriam conservation practice). He did not hear it said again until nearly 30 years later when Margaret Lawrie had it written down for inclusion in a book.[22] Nevertheless, this witness told the court that the 'basic principles of proper conduct' continue to be followed among the Meriam, especially those relating to trespass.[23]

This position concurs with the basic claim made by most of the Meriam; the plaintiffs had built their case around the continuity of fundamental principles rather than outward signs. The way in which most senior Meriam people retain a fidelity to certain basic cultural principles while at the same time professing Christian beliefs is, I believe, expressive of a process noted by Deborah Rose among Aboriginal peoples:

> Most Aboriginal religions are extraordinarily open to accommodating new events and ideas . . . any numbers of permutations, additions, and accommodations are possible as long as the underlying principles are not challenged.[24]

Both Margaret Lawrie, a witness for the defendant, and Jeremy Beckett, an anthropologist called by the plaintiffs who had carried out fieldwork at the Murray Islands between 1958 and 1961, reaffirmed the Meriam witnesses' statements about the continuity of principles of land ownership (the 'golden rule against trespass', as Lawrie called it, about pride in ownership[25]), and in particular, the way in which all Meriam people today feel bound by certain rules of behaviour with respect to land. Dr Beckett recalled being scolded by his Meriam host and made to apologise to the owner of a garden he had walked into uninvited.[26]

## MALO AND MERIAM IDENTITY

The Meriam of the Murray Islands were an especially cohesive group in pre-colonial times. Following his visit to Mer in 1898, Dr Haddon, who led an anthropological expedition from the University of Cambridge, wondered what other grouping living in an area of no more than one and a half square miles in size 'can exhibit such rich variety' in their lives. They enjoyed:

> an active economic life filled with a great variety of small individual and large collective rites . . . The spirit pantomimes emphasised the continuation of life after death. The spirits of their forbears . . . cooperated with the living in promoting present well-being. Finally, all the islanders were embraced within a powerful, awe-inspiring cult which gave them a new feeling of nationality and induced an increased zest for life.[27]

That 'cult', as Haddon called it, was the sacred order of Malo-Bomai, a fraternity which brought together the eight clans of the Meriam in one social body, an identity as one people. In the words of Sam Passi, a descendant of the priests or *Zogo le* of Malo-Bomai, Mer became a centre of exchange of produce and other things; the Meriam also voyaged to show the flag, letting it be known that 'this is our land'.[28]

The identity received its sacred endowment through the myth of Malo-Bomai which consists of two associated narratives. The first recounts the coming of Bomai from Tuger in West Irian. He swam to Boigu Island in the form of a whale, then from island to island in the shapes of different sea creatures, being recognised as a *zogo* or sacred being at each island until he arrived in the form of an octopus at the village of Teker, where Kabur was fishing on the reef. Recognising it as a *zogo* she took the octopus home and gave it to her husband, Dog.

> They hung the basket in the house where that night they saw its two eyes shining like stars. The basket with Bomai was stolen by Dog's two brothers-in-law from Las. Then the people of Las visited Dog and they all sat and smoked *zeub*, the pipe of peace. And Dog and his wife said, 'All right, you keep Bomai here'. So they left the *zogo* there with the people of Las and the trees everywhere became painted with red ochre.

The second narrative is about the coming of Malo.

> Malo, a man with a shark's head, came with four brothers to find his uncle, Bomai, to increase his canoe-party in the central islands. '*Bab nade*? Where is *Bab* [father]?' Some of Malo's party speared him in the back and gave the drums they brought to the local people saying: 'These are the dances you are going to perform'. Then Malo was brought and added on to the original *agud*, Bomai'.[29]

The descendants of the seven brothers of Las who kept Bomai are the Shark brethren of Malo, the dancers of the Malo-Bomai ceremonies. From them are drawn the *Zogo le* or priests of Malo who are entitled to wear the masks of Malo and Bomai. Bomai is the sacred and secret name of Malo, known in past times only by the initiated. At the three-year Malo rites the Shark brethren or *Beizam boai* performed the five dances of Malo at which sacred chants were sung. The fifth and most sacred was for the *seuriseuri*, the star-headed stone club of Malo. In that dance the *seuriseuri* was passed from one dancer to the next: the meaning, Dave Passi explained to me, was that the authority of Malo must continue.[30] The Malo-Bomai order was not a hereditary government, although many Meriam believe it was, including the plaintiff E.K. Mabo.[31]

The myth valorised the land tenure system of the Meriam:

- through the octopus, it united the eight clans, each with its own totem;

- through the long sea journeys, it drew upon the strength of *beizam* to transcend the profane danger of the 'other side' in dangerous sea voyages from Mer in the east to Saibai and the New Guinea coast in the west;
- it raised the possibility of a life after death, a resurrection of mortals (*le*) as *lamar* (spirits of the dead) in the land of immortals, an island known as Boigu in the direction of the setting sun.[32]

Malo-Bomai had a point of origin or sacred centre at the village of Las on the eastern side of Mer Island. At this site the Meriam built the circular sacred house (known as *pelak*) at which the masks were kept. In a semi-circle in front of the sacred house the Malo rites were performed. In the Malo period (which Meriam people today say is not very old, perhaps several hundred years) the sacred centre or cradle of the Meriam identity was known as *mamgiz*, which literally means springs or origin of (common) blood: a symbol of the Meriam as one people.

Malo gave the Meriam a code or law by which to live – a moral order distilled in *Malo ra Gelar*. In the oral tradition this law has many versions each with a common core, as I have described.

Members of the hereditary priesthood were custodians of Malo's teachings, as well as of the sacred masks – the tangible symbols of Malo, the five *seuriseuri* (star-headed clubs) and the *wasikor* (Malo's drum). Where was Malo-Bomai pointing? Dr Haddon had asked himself this very significant question at the end of the nineteenth century. 'I am afraid we are never likely to know', he answered.[33] For when he arrived there with his team of scientists from Cambridge, the missionaries of the London Missionary Society had had the sacred houses burned, and the masks had disappeared. At Haddon's request the Meriam had, with visible reticence, made cardboard masks and the rites were re-enacted.[34] They refused to part with the five *seuriseuri*. Nevertheless, Dr Haddon managed with the help particularly of Jack Bruce, the government teacher, to establish at Cambridge University 'the most complete and fully documented' collection of artefacts 'of any made among native peoples in any part of the world'.[35]

When plaintiff Reverend Dave Passi was asked by defence counsel about the sacred burial site of the mask of Malo, he replied firmly, 'I said, precisely I will not point out where Malo was buried'.[36] In the 67 days of the hearing of Meriam and other witnesses, which included also the arguments put by respective counsel (3,489 pages of transcript), scarcely a word about the Malo religion I have just outlined was heard.

Justice Moynihan regretted that little of pre-contact Meriam society was described by expert or other witnesses.[37] When the opportunity arose to hear a Meriam witness put before the court the 'Malo Law story' or myth of Malo (which that witness's father, Marou Mimi, had recorded in his diary on 16 January 1959), Justice Moynihan said that its 'anthropological importance' is unquestioned, but 'it's of absolutely marginal relevance here, isn't it?'[38] The context and rationale of that statement becomes at least partly comprehensible through an understanding of the Christian era in the Murray Islands, to which I now turn.

## THE MERIAM IN THE CHRISTIAN ERA

When the Haddon party arrived at Meriam in 1898, virtually all the Meriam were professed Christians – according to oral tradition, only one man refused to give up the old religion. The relevance of the religious sensibilities of the custodians of the Malo tradition to this conversion was discerned by Haddon among the newly-won Christians he met: 'the most moral and pious heathen', men with a developed sense 'of the sacredness of religious customs', as he called them, 'are the most likely to be attracted by a higher form of . . . religion'.[39] In his view the priests or *Zogo le* of Malo were not vacant vessels waiting to be filled by the new religion: their own sense of sacredness made them receptive candidates for that which extended and went beyond their own teachings – a religiosity distilled in Malo was a foundation on which to accept a new message. Plaintiff Reverend Dave Passi sees the relationship between Malo and Christianity in very specific terms: 'Jesus Christ is where Malo was pointing', he believes, answering inadvertently a question asked by Haddon. 'The Anglican Church is the fulfilment of Malo', his grandfather had said: 'Here is something of the complexity, the mystery that Malo expressed'.[40] This 'fulfilment' does not mean however, the relinquishing of the Malo tradition. The contrary is the case. Again, Haddon pointed towards this truth when he noted how the most religious of the Meriam 'would not be disposed to treat lightly what had meant so much to them'.[41]

Nor, according to oral tradition, did they. Between 1982 and 1984, Sam Passi, the oldest living male descendant of the line of *Zogo le* of Malo and a deacon of the Anglican Church, explained for me how 'Christianity was accepted so quickly because of Malo-Bomai'; 'From Malo-Bomai to Christianity – mental telepathy':

> You just imagine. Grandfather was a high priest of Malo-Bomai. His second son became one of the first Island priests . . . I appreciate such rules [Malo's Law] from Malo-Bomai. Once you learnt that you can just manage to do something that is written in the New Testament.[42]

He also explained how he, as a descendant of the *Zogo le*, sought to preserve Malo's Law, which his grandfather had taught him before his departure from Mer in 1931 to teach in the Western Islands of Torres Strait. He said to him: 'Go through the law of Malo-Bomai. If you go through them you will know how to go about in this life'. It was he who awakened him to *Malo wali aritarit* as being the seed of the New Testament message: sow the seeds of your knowledge in other places.[43]

When Reverend Canon John Done arrived in the Torres Strait as an Anglican missionary early in 1915, the year the Anglican Church took over from the London Missionary Society (LMS), he visited all the islands and reported his experiences in his diary. 'The people are religious in every sense', he wrote, 'there's a wonderful harvest only waiting and willing to be gathered'.[44] They went over 'without a murmur', Jack Bruce, the school teacher, reported from Mer to the bishop.[45] Within a few years Meriam and other Torres Strait Islander priests were ordained, including Reverend Poi Passi. Reverend Done allowed them to revive the Malo-Bomai dances banned by the LMS. Nothing in his diary would suggest he saw their religious significance for the Meriam. But Sam Passi recalled the old men crying and their joy at their new chant for the *seuriseuri* which 'signifies the life that is handed down from the previous generation to the present one'.[46] The next generation equated important symbols in Anglican and Malo-Bomai rites. They saw in Anglicanism much of the mystery and ritual of Malo; ineffable truth within the Eucharist and a total reverence in the moment of wearing the mask. 'God's People-Line' was present too in the Malo tradition: 'the heritage was passed on all the time . . . but it was more hereditarily grounded'.[47]

## WITHOUT A RELIGIOUS INHERITANCE?

Reverend Dave Passi began his written evidence with the words, 'God sent Malo to Murray Island . . .' The senior defence counsel complained that his proof of evidence was 'a theological notion' reading 'a little more like a sermon' than a statement prepared for a court, and not 'acceptable as evidence'.[48] Passi went on to restate a theological position which he had begun to develop in 1976, a time of cultural revival in colonial outposts. In a sermon he preached in Cairns to commemorate the coming of Christianity to the Torres Strait on 1 July 1871, he compared the two cultures in the light of Christian universalism. 'It came to me very strongly', he told me in 1980. In that moment of insight he saw the two-sidedness of *both* cultures: one brings Christianity and kills with bombs; his own creates the uniqueness of diversities-in-unity through giving and returning, and *at the same time* kills through club, knife and sorcery. Out of this comparison he saw 'the greatness of Malo' – through the symbol of the octopus, Malo brought the feuding Meriam clans together, and Malo's Law taught people to conserve the land. The law was a moral code of respect for the property of one another, a law of cultivation and creativity (Malo plants everywhere). The truth, Passi said, is not easy to cross out, as every Christian knows; Malo survived despite the first wave of missionaries because 'Jesus Christ is where Malo was pointing'. In Malo worship the *zogo* or spiritual power was passed on in the sacred chants, the words, the actions. 'I do not see me infusing Malo into Christianity. I see Christianity as the fulfilment of Malo. Malo came to prepare Murray Island for Christianity and it makes me very proud as a *Zogo le* to see Malo playing that role.'[49]

When Reverend Passi, E.K. Mabo, James Rice and most Meriam witnesses explained to the court what they saw as the positive side of the Malo tradition, they were speaking not only of the way they related to land; they were also grappling with the centre of Meriam identity, what sort of people they are and wish to be in the future. 'Real' Murray Islanders follow Malo's Law, they were saying.

Justice Moynihan was not impressed with the syntheses and theological 'notions' developed by Reverend Passi. Describing him as an 'essentially honest witness', he saw his ideas as 'idiosyncratic', although 'no doubt he is persuaded by the truth of his vision'.[50] He did not reserve the same judgment for E.K. Mabo.[51] Although Reverend Passi had stated that in pre-Christian times, '*gabba gabba* [the stone club] was the justice' meted out by his ancestors towards those who trespassed on the Passi lagoon at Waier Island,[52] the judge saw Reverend Passi, E.K. Mabo and some of the witnesses as selectively choosing what they saw 'as desirable "traditional Meriam" values' in their romanticised version of the Malo tradition;[53] their syntheses were flawed by their selection of features acceptable to themselves and the wider community. Justice Moynihan's own perception of pre-Christian Meriam society was of one 'ruled' entirely by the club; without chiefs, constables or court, a state of anarchy reigned in which the 'best brawler won' – 'for God's sake don't start an all-in brawl with the next village'. He did not see that they were intentionally seeking to draw upon the positive side of the principles of Meriam culture: the life-enhancing side of reciprocity which, as I shall consider later, created the uniqueness and depth of Meriam culture.

For the Meriam who saw a correspondence between Malo's Law and the Old Testament, and for those who saw Christianity as offering a progression from the diversity-in-unity of the eight clans and the 'shell friends' created by Malo,[54] to the 'love everyone' message of universal brotherhood, Malo's Law received *increased* strength.

The context of the inquiry was the argument of the defendant that the way of life of the Meriam had been fundamentally destroyed; any significant relationships and meanings of the past had been severed. For reasons which will now be clear, to all intents and purposes, Meriam society today looks very un-Malo-like; its major religious rituals, its symbols, look exclusively Christian. The Meriam witnesses all said they followed certain principles or rules of conduct and many of them identified these as Malo's Law; they also looked like Old Testament and New Testament law, and in major respects like English law. Under these circumstances, when Sam Passi said, 'They're good laws; they have nothing to do with English law. If you want to be a real Murray Islander, you follow Malo's Law',[55] he was not able to produce evidence convincing to the judge. Given the change in outward signs and the capacity of European perspectives to mistake outward signs for underlying realities, counsel for the plaintiffs did not pursue the reasons why Meriam witnesses felt bound to follow certain stated principles or rules.[56]

There are four broad aspects of the process by which the judge divested the Meriam of their spiritual relationship to land and of the religious legitimation of the total ensemble of their social relationships and meaning systems:

1. their land tenure system was presented to the court in a form which resembled English property rights;
2. Meriam law was built into a *lived social practice* and taken for granted by Meriam people and therefore not open to question;
3. the language of metaphor embodied in mythical legitimations was incompatible with the literal and either/or categories of legal logic;
4. the continuities-in-change which form the idiom of cultural renewal are a recent phenomenon among the Meriam.

Each one of these has several facets to which I cannot do full justice here; but I shall do the best I can and refer those who wish to inquire further to a fuller work.[57]

The first broad area is that the rights claimed by the plaintiffs were, in the court's terms, individual or 'private' rather than communal or public rights. The Meriam claims were accompanied by a clear 'hands off' attitude that made them recognisably private 'property-ish' to an English court: 'What belongs to me is mine, I own it'.[58] It's mine. No doubt about it! Unlike the Yolngu clans of Yirrkala on the Gove Peninsula, they were not claiming communal (native) title, a claim which, as we all know, was rejected by Justice Blackburn on the grounds that communal native title does not exist within the common law.[59] (Serendipitously for the Meriam, the majority of the High Court ruled that common law communal native title exists in [most of] the Murray Islands.) In claiming property on behalf of their families or lineages, the Meriam plaintiffs produced evidence of boundaries to the court, both on paper and in the 'view' (to use the court's word when the Supreme Court of Queensland sat at Mer). They prepared chains of title to allotments showing inheritance of the plots reaching back into the period before annexation, and in some instances written wills were produced. Unlike the Yolngu plaintiffs they could not produce ritual objects of spiritual significance which the Aboriginal plaintiffs had identified in court as their 'title deeds' to lands claimed.[60]

The second area concerns the consequences for the court that Meriam law as a *lived* law is taken for granted by most Meriam; it is a 'system of rules of conduct which is felt as obligatory by the members of a definable group of persons', to use the definition of law given by Justice Blackburn in recognising a system of law among the Yolngu in the *Milirrpum* case.[61] 'It's sort of built in us', 'I was brought up with it', 'it's the cultural way', said the Meriam. They are 'born to it, yes', said Margaret Lawrie of the indissoluble links of the Meriam with their land. There is 'one Golden Rule': respect other people's property.[62] Trespassing is something no Meriam would do, said anthropologist Jeremy Beckett, recalling his early minor transgression of the law.[63]

Thirdly, however similar the Meriam interests in land may have looked on the surface, these interests are embedded in religious legitimations which are manifest outwardly in ways which may appear prosaic and profane. I shall take one example of this 'hiddenness' of sacred meanings. Myths and the moral codes that come from them are usually framed in the language of the everyday; the deeper meaning lies beneath. The myth of Meidu cited in court, which one writer used to denote the 'cultural pride' of the Meriam, says, 'though your people eat from sunrise to sunset, they cannot eat all the feed you provide'. Although this writer sensed that she was stepping on ground vital to the Meriam, she did not see it as a sacred text.[64] The myth of Malo-Bomai says nothing about rights to land or sea; yet the journeys of the culture heroes across Torres Strait from west to east and their creation of a sacred centre at Las on the eastern side of the Mer is a statement about the sacred character of land tenure. In court the language of metaphor was mistaken for a literal statement: *Malo tag mauki mauki* doesn't say the land is handed to the eldest son, senior defence counsel complained. Nor, in a literal sense, does it.

A fourth way in which the Meriam were divested by the court of the religious grounding and the spiritual side of their relationship to land has its context in the non-linear changes in Meriam culture, its waning and waxing over the period of colonisation and decolonisation; in relation to sea property Dr Johannes, a marine biologist called by the plaintiffs, saw 'a reawakening cultural pride' among the Meriam comparable to that he had observed in Pacific islands.[65]

By the time Jeremy Beckett, the first anthropologist to follow the Haddon team, undertook field work at Mer between 1958–1961 (a gap of 60 years), the culture had waned. As Beckett reflected a quarter of a century later, the 'centre of gravity' of his study lay in the transitional period when the tide was about to turn on the 'old colonial regime'.[66] Looking back in 1994 on the syntheses made by cultural leaders such as Reverend Dave Passi, he notes that the apparent absence of the idea of Malo as precursor of Christianity among the Meriam in 1961 does not preclude the possibility 'that its seeds were there, waiting for a more liberal climate such as the 1980s offered'.[67] In the years between 1978 and 1983 those who took on the responsibilities of custodians of Meriam culture were expressing exactly the same principles in relation to the Malo tradition as they did in court. They could have been mistaken for a different people to those whom Beckett had written about in 1963.[68] In the period in which the case began and proceeded, the doldrums of spiritual weariness and lack of confidence were disappearing.[69]

Sadly, the perceptions Beckett brought to the court did not discern that such seeds were sown deeply among the Meriam. He seems to be unaware of the power of a religious cult (in this case Malo-Bomai) to expand an older totemic culture.[70] The apparent absence of an integrative institution helped create Justice Moynihan's picture of pre-colonial Meriam society as a one-sided 'tribal anarchy' where 'disputes are resolved by having a brawl or avoiding a brawl'.[71] His Honour acknowledges a debt to the evidence given by Dr Beckett on the motif of pre-colonial Meriam life as a competition for resources 'in a potentially volatile social environment'.[72] This may ignore the two sidedness in pre-colonial Meriam society and lead to a picture of a rough and ready 'primitive secularism'.[73]

## THE STRENGTH OF THE MERIAM

The argument of this lecture has been that Meriam social life is legitimated religiously, and that if one fails to see a continuity of underlying principles from the time of Malo into the Christian era one may take from Meriam people a religious sensibility which pervades every aspect of their lives. Their relationship to land is both an expression of this and at the same time its ongoing confirmation. I am arguing that far from destroying the well-springs of Meriam culture, and notwithstanding that Christian missionaries destroyed the Malo-Bomai order as an institution, the richness and uniqueness of Meriam culture today and its strength to endure arise from the cumulation of the structures and meaning systems of the past. I shall illustrate this through the examples of plaintiff James Rice and witness Gobedar Noah; both are professed Christians active in their respective churches (there are five churches on tiny Mer Island) and Mr Noah, who has lived in Townsville for some twenty years, is a Christian pastor.

When James Rice was confronted by the defendant's senior counsel in court he drew strength from his totem *dabor*, a great warrior fish with sharp teeth.[74] After giving his evidence he talked freely; sitting on his own land he reflected upon the significance for him of the naming sequence of his genealogy:

> This area, this land is ours. Our ancestors were living here. There were no white people here . . . I know my boundaries; I know my areas. I can name them where the ancestors been naming all these places. These are not any white people's names . . . I say Bazmet – this is my ancestor's name. And this land belongs to my ancestors.[75]

He is pointing to a sacred endowment, in this case a garden plot which was his 'grandma's wedding present',[76] to a cultural pride which is multiply valorised: through totemic ancestors, through Malo and the Law, and reconfirmed by Christianity. Very importantly, and in

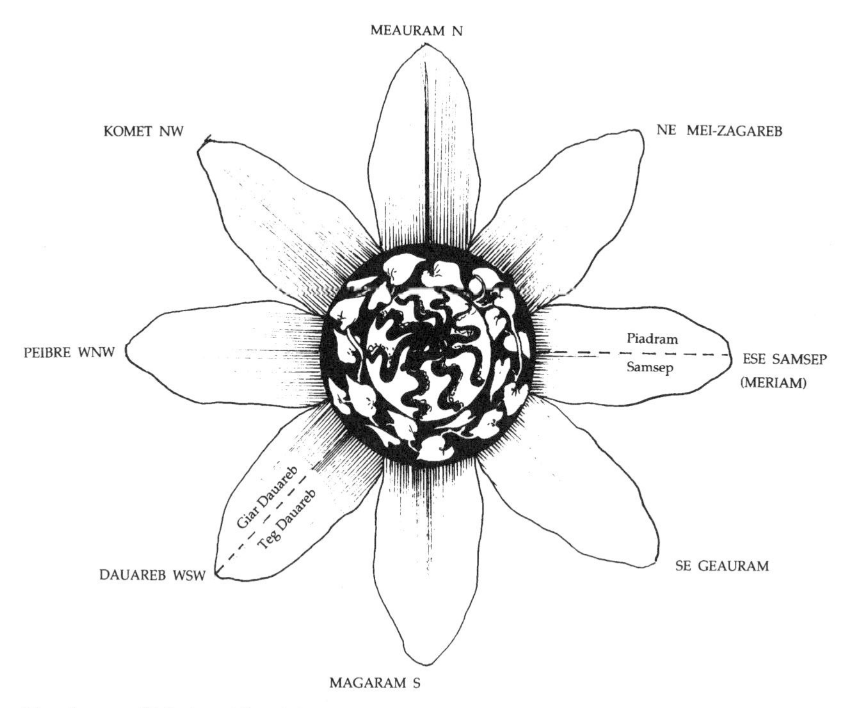


The flower of Meriam identities.

contrast to the conclusions of successive anthropologists,[77] far from effacing the prior deity, contemporary Meriam meaning systems are built out of and derive their strength from the substratum of religious truths which 'succeeded' one another. Meriam identity and belief is layered; the diversities-in-unities about which Reverend Dave Passi speaks are the cultural motif of the Meriam. Elsewhere I have depicted the cultural ensemble of Meriam identity in graphic form.[78] The image shown here is the flower of Meriam identities.

Its strength has other dimensions integral with land: totems or *lubabat*, the wind that blows in their particular quarter (or eighth), the waxing or waning phases of stars. So the waning phase of Venus as the Evening Star (*Kek*) belongs to a nameholder in Komet, a clan facing north-west; Komet wind or season is north-west. Mr Depoma, a man who challenged Koiki Mabo's land boundaries at Sebeg village (Komet territory), has Komet totems of sardine and others. He also has his mother's totems: 'When I see the tern, it makes me cry because I am thinking of my mother'. Reverend Passi's totems are frigate bird and turtle; in the time of the south-west season where his land at Dauar is situated (west-south-west) the wind 'blows' the frigate bird, a bird which soars high and swoops down on its prey. Reverend Passi and his family assure me that this behaviour is consistent with that of his ancestor Koit Number One, the oldest male descendant of the seven brothers of Las who kept Bomai, a *Zogo le* or priest of Malo, who went to conquer Dauar Island. That does not stop Reverend Passi saying with Christ, 'Love everyone', nor his grandfather saying to the nineteen-year-old eldest brother Sam as he left Mer, 'Look at my hands, the hands of love'.[79]

'Comes from', whether land or totem or wind or star, denotes a tie to sacred ancestors; so people speak of all these with joy and reverence. For these two words signify an indissoluble tie with the past, and in consequence, a responsibility which often seems to dissolve any distinction between past, present and future. The Meriam explained in court how they came to know their land: 'Father said then at Dauar, "This is our boundaries, this is our land, this is our reef". Grandpa used to tell the whole story, come back and tell the whole story again'.[80] 'My dad told me', said Mr Noah, '"If I am gone, you have every right and all the responsibility for my land as my eldest son". I own it as willed by my father', he said of his land.[81] That right to land is a sacred right. In Meriam tradition spoken words create an indissoluble tie between one generation and the next. Even in the era of written wills, which encompassed the Meriam in statutory form in 1965,[82] words still carry the greater authority. The authority of the words of the man who comes first (father) as they *pass over* to the son who comes 'behind', embodies a transcendence; it is a joining relationship of a primordial kind. When Gobedar Noah says, 'In Meriam ways, white man say verbally, if it is passed on by words it is sealed',[83] he is invoking a sacred trust, something akin to 'plighting a troth' in European tradition. In passing over every right with all the responsibility, the father is speaking from the heart of a reciprocal system of rights and responsibilities. To own is a right; covalent with it is the obligation to share its resources with others associated in that right. The undetachability of rights and responsibilities is reflected in language: in court this witness said, 'I can order someone to get out of my land, no doubt at all' because of my responsibility (as well as my right) to it.[84] The naming process handed down by forebears exerts a moral force on each generation, the responsibility to respond to the land, as Nancy Williams has noted about Yolngu people.[85] Meriam rights to lands claimed – the sphere of ownership in English law – were determined as fact in respect to some lands claimed by two of the three plaintiffs.[86] The responsibility side, encompassing the spiritual aspect referred to by Justice Blackburn as 'belonging to the land' and taken by him to be non-proprietary,[87] was not recognised as fact among the Meriam. Yet the very right to say 'hands off' is part of the Meriam 'way' of 'following in the footsteps'; whether this is expressed through the naming process of lands trod by the feet of ancestors and invested with their spirits or whether the more abstract and metaphorical form of Malo's Law – 'stars follow their own course' – is invoked, there is an awareness of a 'people-line' which gives a transcendence to relationships with land, to other humans and to all living things.

The Meriam are positioned spatially in relation to one another through their ownership of land; spatial location is primary for the Meriam cultivators – the same word *ged* is used for the uterine 'home-land' of an unborn infant and for land. They are also positioned in relation to natural cycles (I have called this 'cosmic positioning').[88] The complementary obligation that accompanies the right to be on lands 'betrothed' and bequeathed is an obligation to look after the land – habitat is perhaps the right word. As I have said, each aspect carries its own sacred significance. *Eburlem es maolem*, Malo's commandment to conserve, is an injunction to nurture what English speakers call the environment: it is 'natural' for the Meriam to 'read nature' as a book, as Sam Passi says. Frankfort and others refer to this kind of relationship with nature as an I-Thou one, where Thou is a living creature, not an it. Theirs is an elegant exposition of reciprocal confrontation, in the mode of the face-to-face, the personal rather than abstract mode, of the you-to-me:[89]

> Any phenomenon may at any time face him, not as 'It', but as Thou'. In this confrontation, Thou' reveals its individuality, its qualities, its will. 'Thou' is not contemplated with intellectual detachment; it is experienced as life confronting life, involving every faculty of man in a reciprocal relationship. Thoughts, no less than acts and feelings, are subordinated to this experience.[90]

The watchword is discernment in the process of life confronting life. When Malo came, the possibilities of that life were enhanced; the culture heroes gave the Meriam a sacred centre, a cradle of civilisation at Las.[91] That space and the *Zogo le* of Malo had their origins on the eastern side of Mer. If the Malo religion brought the possibility of a transcendence of death, like other Melanesian religions it also led people back into this world, not away from it in the contemplative style.[92] Again, Deborah Rose's insights into the way in which Yarralin Aboriginal people 'do not see a barrier between themselves and the cosmos' are evocative of the Meriam:

> Where mysticism in the great traditions leads people out of this world and towards a transcendent experience of unity beyond, Aboriginal religion leads people into this world and toward an immanent experience of unity in the here and now.[93]

This returns us to 'Malo sows everywhere', Malo providing the example to sow, to exchange with others and to harvest in an ongoing cycle of reciprocities. You will recall that this message given to the young Sam Passi by his grandfather was 'Stand firm on Malo Law' – yes, go to far away (Western) islands and offer them our message; and Sam's advice to the young Mabo as he set off on what turned out to be a long, singular and fateful journey. Those messages embodied the terms and the spirit of giving and returning, that is, of reciprocal exchange. Koiki Mabo learnt what the *Kole* (white man's) culture had to offer; he met moral Europeans with whom he could exchange. Of the two he mentioned by name to me in 1980, each played a significant role in the case: one was an organiser of the conference in 1981 at which plans for the case crystallised; important insights from the historical research of the other were relied on by High Court justices in the difficult process of regaining the integrity of the common law.[94] It is this process of reciprocity, which still remains the central motif of Meriam society (although highly endangered), that strikes a chord of responsiveness among (some) European Australians: an exchange of what each has to offer – cultural differences – among equals. Once again, Deborah Rose's conclusions about Aboriginal people she worked with in the Northern Territory are discerning of a logic of dialogue characteristic of Meriam people:

> Founded in the belief that Law is everywhere, people hope that others will recognise the key events and find their own strong stories which, as they implement them in their own lives and places, will answer back in affirmation.[95]

As I have argued in a larger work,[96] it is the positive side of the principle of reciprocity so central to Meriam society, today in real danger of being lost to the Meriam, which is resonant with the principles which lie at the centre of a capacity for moral behaviour among (some) European

Australians, a type of reciprocal relation which Koiki Mabo was seeking: the search for the 'moral European' who would act reciprocally on equal terms, which Kenelm Burridge noted in a colonial millenarian myth among Tangu of New Guinea.[97]

## A SECOND CATEGORY OF LAW IN AUSTRALIA

In this lecture I have given the religious background and foundation to Malo's Law in court and its espousal and elaboration by the Meriam as an expression of a religiously grounded and religiously meaningful society. The Meriam tried to convey the moral basis of their society. The presiding judge was not able to appreciate the religious nature of their social life, the spiritual side of their ties to land and sea.

However, in a much broader sense the High Court recognised interests in land 'of a kind unknown to English law', the words of Lord Denning speaking for the Privy Council in the case of *Adeyinka Oyekan v Musendiku Adele* (1957).[98] In the judgment known as *Mabo (No 1)* of 8 December 1988, the majority ruled that traditional rights in land, assumed to exist for the purposes of the legal argument at that stage, were both different from and broadly equivalent to rights to English law enjoyed by other Australian citizens; to deprive the traditional owners of those rights would contravene s10(1) of the Racial Discrimination Act,[99] thus recognising for the first time in Australia the possibility of two categories of law. On 3 June 1992 the High Court addressed this issue further. In speaking to the question identified by Justices Deane and Gaudron as a 'moral claim to nationhood',[100] the majority identified that second category of law as 'communal native title' (a category which Justice Blackburn had ruled did not exist in the common law).[101] Justice Brennan defined native title as 'the interests and rights of indigenous inhabitants in land' which may be 'communal, group or individual' and whose nature and incidents are given by 'the traditional laws acknowledged by . . . the indigenous inhabitants'.[102] Malo's Law was not identified as a matter of fact by Justice Moynihan; however, the existence of a 'native system of law' was taken to exist by the High Court majority. What that means for Meriam, or Yolngu or Yarralin people (to take the two Aboriginal groupings I have been referring to), will be as strong (or as minimal) as the strength of the stories they have to offer. The practical context includes new as well as old moves back towards *terra nullius*. Powerful currents are moving to undermine those forms of relationship to land which Reverend Passi and other custodians of Meriam traditions identify as the sacred endowment of their 'natural inheritance'. He told senior defence counsel in court:

> I am born into the ownership of this land. It is against our traditional law that we sell the land . . . that is trespassing against Malo's law.[103]

## NOTES

1 *Mabo and Others v The State of Queensland and the Commonwealth of Australia*, in the High Court of Australia, Number 12 of 1982; Statement of claim by five Murray Island plaintiffs, 20 May 1982 (hereafter 'Statement of Claim').

2 *Mabo v Queensland*, 3 June 1992. Judgment per Brennan J, *Australian Law Journal Reports (ALJR)* 66 (1992), p. 437.

3 Judgement per Deane and Gaudron JJ, *ALJR* 66 (1992), p. 454.

4 *ALJR* 66 (1992), p. 482.

5 Flinders estimated the population at 700 from the numbers of men in their canoes and 'sitting upon the shore' on 30 October 1802. (M. Flinders, A *Voyage to Terra Australis*, 2 volumes, G. and W. Nicol, London, 1814, vol. 2, p. 111.)

6 W.E.H. Stanner, *On Aboriginal Religion*, Oceania Monograph 11, University of Sydney, Sydney, 1963, p. 14.

7 Mr Justice Moynihan heard evidence from Meriam and expert witnesses in the Supreme Court of Queensland over a total period of 67 days between October 1986 and September 1989; the evidence was recorded in 3,489 pages of transcript. See 'Determination pursuant to reference of 27 February 1986 by the High Court to the Supreme Court of Queensland to hear and determine all issues of fact raised by the pleadings, particulars and further particulars' in High Court action B 12 of 1982, 16 November 1990; hereafter 'Determination'.

8 M. Eliade, *Australian Religions: An Introduction*, Cornell University Press, Ithaca, 1973, p. 62.

9 'Determination', p. 12.

10 'Determination', p. 155; see also p. 170. For an analysis of the Determination with respect to Meriam culture, see N. Sharp, 'No Ordinary Case: Reflections on Mabo (No. 2)' in *Essays on the Mabo Decision*, Law Book Company, North Ryde, 1993, pp. 23–38; N. Sharp, *No Ordinary Judgment: Mabo, the Murray Islanders' Land Case*, Aboriginal Studies Press, Canberra, 1996, chapter 7.

11 W.E.H. Stanner, 'Some Aspects of Aboriginal Religion', Charles Strong Memorial Lecture, 1976, see Chapter 1 above.

12 Per Brennan J: 'Native title has its origins and is given its content by the traditional laws acknowledged by and the traditional customs observed by the indigenous inhabitants', *ALJR* 66 (1992), p. 429.

13 'Statement of Claim', p. 2.
14 Passi's claim was made on behalf of an extended family group.
15 Marwer Depoma appeared as a witness for the defendant to dispute the boundaries of land claimed by E.K.Mabo at the village of Sebeg on Komet land (Supreme Court of Queensland, Transcript (hereafter TQ), p. 1211).
16 TQ, p. 1574. See also TQ, p. 1662: '. . . that's why this [test] case here [is] for Meriam people'.
17 TQ, p. 1893.
18 Douglas Bon, TQ, p. 2398.
19 Diaries in the keeping of his daughter-in-law, Mas village, Mer Island (read by the author 20 December 1993).
20 M. Lawrie, *Myths and Legends of Torres Strait*, University of Queensland Press, St Lucia, 1970.
21 *Mabo v Queensland*, Affidavit of Patrick J. Killoran, 16 August 1982, Eighth Sheet, 14(c).
22 TQ, p. 2508: 'It was such an unknown concept that it created great interest', he continued, saying that it had stayed very alive and active in people's minds; but it was 'not of great interest to me'. Haddon had recorded the practice of placing a taboo on a garden in 1908. (See A.C. Haddon (ed.), 'Sociology, Magic and Religion of the Eastern Islanders', pp. 248–49 of Vol. 6 (1908) of *Reports of the Cambridge Anthropological Expedition to Torres Straits*, Cambridge University Press, Cambridge, 1904–1935.)
23 TQ, p. 2508.
24 Deborah Bird Rose, *Dingo Makes Us Human: Life and Land in an Aboriginal Australian Culture*, Cambridge University Press, Cambridge, 1992, p. 207.
25 TQ, pp. 2608, 2610; see also Lawrie, *Myths and Legends of Torres Strait*, p. xxi.
26 TQ, p. 2235.
27 Haddon (ed.), 'Sociology, Magic and Religion of the Eastern Islanders', p. 183.
28 Cassette 105/AB/M1/82; 'Book of Islanders', p. B 148. (The 'Book of Islanders' is compiled from cassette recordings (Cassettes 001–138) made by Nonie Sharp in the Torres Strait Islands and Cape York Peninsula, 1978–84, and is printed in Vol. 2 of Nonie Sharp, 'Springs of Originality among the Torres Strait Islanders', PhD Thesis, La Trobe University, 1984.)
29 Sam Passi, Cassette 135/AB/T1/3/84 in possession of the author; see also N. Sharp, *Stars of Tagai: The Torres Strait Islanders*, Aboriginal Studies Press, Canberra, 1993, p. 29. Most importantly, as Sam Passi said, Bomai came first; of great importance too was that at Teker, Kabur was fishing on the reef. (From notes of conversation with Gobedar Noah, Townsville, 7 December 1993). In the version written by Aet Passi for the Cambridge linguist Sidney Ray, there is only one narrative (*Reports of the Cambridge Anthropological Expedition to Torres Straits*, Vol. 3, 'Linguistics', edited by S.H. Ray, 1907, pp. 233–39); see also Haddon

(ed.), 'Sociology, Magic and Religion of the Eastern Islanders', pp. 337–44; Lawrie, *Myths and Legends of Torres Strait*, pp. 326–36.

30 Sharp, *Stars of Tagai: The Torres Strait Islanders*, p. 108.

31 See Rivers in Haddon (ed.), 'Sociology, Magic and Religion of the Eastern Islanders', pp. 178; E.K. Mabo, TQ, pp. 1014–15. Senior Meriam like Sam Passi emphasise that they were not rulers; but they had warriors to fight for them ('Book of Islanders') and men known as *mogor*, who carried out punitive actions (Haddon (ed.), 'Sociology, Magic and Religion of the Eastern Islanders', pp. 311–12).

32 See Sharp, *Stars of Tagai: The Torres Strait Islanders*, pp. 60–77; see also note 54, below.

33 Haddon, 'Sociology, Magic and Religion of the Eastern Islanders', p. 44.

34 Haddon, 'Sociology, Magic and Religion of the Eastern Islanders', p. 289.

35 D.R. Moore, *The Torres Strait Collections of A.C. Haddon: A Descriptive Catalogue*, British Museum, London, 1984, p. 38.

36 TQ, p. 2027.

37 'Determination', pp. 44–45.

38 TQ, p. 1163.

39 Haddon, 'Sociology, Magic and Religion of the Eastern Islanders', p. xix.

40 Recording made in 1980; 'Book of Islanders', p. B 125; Sharp, *Stars of Tagai: The Torres Strait Islanders*, p. 82.

41 Haddon, 'Sociology, Magic and Religion of the Eastern Islanders', p. xix.

42 'Book of Islanders', pp. 1354–1369, 142–150; *Stars of Tagai: The Torres Strait Islanders*, p. 82.

43 Sharp, *Stars of Tagai: The Torres Strait Islanders*, p. 82.

44 Rev. J. Done, Diaries and Personal Papers, 1915–1926. Manuscript in possession of his son, T.E. Done, NSW.

45 As cited in Gilbert White, *Round about the Torres Straits: A Record of Australian Church Missions*, Central Board of Missions, London, 1917.

46 Like his younger brother, Reverend Dave, Sam Passi explains the symbolism of the *seuriseuri* dance as sacred succession: it 'means that tradition must be left to someone who comes behind him' (Sharp, *Stars of Tagai: The Torres Strait Islanders*, pp. 251ff).

47 Dave Passi (Kebi Bala) in Sharp, *Stars of Tagai: The Torres Strait Islanders*, pp. 111 and 108.

48 TQ, p. 1887.

49 See Kebi Bala in Sharp, *Stars of Tagai: The Torres Strait Islanders*, p. 108.

50 'Determination', p. 206.

51 'Determination', pp. 170–72. Nor did he accept E.K. Mabo's claims to adoption by Benny Mabo ('Determination', pp. 199, 204, 204A–204J).

52 'Determination', p. 63.

53 'Determination', p. 63. Reverend Passi, Justice Moynihan concluded, showed 'a propensity for a selective', if honestly intentioned, reconstruction of the past (p. 206).

54 Shell friends were known as *wauri tebud*. *Wauri* was the Meriam name for the sea voyages they undertook for gift exchange and trade. See

Haddon, 'Sociology, Magic and Religion of the Eastern Islanders', pp. 186–87. See Sharp, *Stars of Tagai: The Torres Strait Islanders*, pp. 63–67, for a discussion of the connection between *wauri* voyages and the sacred order of Malo-Bomai. *Wauri* is the cone shell (*conus litteratis*).

55 TQ, p. 1115.
56 See TQ, pp. 3467–74.
57 See Sharp, *No Ordinary Judgment*, especially Chapters 3–7.
58 TQ, p. 2146.
59 *Milirrpum v Nabalco Pty Ltd and the Commonwealth of Australia* (1971), Judgement, *Federal Law Reports*, p. 273; see also J. Hookey, 'The Gove Land Rights Case: A Judicial Dispensation for the Taking of Aboriginal Lands in Australia?', *Federal Law Review* 5 (1972), p. 88, on the claim to communal rights in land 'despite their apparent un-Englishness'.
60 N.M. Williams, *The Yolngu and their Land: A System of Land Tenure and the Fight for its Recognition*, Australian Institute of Aboriginal Studies, Canberra, 1986, pp. 159, 191 n4.
61 *Milirrpum v Nabalco* (1971), p. 266.
62 TQ, p. 2629A; TQ, pp. 2601, 2606, 2610.
63 TQ, p. 2235.
64 TQ, p. 2620; compare Lawrie, *Myths and Legends of Torres Strait*, pp. 314–15 n3.
65 TQ, p. 2791.
66 J. Beckett, *Torres Strait Islanders: Custom and Colonialism*, Cambridge University Press, Cambridge, 1987, p. 21.
67 J. Beckett, 'The Murray Island Land Case and the Problem of Cultural Continuity', in W. Saunders (ed.) *Mabo and Native Title: Origins and Institutional Implications*, Research Monograph, number 7, Centre for Aboriginal Economic Policy Research, Australian National University, Canberra, 1994, p. 19.
68 J.R. Beckett, 'Politics of the Torres Strait Islands', PhD thesis, Australian National University, 1963.
69 Evidence of this revival was already visible in Lawrie's *Myths and Legends of Torres Strait* (1970); see H. Kitaoji's works: 'Culture of the Torres Strait People', *Arena* 50 (1978), pp. 54–63; 'Meriam Perceptions of Themselves and Those around Them: Cognitive Ordering after One Hundred Years of Culture Contact', paper presented to Australian Anthropological Society Conference, University of Queensland, St Lucia, Queensland, 1980.
70 In his seminal study of the Hero Cult of I'wai (crocodile) among the Koko Ya'o, a sandbeach people on the north-eastern seaboard of Cape York Peninsula, anthropologist Donald Thomson draws attention both to the inclusion of *abstract*, non-material things like dances as totems; and the integrative role of the cult 'in establishing a common tribal centre . . . and so providing the basis for tribal, as distinct from clan, solidarity' (D.F. Thomson, 'The Hero Cult, Initiation and Totemism on Cape York', *Journal of Royal Anthropological Institute of Great Britain and Ireland* 63 (1933), p. 459). These two qualities of I'wai resemble closely those of Malo-Bomai, as does the belief in a life after death (p. 493).

71 TQ, pp. 1807–1808; 'tribal anarchy' is Beckett's expression ('The Murray Island Land Case and the Problem of Continuity', p. 16.)
72 'Determination', p. 170.
73 This position, I have argued, has its origins in a generalisation to all humankind, of a Hobbesian essentialist view of human nature (Sharp, *No Ordinary Judgment*, Chapters 6 and 7).
74 Author's notes of conversation, Mer, 1989.
75 *Land Bilong Islanders*, documentary film, Yarra Bank Films.
76 TQ, p. 1530.
77 See Beckett 'Politics of the Torres Strait Islanders' and *Torres Strait Islanders*; a contrasting position is taken by Sharp, 'Springs of Originality among the Torres Strait Islanders' and *Stars of Tagai*.
78 See Sharp, *Stars of Tagai*.
79 Sharp, *Stars of Tagai*, p. 82.
80 TQ, p. 1531.
81 TQ, p. 2108, see also TQ, p. 2167.
82 Torres Strait Islanders Act (Qld).
83 Author's notes of conversation, Townsville, 7 December 1993.
84 TQ, pp. 2146–47.
85 Williams, *The Yolngu and their Land*, p. 73.
86 See 'Determination', pp. 213, 221; Mabo (No 2), High Court of Australia, 3 June 1992, pp. 454–55.
87 *Milirrpum v Nabalco* (1971), pp. 270–72.
88 Sharp, *Stars of Tagai*, pp. 60, 121.
89 See Sharp, *Stars of Tagai*, Chapter 3.
90 H. Frankfort, H.A. Frankfort, J.A. Wilson, T. Jacobsen, and W.A. Irwin (eds) *Before Philosophy: The Intellectual Adventure of Ancient Man: An Essay on Speculative Thought in the Ancient Near East*, University of Chicago Press, Chicago, 1946, p. 6.
91 Kitaoji ('Culture of the Torres Strait People', p. 68) concludes that 'a cradle of civilisation' is absent among the Islanders of Western Torres Strait. Eliade (*The Sacred and the Profane*, p. 44) discusses the Hebrew tradition where the creation of the world is like an embryo which grows from the navel, its central point, from where it spreads out in all directions.
92 The 'this-worldly' concern of Melanesian religions led some anthropologists to reduce Melanesian religious systems ethnocentrically to technologies. Thus Lawrence saw 'the exchange of goods and services' reflected in their social values and epistemological assumptions which express 'the significance of material culture in their lives'; 'anthropocentrism and materialism were undisguised' in a religion which was 'above all a technology' (P. Lawrence, 'Where God is Managing Director!', *New Guinea* 2 (1967), p. 28).
93 Deborah Bird Rose, 'Consciousness and Responsibility in an Australian Aboriginal Religion', in W.H. Edwards (ed.) *Traditional Aboriginal Society*, Macmillan, Melbourne, 1987, p. 268.
94 See Sharp, *No Ordinary Judgment*, Chapters 2 and 9.

95 Rose, *Dingo Makes Us Human*, p. 235.
96 Sharp, *No Ordinary Judgment*, Chapter 11.
97 K. Burridge, *Tangu Traditions: A Study of the Way of Life, Mythology, and Developing Experience of a New Guinea People*, Oxford University Press, Oxford, 1969, pp. 407–8.
98 *Weekly Law Reports* 1 (1957), p. 876. Justice Hall used similar words in the case of Calder v Attorney-General of British Columbia (1973), *Dominion Law Reports* 34 (1973), p. 145.
99 Section 10(1) of the Commonwealth Racial Discrimination Act (1975) is based on Article 17 of the Universal Declaration of Human Rights (1948) which upholds the universal right to own property and not to be dispossessed of it arbitrarily. The reason the court was asked to assume that Meriam rights existed is that the facts were awaiting determination by the remitter court. Each of the minority judgements argued that the equivalence of Meriam rights to those of English law would have to be shown before inequality before the law could be demonstrated. See Sharp, *No Ordinary Judgment*, Chapter 8 and the section titled 'Not "Any Sort of Custom": The Minority Perspective' of Chapter 9.
100 *Mabo v Queensland* (1992), Deane and Gaudron JJ, p. 482.
101 *Milirrpum v Nabalco* (1971), p. 273; see also Deane and Gaudron JJ (1992, p. 456).
102 *Mabo v Queensland* (1992), per Brennan J, p. 429.
103 TQ, p. 2044 (typographical errors corrected by author).

# INDEX